Welcome to the EVERYTHING® series!

These handy, accessible books give you all you need to tackle a difficult project, gain a new hobby, comprehend a fascinating topic, prepare for an exam, or even brush up on something you learned back in school but have since forgotten.

You can read an *EVERYTHING®* book from cover-to-cover or just pick out the information you want from our four useful boxes: e-facts, e-ssentials, e-alerts, and e-questions. We literally give you everything you need to know on the subject, but throw in a lot of fun stuff along the way, too.

We now have well over 100 *EVERYTHING®* books in print, spanning such wide-ranging topics as weddings, pregnancy, wine, learning guitar, one-pot cooking, managing people, and so much more. When you're done reading them all, you can finally say you know *EVERYTHING®*!

FACTS
Important sound bytes of information

ESSENTIALS
Quick handy tips

ALERT
Urgent warnings

QUESTIONS?
Solutions to common problems

THE EVERYTHING® Series

Dear Reader,

I'm so excited that you have chosen this book to support you in your personal commitment to bring more health and wellness into your life. I truly hope that the information you find here not only helps you get started, but also encourages you to keep up with your exercise activities. Feeling the strength in your muscles, lifting things easily, standing tall or even having that overall tired feeling after a beautiful day of outdoor fun—these are the great and simple joys of life.

As you continue your journey of a healthy and fit lifestyle, I hope you experience these and many other joys and pleasures often in the days ahead.

Feel free to write to me at *SArcherJD@aol.com* or visit my Web site at *www.shirleyarcher.com*. I'm always happy to hear from my readers, especially when I learn how I have helped or can do more to help you become a stronger and more fit person.

In fitness and in health,

Shirley Archer

THE
EVERYTHING®
WEIGHT TRAINING BOOK

Tone, shape, and
strengthen your body—
look your best in no time

Shirley Archer

Adams Media Corporation
Avon, Massachusetts

EDITORIAL
Publishing Director: Gary M. Krebs
Managing Editor: Kate McBride
Copy Chief: Laura MacLaughlin
Acquisitions Editor: Bethany Brown
Development Editor: Lesley Bolton

PRODUCTION
Production Director: Susan Beale
Production Manager: Michelle Roy Kelly
Series Designer: Daria Perreault
Layout and Graphics: Arlene Apone,
Paul Beatrice, Brooke Camfield,
Colleen Cunningham, Daria Perreault,
Frank Rivera

An Everything® Series Book.
Everything® is a registered trademark of Adams Media Corporation.

Published by Adams Media Corporation
57 Littlefield Street, Avon, MA 02322 U.S.A.
www.adamsmedia.com

ISBN: 1-58062-593-2
Printed in the United States of America.

J I H G F E D C B

Library of Congress Cataloging-in-Publication Data
Archer, Shirley J. S.
The everything weight training book : tone, shape, and strengthen your body,
look your best in no time / by Shirley J. S. Archer
p.   cm.
Includes index.
ISBN 1-58062-593-2
1. Weight training. 2. Bodybuilding. I. Title.
GV546 .A73   2002
613.7'13–dc21   2001053592

Illustrations by Barry Littmann.
Photos courtesy of Dimitre Photography.

*This book is available at quantity discounts for bulk purchases.
For information, call 1-800-872-5627.*

Visit the entire Everything® series at everything.com

Dedication

This book is dedicated to every person, male or female, regardless of shape, size, or level of ability, who wants to be strong both on the inside and out. Believe in yourself. With commitment and good instruction, which I hope this book provides to you, you can achieve your goals. Just keep going. Every bit counts (and every rep, however humble, counts too).

Acknowledgments

I'd like to thank everyone who helped support me on this project and breathe life into this book. Thanks especially to Bethany Brown, editor, for her understanding and support; to Carol Roth, my agent, for always encouraging me; to Lea Ann and Marirose at m.rose Sportswear for their support and wonderful sportswear; to Andrea Goodman at Reebok for her support and for providing footwear and apparel; and to my friends, colleagues and many students, especially Paul, Jane, and Monica. Thanks to Mike Spezzano at the YMCA of the USA for sharing his time to demonstrate exercises and to Darren and Sandy at the Lakeview YMCA in Chicago for letting us shoot in their facility. Thanks to the people at Bunim/Murray Productions and the great crew of Real World Chicago and thanks to Georgia, Anthony, Ken, Mia, and Frank for their loving support. Thanks to my mother for always believing in me and loving me. And, most of all, thanks to my many readers and students. Here's to your continued health, fitness, and joy in all that you do.

Contents

CHAPTER 1

Weight Training Is for Every Body

What's all the buzz about weight training? Study after study points to the critical importance of weight training to improve fitness and health. And, everyone can do it. You can achieve strength gains with weight training at any age. It doesn't matter what level of fitness you're at when you start. Weight training no longer belongs only to big, bulky "strong" men. Weight training belongs to everybody, including your kids and your grandmother.

What Is Weight Training?

Weight training is a method of building muscle strength and endurance over time through the use of resistance in progressively increasing amounts. When you condition your muscles, you train to increase muscle strength or muscle mass or both. Weight training uses resistance to achieve this conditioning response.

Why Weight Train?

Different people weight train for different reasons. But everyone wants results. Following are some reasons people train:

- Body builders weight train for competitions.
- Athletes of all ages, including kids and teens, weight train to improve sports performance and prevent injury.
- Individuals who have injuries weight train to rehabilitate.
- Individuals who need surgery for orthopedic concerns weight train to "prehabilitate."
- People of all ages weight train to firm up and improve muscle tone.
- People weight train to gain the energy and strength to do all the other fun activities, like traveling or playing sports, they want to do in their lives.
- People weight train to improve appearance.
- Recreational sports enthusiasts weight train to prevent injuries and to get in or stay in shape for their game.
- Some adults weight train so they can walk up stairs, carry bags of groceries, and play with children or grandchildren.
- Some adults weight train so they can successfully live independently without physical assistance.
- Other adults weight train to improve bone health.
- Some people weight train because they know it's good for their health.

ESSENTIALS   Why do you want to weight train? It's important to know your reasons for wanting to train, since this fuels your initial motivation. As you start reaping results, your motivation may change. That's okay. It happens with lots of people. It's still important to identify why you want to start.

Whatever your reasons, weight training is a great activity that will change your life. If you stick with your program over time, you'll realize so many benefits. You may even forget why you started in the first place. It won't even matter anymore. You will have found the joy of weight training.

One person who found the joy of weight training is twenty-four-year-old Anna: "I strength train to stay in shape and to stay healthy. I used to be someone who only did cardio workouts. Cardio, cardio, and more cardio. Last spring I strained a ligament in my left leg, not because I was out of shape but because I was overworking some muscles during my workouts while neglecting others. Due to my injury, I had to stop exercising for four weeks. I was miserable! When I started exercising again, I was much weaker than before.

"I started strength training to overcome my injury and to regain my strength. I'm so happy with the results. After only a couple of months, I felt better and stronger than ever. Strength training has made me much more aware of my body, my different muscle groups, and how I use all of them. Today I continue to strength train both to assure that I don't injure myself again and to keep this great feeling!"

Weight Training Benefits

In medical circles it has been said that if exercise were a prescription drug, it would be the most widely prescribed medicine. Regular exercise provides so many benefits for so many people, it's hard to believe that more people are not more active. You may feel you need more information, tools, and support to get going. But once you do, you'll be thrilled by the many positive changes that will take place in your life. Weight training is a great place to get started with your exercise program. Once you start feeling stronger, you'll want to do so many things, no one will be able to slow you down.

Following are some of the many benefits of weight training:

- Burn more calories and effectively manage weight for the rest of your life.
- Exercise time can be used efficiently and effectively.
- Strengthen bones.
- Strengthen muscles.
- Increase energy.
- Feel more confident and improve your self-esteem.
- Improve joint stability.
- Improve balance.
- Reduce your risk of injury.
- Enhance your athletic power.
- Improve your posture, muscle tone, and overall appearance.
- Reduce or eliminate lower back pain.
- Reduce your risk of disease.
- Slow down the aging process.
- Have more fun.
- Manage stress effectively.
- Sleep better.

When you combine all of these benefits, your life is improved in so many ways, physically and emotionally, it can only add up to a better quality of life. The ability to do things for yourself, coupled with more energy and confidence, can brighten anyone's day.

Why You Need Weight Training

Functional fitness is a popular exercise buzzword these days. What are people talking about? Although intuitively you know that exercise is good for you, the concept of the importance of fitness to health is a more recent distinction in scientific research. The historical focus on fitness related to how it could improve athletic performance.

More and more research studies show that a certain level of fitness is necessary just to get through your day successfully. This is different from the fitness pursued by recreational or professional athletes. This is fitness for living, referred to by researchers as "functional fitness."

You need functional fitness, even if you never play sports. Functional fitness is generally considered to be your ability to perform light, moderate, and strenuous recreational, household, daily living, and personal care tasks. These functional activities vary widely depending upon your health, lifestyle, activity level, and occupation.

FACTS

According to Cathy A. Maloney-Hills, a licensed physical therapist at Courage Center in Golden Valley, Minnesota, "Functional activities can be as basic as walking, moving in and out of chairs, lifting, carrying, cleaning, cooking, dressing, yard work, housework, or shopping. Higher-level activities incorporate high demand occupational tasks, recreational, or athletic activities, such as playing golf or tennis or hiking. The list can be limitless, depending upon an individual's activity level and independence within or outside of the home."

Research shows that people who maintain muscular strength over the years seem to have fewer functional limitations as they age. In other words, the more strength you have and keep, the more activities you are able to do in life. And, the more activities that you can do, the more you can enjoy yourself.

Strength is not the only component of fitness that is important. You need to achieve and maintain cardiovascular endurance, flexibility, muscle endurance, and a healthy body weight. Muscular strength and endurance, however, are important to attain these other aspects of fitness.

For example, if you are not strong enough or do not have enough endurance to take a walk, it's difficult to maintain cardiovascular fitness.

Similarly, if you have no energy for exercise, it's difficult to maintain a healthy body weight.

"Strength training is not a contest. It's good for everybody. Most men and women do not have the genetic ability to gain large muscle mass. Another myth is that strength training is expensive, time consuming, and complex. In fact, it shouldn't take more than thirty minutes per session," says James Peterson, Ph.D., Sports Medicine Consultant in Monterey, California.

Strength training, therefore, is key to maintaining overall health and independence over a lifetime. The loss of functional abilities usually does not occur overnight. Physical limitations, instead, develop slowly over periods of time, as a result of our everyday habits.

ALERT

Evidence from research suggests that much of what we used to think was due to age really results from inactivity. With regular practice, everyone, even people in their nineties, can improve flexibility, range of motion, balance, and agility.

One day, you move through your day with ease. Another day, years later, you realize you can't touch your toes. You can't walk up a flight of stairs. The idea of doing a cartwheel seems terrifying, not fun. Now, you may never have enjoyed cartwheels. That's not the point.

The point is you notice that you're no longer able to do things you used to do easily. And, you may no longer be able to do things that you used to enjoy. According to statistics from the National Center for Health, approximately 50 percent of American adults cannot even carry a ten-pound bag of groceries.

It doesn't have to be this way. And, it's not your fault. This lack of functional strength reflects the lack of natural activity in your daily life. Technology and the conveniences of modern living eliminate much of your need for physical labor to get through your daily tasks.

Unless you have a job that is physically demanding, you're not likely to be required to move a lot to get through your day. Although labor-saving devices are convenient, your body still needs a minimal amount of physical activity each day to stay healthy. There is a point at which you can begin to conserve too much energy. We all need to take steps to put activity back into our lives.

One important principle of fitness is "use it or lose it." We lose the ability to do things if we no longer do them. Therefore, getting in shape is a project that's never done. Because once you're "in shape" then you need to work to stay that way. Being active is simply part of a healthy lifestyle. The good news is that the process is fun when you find things that you enjoy doing.

Remember, you're never too old to begin weight training. Studies show that adults over the age of seventy have made significant increases in muscular strength from regular training. And, anything you do is better than nothing. Increasing your daily level of activity and adding a strength-training program are excellent ways to promote your health and well being.

ESSENTIALS   Longitudinal studies show that older adults who exercise compared with sedentary adults of the same age are effectively at a biological age of as much as ten to twenty years younger. So, get moving! It will do you and your body a world of good.

Lean Body Math

After age thirty, both men and women tend to lose $\frac{1}{3}$ to $\frac{1}{2}$ pound of body mass per year. One pound of lean body mass burns approximately fifty calories per day. One pound of fat mass burns approximately two calories per day. The caloric energy burn of one pound of lean body mass over one year equals 18,250 calories. One pound of fat equals 3,500 calories. A loss of $\frac{1}{3}$ pound of lean body mass per year equals a loss of approximately 6,000 calories. This equals to about 2 pounds.

If you maintain your current level of activity and food intake, if you do not do something to maintain or increase your lean body mass as you age, you're likely to gain around 2 pounds per year.

FACTS

"Many of us on the road to adulthood lose that childhood instinct to run and jump, to skip with joy, to walk briskly through crisp autumn leaves. But it is movement, in assorted styles and speeds, on a regular basis, that is critical to maintaining our astoundingly complicated and wonderful bodies." John W. Farquhar, M.D., Founder and Former Director of the Stanford Center for Research in Disease Prevention, Stanford University School of Medicine, Palo Alto, California

Benefits of Regular Physical Activity

Regular physical activity performed on most days of the week reduces the risk of developing or dying from some of the leading causes of death in the United States. According to a 1996 report of the U.S. Surgeon General, the U.S. Department of Health and Human Services, and the National Heart, Lung, and Blood Institute, regular physical activity improves health in the following ways:

- Lowers LDL or "bad" cholesterol
- Increases HDL or "good" cholesterol
- Lowers triglycerides, another form of fat in the blood stream
- Reduces risk of developing diabetes
- Reduces risk of developing high blood pressure and heart disease
- Helps lower blood pressure in people who have high blood pressure
- Reduces risk of developing colon cancer
- Reduces feelings of depression and anxiety
- Helps manage weight
- Helps build and maintain healthy bones, muscles, and joints

Here's the testimony of sixty-one-year-old Lowell: "Fitness came naturally to me as a youth. I was a high school sprinter and enjoyed canoeing, hiking, bicycling, and skiing. In my mid forties I realized that I wanted to feel stronger and have more endurance. I joined organized aerobics classes to stay on track.

"When I turned fifty, I felt my upper body strength slipping away. My legs were doing okay but I couldn't lift things like I used to. I joined a circuit weight training class and regained my upper body strength.

"I was surprised at how much it helped my bicycle riding. Last summer, at age sixty-one, I rode my bicycle across the country. I became a certified instructor and now lead circuit weight training classes. Aerobics and weight training will be an important part of my weekly schedule for the rest of my life. Also, I plan to keep up my bicycling, hiking, and skiing."

Weight Training Myths

Despite all the well-founded reasons to weight train, many myths surround the subject. Here are some of the major ones:

Weight training makes you big. Many people, both male and female, will never get "big" from weight training. Developing large, bulky muscles results from hard training and hormones.

Weight training requires hours in the gym. Visible results from weight training can be achieved in as little as twenty-five minutes, twice a week.

As we get older, we get weak and there's nothing anyone can do about it. Much of the loss of the ability to move that we associate with age or with chronic illness is really the result of inactivity. Muscles shrink and become weak if they're not used.

QUESTIONS?

What have you got to lose?
Fat! What will you gain? Muscle, strength, endurance, stronger bones, and higher metabolism. What better reason do you need to start weight training today?

Reasons to Start Today

Many people are looking for a magic bullet. They keep searching and searching for a new formula that will provide a "perfect" body in an instant. Fad diets, expensive supplements, and exercise equipment that gathers dust all illustrate this principle. And, as we all well know, none of these gimmicks alone can provide lasting, effective, and healthful results.

Some people don't look for a solution at all. The years go by and other priorities come before regular exercise. It happens easily. Money is invested in retirement accounts with plans for the security and comfort of the golden years. But, no investment has been made in the "physical" account. So, when it's time to enjoy your retirement years, you find yourself without the physical energy or ability to do things that are enjoyable. You need to plan for your physical future.

A strong, fit, toned, and healthy body can be yours for a lifetime. And, it's the product of a healthy lifestyle. Your lifestyle is the way you tend to live each and every day. A healthy lifestyle combines good nutrition, consistent exercise, a physically active approach to living, an effective method to manage stress, a positive attitude, and a sense of balance in blending different facets of life.

Most importantly, a healthy lifestyle is a process. It's a commitment you make to yourself and to those you love and who care for you each and every day. And, as you choose to live healthfully each day, you reap rewards. You get stronger, you feel more energetic, and your outlook on life improves. However, the rewards are not an endpoint. They simply represent that you are on a healthy path—a path you'll hopefully stick with for the rest of your life.

So, there's no reason to wait. With weight training, as with many endeavors, each day is the first day of the rest of your life. Some weeks you will stick to your schedule. Other weeks, you won't. Some days you're filled with energy and enthusiasm. Other days, you're barely able to pull yourself out of bed.

The important thing is that you keep on going. Over time, your strength training becomes so much a part of your life, you miss it when you're not able to do it. And, you find the time because it's important to your life.

CHAPTER 2

Stop Dieting for Life

You probably want to give up dieting. Studies show that the most effective method of long-term weight management combines exercise and good nutrition. Weight training provides a critical foundation for your exercise program. For every pound of muscle you gain, there is an increase of about thirty to fifty more calories burned a day.

Body Composition and Basal Metabolic Rate

It's not the shape or weight of the package that's important, it's the percentage of fat mass and lean mass. Your body consists of lean body mass and fat mass. Weight training increases your percentage of lean body mass. Muscles are part of your lean body mass. Your percentage of lean body mass and the rate that your body burns calories, even at rest, are directly related. Our bodies are always consuming energy, even when we sleep.

FACTS

Your resting metabolic rate, or metabolism, is the amount of calories your body burns when you are at rest. This is the number of calories you burn to simply be alive. Metabolism is affected by genetics and by percentage of muscle mass. Muscles are active tissue and require lots of energy. The more muscles you have, the more calories you burn, even when you do nothing.

Muscles Are Calorie Burning Engines

When you increase your muscle mass, you elevate your resting metabolic rate. This means that all other things being equal, your body will burn more calories even when you are doing nothing. Isn't it great to know that you will burn more calories even when you're sleeping?

Studies show that for every additional one pound of muscle mass that you gain, your body may burn up to thirty to fifty more calories per day. For example, if you work hard and gain 5 pounds of lean body mass from weight training, you may burn up to an additional 250 calories per day.

In one week, that equals 1,750 calories. One pound is equal to 3,500 calories. So, in two weeks, after you have increased your lean body mass, if you maintain your same level of activity and food consumption as before, you could burn up to one pound of excess fat. Muscles burn energy. When it comes to calories, you want your body to be a fuel guzzler.

SSENTIALS Strong muscles give you energy to get up and go. When you get stronger, you're also likely to become more active. As your strength increases, all of your daily activities will seem easier. This increased activity boosts your metabolism and increases the number of calories that you burn.

It's Good to Be Dense

Muscle mass is not only metabolically more active than fat, it's also denser. That means that pound for pound, muscle takes up less space on your body than fat. And, with respect to mass, muscle weighs more than fat.

That's why athletes often fall into the category of "overweight" on traditional height and weight charts or even in measurements using the body mass index, or BMI. This extra muscle mass, however, is positive. These athletes do not necessarily need to lose weight.

When you first start weight training, don't be surprised if you actually gain weight. This is a normal reaction for many people. The average person starting an exercise program may gain 3 to 5 pounds. If you're among these people, you've successfully gained lean body mass or muscles. Congratulate yourself. You deserve a pat on the back for all your hard work!

This gain of lean body mass is good, since muscle is metabolically more active. Remember, your muscles are calorie guzzling machines. The calorie burning effects of this change in your metabolic rate, however, take place over time. Be patient. It's likely that your excess fat was not gained in one week and therefore will not be completely lost in one week either. Give your body time to change. Give your body time to burn off some of its stored energy, otherwise known as fat.

It's Possible to Be Thin and Overly Fat

People often don't realize that it's possible to be both thin and fat. A person may be small in size, yet have a very low percentage of lean body mass. What is important to remember for healthy weight management is that it's not the size or shape of the body that matters, it's the relationship of lean mass to fat mass. Strength training is important to everyone, not only larger sized individuals, because we all need to be strong. And, it's possible to be thin and weak.

Healthy bodies come in *all* shapes and sizes. It's important to remember that your goal to get in shape does not mean you need to become a size two or look like a cover model. Today's typical female model is 20 percent smaller than the average woman. Only 2 percent of women in America can maintain a typical model's physique without resorting to unhealthy or eating disordered behavior.

Healthy bodies come in various shapes and sizes. Just as we are not all tall, we are not all genetically predisposed to have a small frame. Look at pictures of elite athletes. Some of them are very large in size, others are small. However, many of these athletes have a healthy fat to lean ratio and are at a healthy weight for their body type.

Weight Training Keeps You Strong and Healthy

Weight training helps you build lean body mass and prevent the loss of the lean body mass that you have. If you combine your weight training with regular cardiovascular exercise, an active lifestyle, and healthy nutrition, when you lose weight, you are likely to lose mostly fat weight. And, you're much more likely to keep it off for good.

Studies show that regular physical activity combined with good nutrition is *the most effective* method to ensure long-term weight management.

As a testimony to her perseverance, thirty-three-year-old Anne recalls, "I started strength training one year ago, mainly to feel stronger. I was also concerned about my health. I had always been fat, but healthy. Last spring, at a routine doctor's appointment, I discovered my blood pressure was getting high, as was my blood glucose level.

"The benefits of my weight training and generally increased activity level did not appear immediately—it took a little while. I'm glad I stuck with it. It took months to see visible results, but when it happened, wow!

The Continuous Weight Gain Cycle

We naturally lose lean body mass as we age. After the age of thirty-five, both men and women typically lose $\frac{1}{3}$ to $\frac{1}{2}$ pound of muscle each year. In addition, they gain an equal amount of body fat. One-third to one-half pound may not seem like much; however, because it's metabolically active, its effect is multiplied exponentially. Just as you may burn thirty to fifty calories more per day for every pound of lean body mass that you gain, you will also burn fifteen to twenty-five calories less per day for every half pound of lean body mass that you lose.

This can equal as much as 175 calories per week, or 9,100 calories per year. Remember: one pound equals 3,500 calories. If your activity and consumption levels remain exactly the same, you could gain 2.6 pounds per year. Over ten years this equals 26 pounds. Suddenly, it's easy to see how excess weight piles on.

E

FACTS

How does 100 extra calories a day add up? Each day, you burn calories to stay alive and to do activities. Excess calories are stored in the body as fat. An excess of 3,500 calories equals one pound of fat. If you consume 100 more calories per day than your body uses, that adds up to 36,500 excess calories in one year. Therefore, you could gain approximately 10 pounds of body fat in one year.

And, it doesn't stop there. As you lose your lean body mass and replace it with fat, you become weaker. As you become weaker and have less energy, you also tend to become less active. The same activities you did before now leave you feeling more tired, so you slow down, move less, and sit more. Because of your reduction in activity, you gain even more weight. It becomes a continuous cycle of weight gain.

So, how do you stop it? Weight training. It really is that simple. Find a method of strength training that you can fit into your weekly lifestyle. It can take as little as twenty-five minutes, two days a week. Not only will you feel stronger, look better, have more energy, and stand taller, you will also be reversing the weight gain cycle. And, you'll start feeling like your energetic self again.

Get off the Yo-Yo Diet Highway

What happens when you crash diet and don't combine your reduction in food consumption with physical activity? You're likely to lose lean body mass or muscle tissue. And, if you fall off your diet and back into old eating habits, unless you're active, you're likely to add back body fat instead of muscle.

The result of your short-term dieting efforts is that you think you're back where you started. But, you're not! In fact, you're likely to have a higher percentage of body fat than you did before your crash diet.

This loss in lean body mass has consequences. Your metabolism slows down. What that means is that you'll burn fewer calories for the same level of activity. Therefore, it will be even easier for you to gain weight than it was before. Get the picture?

ALERT

Yo-yo dieting is a no-win situation. Some studies suggest that yo-yo dieting can increase your risks for heart disease, stroke, or diabetes. The evidence to date, however, is not conclusive—but why risk it?

The only approach to weight management that makes long-term sense is to improve your nutritional habits and exercise regularly. And, weight training is an important part of your exercise program. Strength training will build that essential lean body mass to rev up your metabolism and help stop those extra pounds from creeping on.

Body Composition

Body composition refers to the percentage of fat and percentage of fat-free body mass that makes up your total body weight. Fat-free mass, also known as lean-body mass, consists primarily of muscle tissue, bones, and blood, essentially all the rest of your body that is not fat.

Research suggests that the ideal percentage of body fat for men is 15 to 18 percent. For women, the ideal range of body fat is 22 to 25 percent. It's important to remember that these are suggested ranges.

Some individuals with a higher percentage of body fat who are regularly active may still be considered at a healthy weight.

According to a study by Dr. Steven Blair at the Cooper Institute on male subjects, those who were thin and sedentary had a higher risk for disease than those who were "overweight" and physically active. Regular physical activity seems to be an important factor in maintaining long-term health.

When you begin your weight training program, you might want to measure your body composition. This way, you'll have a baseline against which to measure the effectiveness of your training program over time. You can see how much muscle mass you have when you get started. Every six weeks or so, you can check to see how much more muscle mass you have developed. If you're a person who is motivated by numbers, this can be a concrete way to stay excited about your progress.

Can Weight Training Affect Body Composition?

You bet. Genetics largely determines your height and body type, such as whether or not you are short or tall or have a small, medium, or large frame. You have very little control over these physical characteristics.

In contrast, genetics plays a smaller role in metabolism and the tendency to gain fat. For example, as we get older, most of us experience a decrease in muscle size and an increase in body fat and total body weight. Although this is the norm for the majority of the American population, since the American population continues to grow larger, environmental factors seem to be playing a role.

By starting a weight training program and combining it with good nutrition and more physical activity, you can change this tendency to lose muscle and add weight. Instead, you can add muscle and stabilize your weight.

Weight Training and the Average Woman

The average American woman is 5 feet, 4 inches tall. She weighs 135 pounds. She has 26 percent body fat: 50 pounds of muscle and 35 pounds of fat.

Research shows that with two months of regular strength training, two times a week, and proper nutrition, subjects experience a reduction of about 12 pounds of fat and the addition of 3 pounds of muscle. Total weight loss was 9 pounds.

For our new strength-trained woman, this means that after two months of sticking with her weight training program, she weighs 126 pounds. She has 18 percent body fat: 53 pounds of muscle and 23 pounds of fat.

Not only has she lost weight and gained strength, but she's also more energetic with a firmer, more toned appearance. Strength training exercises affect both muscles and fat. It's the best method of exercise to improve your body composition and your appearance for people of all shapes and sizes.

Talking about her own experience, thirty-four-year-old Kim says, "I initially started strength training in 1995—I was 35 pounds overweight and didn't feel good with the extra weight I was carrying. Plus, I felt weak and tired most of the time.

"With minor modifications to my diet, along with strength training, I've lost the 35 pounds in three years. That may seem like a long time, but I've kept the weight off since then (three years now). Strength training has improved my posture, self-image, and best of all, energy level.

"I've increased my over all strength at least three times. This is the best I've felt since I was 17! And the best part? I can now fit into my bikini when it's time to hit the beach, and feel good about it!"

CHAPTER 3

Understanding Weight Training Principles and Terms

You know weight training is good for you. You know weight training enables you to achieve physical goals. But, how does it work? Here's the bottom line. Weight training is a method of building muscle strength and endurance over time through the use of resistance in progressively increasing amounts.

Strength Versus Endurance

Muscle strength refers to the maximal amount of weight your muscles can lift in one repetition. Training to develop strength uses heavy weights for few repetitions to reach muscle failure. Muscle endurance refers to a muscle's ability to continually lift weight over a period of time. Training to develop endurance is achieved by lifting lighter weights for more repetitions.

Men generally are physically stronger than women because they have more muscle mass. When you compare muscle cross-sectional areas from a man and woman, no strength differences exist. Muscle quality, therefore, is not related to gender.

Your muscles develop in response to how you train them. This is called the *principle of specificity*. What you train is what you get. For example, if you emphasize strength with heavier weights and fewer repetitions to muscle failure, your muscles will get stronger. This principle is sometimes described as SAID (Specific Adaptation to Imposed Demands).

Why Does Weight Training Work?

Weight training works because muscles adapt to stress. This is called the *overload principle.* Your muscles develop strength and endurance when you increase the amount of resistance. Muscles also develop strength and endurance as you increase how often you challenge them and how long you push them to endure an activity.

ESSENTIALS   In weight training, "failure" is a good thing. In fact, it's one of your goals. When you exercise, you want to push your muscles to failure. When you challenge your muscles to that level, that's how they become stronger.

For example, when your muscles are challenged to lift something heavier than they are used to, they respond by growing stronger to meet the challenge. Isn't it great to know that your body is working with and for you? This is true even if your body is over ninety years old.

The human body is remarkably resilient. And, if you combine your mind with your muscle, you will accelerate your results.

If your muscles are reasonably challenged, they respond by building tissue and becoming stronger. A reasonable challenge is a load that is somewhat heavier than your usual load. This is unique to each individual. An unusually heavy load would *not* be a reasonable challenge. What is "light" or "heavy," therefore, is relative to what you do in your daily life. It has nothing to do with what your friends, neighbors, or even your family members do, just you.

If a muscle is overly challenged, it becomes injured and weaker. This is not desirable. You can avoid it. Apply the correct amount of stress. You'll create a positive training response. Train intelligently, and you'll keep on training. If you're overly aggressive, unrealistic, or simply careless, your body will stop you very quickly. The body has its own wisdom. And, it will take steps to protect you, sometimes even from yourself.

To positively stress muscles over time it's important to increase weight gradually and systematically. This is the *principle of progression*. Weight training takes time. Visible results don't happen overnight. "Invisible results," however, do occur as you train consistently. Your joints become stronger. Your neuromuscular system develops. This is all part of the "inner workout."

Your Training Program

The American College of Sports Medicine (ACSM) recommends that you train a minimum of two times a week. Why at least twice a week? You need to stimulate your muscles regularly to gain improvements. Why not more frequently? You *can* train more often, but research shows that increasing the frequency of training results in a minimal amount of additional improvement relative to the additional time investment.

In other words, the most bang for your buck comes from those first two days a week. More days of exercise will give you more bang, just not as big a bang. To quantify this difference, according to research studies, training two days a week may produce only 75 percent of the gains that a three day a week program would. So it's really up to you and what you want. The bottom line is that a minimum amount of strength training will result in significant health and fitness improvements.

"Work In" as Much as You "Work Out"

As with many things in life, when it comes to weight training, more is not necessarily better. Muscles need at least forty-eight hours in between training sessions to recover and repair. (The one exception is the abdominal muscle group, which can be exercised every day.) If you're training your entire body daily, your muscles will not have time to build new tissue. You could be overtraining. Many advanced bodybuilders divide their body parts into two groups and exercise them alternately on consecutive days. This is known as working a "split routine."

SSENTIALS

Research shows that exercise sessions over one hour in length tend to have high drop-out rates. You can efficiently do one set of eight to ten exercises for the major muscles in your body in twenty to twenty-five minutes. Keep it short and you're likely to keep it up.

Strength training works because it places stress on your muscles. This stress causes microscopic injury to your muscle cells. During your rest period, your cells repair this damage. Through repair, your muscles become stronger. If you don't allow your body time to recover, the next time you workout, you'll be placing more stress on already damaged muscle cells. Overtraining slows your progress and can lead to injury. Signs and symptoms of overtraining are decreased performance (you can't lift as much as usual), difficulty in maintaining good form, chronic fatigue, muscle soreness and damage, increased incidence of injuries, joint aches and pains, reduced ability to concentrate, lower self-esteem, increased sensitivity to stress, increased occurrence of illness, decreased rate of healing, and disturbed sleep.

The good news is that rest and recovery time need to be part of your weekly workout schedule. Don't you love it when you can sit on the couch and tell people that it's part of your training program? And, it is. Actually, you're "working in," which is equally important and often neglected. You're allowing the inner process of tissue rebuilding and repair to occur. This is essential to increase your strength and get results.

On the other hand, if you take too much time off between sessions, your muscles will not continue to get stronger without continued stimulation. You will gain new tissue immediately following your last session. But if you spend too much time on the couch, this tissue will atrophy, or shrink.

QUESTIONS?

Can I build muscle strength by doing aerobics?
Aerobic training increases aerobic power. Aerobic training or "cardio" does not build muscle strength or size. Only strength training increases muscle strength. Intense "cardio" training can actually inhibit the benefits of resistance training.

Intensity: Middle of the Road Is Best for Most

The intensity of your training relates to your effort level. This is based on training volume. The volume of your training is measured by repetitions (reps), sets, and resistance. All strength-training exercises are defined by these factors. A moderate program consists of eight to ten exercises that include the following major muscle groups:

- **Chest:** pectoral muscles
- **Shoulders:** deltoid muscles, rotator cuff, scapular stabilizers, trapezius
- **Arms:** biceps, triceps, forearm
- **Back:** latissimus dorsi, erector spinae, trapezius
- **Abdomen:** rectus abdominis, obliques, transversus
- **Legs:** gluteals, quadriceps, hamstrings, calves

Weights Versus Reps

When it comes to counting reps to muscle failure, lifting a very heavy weight that can only be lifted a few times would be considered high-intensity training. Very heavy lifting is only appropriate for athletes and experienced exercisers. Athletes perform very heavy lifting to produce strength and power gains.

For most people, a moderate intensity approach minimizes injury and produces results. Performing eight to twelve repetitions to muscular failure is considered moderate intensity. By performing between eight to twelve repetitions, you strike a balance between building muscle strength and endurance.

When you select your level of weight for each exercise, make sure that you are feeling challenged, but not overwhelmed. If you can perform 15 repetitions of an exercise easily, that's a sign that your weight is too light. If you can't do 8 reps, then the weight is too heavy. Always start light and increase weight in the smallest possible increments. Don't try to force a lift. You may injure yourself.

FACTS

Your large muscles can lift much heavier weights than your small muscles. Your leg, thigh, and buttock muscles are probably the strongest in your body because you tend to use them more throughout the day. Daily activities don't generally require that you use your upper body a lot and, consequently, your arm and shoulder muscles are much smaller. Your weight level will be much lighter for these smaller, weaker muscles.

After you've selected a safe weight level, execute your reps with good form. Breathe throughout the exercise. Maintain good posture. Remember, what you train is what you get. Stand up straight! Perform your movements through as full a range of motion as possible. Move with control. Use the same speed of movement throughout the exercise. Don't speed up as you lower your weight. That means gravity is assisting you; you're not working your muscles fully.

If one repetition represents the maximum amount of weight that you can lift for an exercise, how hard are you working when you do fewer reps to fatigue?

- 1 rep = 100 percent
- 2–3 reps = 95 percent
- 4–5 reps = 90 percent
- 6–7 reps = 85 percent
- 8–9 reps = 80 percent

- 10–11 reps = 85 percent
- 12–13 reps = 70 percent
- 14–15 reps = 65 percent
- 16–20 reps = 60 percent

As you can see, it's more difficult to work at a higher level of intensity. To achieve results, your efforts need to be at least 65 percent.

Progressing Your Program

As you start feeling stronger, you may be tempted to quickly increase your weight loads. Resist the temptation. Before you increase the weight level, increase the number of your repetitions. If you're performing all twelve of your repetitions with good form, then bump up your weight. The rule of thumb is to increase your weight by roughly five percent. Listen to your body. Let your muscles be the judge. You don't want to increase your weight levels so much that you injure yourself or experience excessive muscle soreness.

Add a conservative amount of weight and see how it feels. Trust your body. If it feels within a comfortable range for you, it's likely to be a good increment. If it feels like too much, it probably is. You also want to change your exercises to challenge your muscles in different ways. Muscles need variety. Keep stimulating them. Your mind will also appreciate the change. If your program feels boring to you, your body is probably bored, too. Time for a change.

Keep in mind that life is not a straight, linear progression. Wouldn't life be easy if it were? But it would also probably be dull, so we learn to appreciate the peaks and valleys. Along the same lines, when you train, some days you may feel strong and full of energy. On other days, you may simply feel tired. That's normal.

Sometimes you may get sick. You may go on vacation. You may miss your workouts for any number of reasons. You're likely to lose some strength during these times. That's normal. Just get right back into your workout schedule. It's the consistency over your lifetime that will pay the most dividends. And, it's easier the second, third, and fourth times around, because your muscles have a "memory." Just don't let them forget for too long. Avoid overtraining and "over-recovery."

Some Gym Rat Lingo

Alignment: Alignment refers to posture. Yes, all those old rules about standing up straight and pulling your stomach in do apply.

Failure: Failure, believe it or not, is a good thing in weight training. It means that you have repeated an exercise enough times and with enough weight that the working muscles cannot do another complete movement.

Form: You may hear people ask, "How's my form?" or hear trainers say, "Watch your form." These may not be the come-on lines that you think. When you exercise, it's important to perform an exercise and maintain good posture and alignment. It's also important to move smoothly and with control. *Good form* refers to executing an exercise properly.

Free weights: Free weights include the dumbbells and barbells that you can adjust by adding or removing plates on the ends. Using free weights requires you to challenge your ability to stabilize and balance yourself while doing movements with extra weight.

Hydrate: Gym rats frequently say that they need to hydrate. This simply means they need to drink fluids.

Machines: All the equipment that you stand on, sit on, or move against. "Cardio equipment" includes those machines where you warm up to get your heart rate going, such as the exercise bikes, stair climbers, or treadmills. "Weight machines" are the ones where you can adjust the weights and challenge your muscles in specific positions.

Plates: These are not for dinner. Weight plates allow you to add weight to your dumbbells or barbell in increments as you get stronger.

Recovery: This does not refer to a rescue operation. Although when you're just starting out, your recoveries may provide a rescue. Recovery refers to resting in between working. For example, you can recover in between sets of exercises. Or, you can recover by taking one to three days off between workouts to give your muscles a chance to repair.

Rep(s): Also known as *repetition(s),* a rep is one completely executed exercise movement. For example, one push-up is one rep.

ROM: ROM stands for *range of motion.* It means how far you can move a limb around a joint. For example, when you circle your arm backwards as if you were doing a back stroke, the largest circle you can make is your active ROM. You want to do your exercise movements as fully as you can within your ROM.

Set(s): A group of reps done without stopping. Exercises are generally organized into a certain number of reps before you can't do any more.

Spot: A spot or spotter (person who spots) prevents you from going beyond your natural range of motion to avoid injury. For example, when you are new to an exercise or working with a heavy weight, it's a good idea to have someone "spot" you to guide the movement and serve as a safety net.

Warm-up: A warm-up is that thing you do when you first arrive dressed for your workout. After you finish saying your hellos, you can politely excuse yourself and say, "I have to go warm up." This means you will be doing some type of rhythmic movement that stimulates you to start breaking out in a sweat.

Warmdown: Also known as a *cooldown,* a warmdown is the reverse of your warm-up. When you're ready for your final stretch, you can tell your friends, "This has been great. I've got to go warm down now."

Workout: Your workout refers to your specific plan of exercises. For example, you may do a specific sequence of twelve exercises, one set each, for a total body workout. That would be your workout or program.

Types of Weight Training

Besides varying the number of reps and sets and varying your exercises, it's a good idea to include different modes of weight training. Combine free-weight exercises with machines. Mix up your program. Every type of exercise challenges your muscles in slightly different ways. For variety, take your workout to the pool. When you're on the road, train with rubber tubing and bands. All of these methods have value and keep your program fun, interesting, and effective.

The various types of weight training include:

- Free weights, dumbbells, barbells
- Machines
- Cables
- Resistance bands and tubing
- Body weight
- Water

Balanced Muscle Development

Our muscles exist in relationship to each other. For example, the biceps muscle in front of your upper arm works together with the triceps muscle in the back of your upper arm. When the biceps contract, your elbow bends or flexes and your triceps lengthen. When the triceps contract, your elbow extends your forearm and your biceps lengthen. The biceps and triceps, therefore, are opposing muscles.

A muscle imbalance occurs when one side of the opposing group dominates the other due to greater strength. Muscle imbalances contribute to poor alignment and to injuries. That's why it's important to train your muscles as a group. If you train the front of your legs, then you need to train the back of your legs. If you train your chest, also train your back.

ALERT

The most common example of muscle imbalance is focusing on training abdominals. In order to strengthen the mid-section, it's equally important to train the muscles in back as well as in front. If you only train abdominals, you can set yourself up for injury, postural misalignment, and potential back pain.

When beginning a strength-training program it's important to assess your baseline strength levels. Focus should be placed on all of the major muscle groups including arms, shoulders, chest and upper back, abdominal and lower back, upper and lower legs. To help you move, your muscles work together. Don't just focus on sit-ups and forget everything else. Your body is only as strong as its weakest link. Train the whole picture.

CHAPTER 4
Get Ready Tips

All you need to do is take your first step. As you get started, remind yourself of these key points: think about your exercise program, educate yourself about weight training, make a commitment to yourself, learn the skill of weight training, realize that new habits take time.

Check with Your Health Care Provider

Before you begin this, or any exercise program, it's a good idea to check with your health care provider. In particular, if you have not been active, are over the age of thirty-five, or have specific medical conditions, you should consult your physician.

Specific medical conditions include:

- High blood pressure
- Heart trouble
- High cholesterol
- Family history of stroke or heart attacks
- Frequent dizzy spells
- Extreme breathlessness after mild exertion
- Arthritis or other bone problems
- Severe muscular, ligament, or tendon problems
- Obesity
- Diabetes
- Other known or suspected diseases or medical conditions, including back problems

PAR-Q and You

The following Questionnaire, known as the PAR-Q (Physical Activity Readiness Questionnaire), designed for people aged fifteen to sixty-nine, will help you determine if you may need medical supervision.

Regular physical activity is fun and healthy, and increasingly more people are starting to become more active every day. Being more active is very safe for most people. However, some people should check with their doctor before they start becoming much more physically active.

If you are planning to become much more physically active than you are now, start by answering the seven questions in the following box. If you are between the ages of fifteen and sixty-nine, the PAR-Q will tell you if you should check with your doctor before you start. If you are over sixty-nine years of age and you are not used to being very active, check with your doctor.

Check YES or NO

YES ❑　NO ❑　1. Has your doctor ever said that you have a heart condition and that you should only do physical activity recommended by a doctor?

YES ❑　NO ❑　2. Do you feel pain in your chest when you do physical activity?

YES ❑　NO ❑　3. In the past month, have you had chest pain when you were not doing physical activity?

YES ❑　NO ❑　4. Do you lose your balance because of dizziness or do you ever lose consciousness?

YES ❑　NO ❑　5. Do you have a bone or joint problem that could be made worse by a change in your physical activity?

YES ❑　NO ❑　6. Is your doctor currently prescribing drugs (for example, water pills) for your blood pressure or heart condition?

YES ❑　NO ❑　7. Do you know of *any other reason* why you should not do physical activity?

Please note: If your health changes so that you then answer "yes" to any of the PAR-Q questions, tell your fitness or health professional. Ask whether you should change your physical activity plan.

Informed Use of the PAR-Q: The Canadian Society for Exercise Physiology, Health Canada, and their agents assume no liability for persons who undertake physical activity, and if in doubt after completing this questionnaire, consult your doctor prior to physical activity.

Reprinted from the 1994 revised version of the Physical Activity Readiness Questionnaire (PAR-Q and YOU). The "PAR-Q and YOU" is a copyrighted, pre-exercise screen owned by the Canadian Society for Exercise Physiology, Inc.

If you answered yes to any questions, talk to your doctor by phone or in person *before* you start becoming much more physically active or *before* you have a fitness appraisal. Tell your doctor about the PAR-Q and which questions you answered "yes." You may be able to do any activity you want—as long as you start slowly and build up gradually. Or, you may need to restrict your activities to those that are safe for you. Talk with your doctor about the kinds of activities you wish to participate in and follow his/her advice. Find out which community programs are safe and helpful for you.

If you honestly answered no to all questions, you can be reasonably sure that you can start becoming much more physically active (beginning slowly and building up gradually is the safest and easiest way to go), and you can take part in a fitness appraisal (this is an excellent way to determine your basic fitness so that you can plan the best way for you to live actively). Delay becoming much more active if you are not feeling well because of a temporary illness such as a cold or a fever—wait until you feel better; or if you are or may be pregnant—talk to your doctor before you start becoming more active.

Ready to Go

You have a clean bill of health or you're fully informed of the specific exercise precautions that are relevant to your unique health situation. You're probably eager to start picking up those weights. Before you rush into any training setting, there are a few more items that are important for you to know.

Weight training, like any type of physical activity, has a risk of injury. Frequently remind yourself that "No pain equals no pain." You do *not* need to hurt yourself to get stronger. In fact, you should not hurt yourself. The pain of injury is a distinct sensation from the feelings of pushing yourself for a physical challenge. You'll find in this book as much information as possible to help you avoid the pain of hurting yourself. Your training program should be safe, effective, and fun.

As you train, it's important to understand the difference between "good" pain and "bad" pain. Bad pain is your body's way of letting you know that something is wrong. If you move in any way and get an immediate "stop it" response from your body, listen to it. Any type of sharp or severe pain is a signal not to continue with that movement.

"Good" pain, in contrast, is not really pain but rather the discomfort associated with fatigue. Another way to distinguish good from bad pain is that good pain tends to be a generalized feeling, rather than a specific pain. Good pain means your body is tired, because your muscles have worked hard. That is positive stress that will strengthen your body. As you grow to love and enjoy your workouts, this sense of fatigue will not even feel like pain. Instead, your muscles will feel awake and alive and glad to be used. You may even start to look forward to that feeling.

ALERT

Do not, under any circumstances, wear rubber or plastic garments when you exercise. These garments prevent the natural evaporation of perspiration that is essential to regulate your body temperature. These outfits do not enhance weight loss and are dangerous.

Dress for Weight Training Success

What you wear when you work out is important to your training success. This isn't a fashion issue, although fun clothes in bright colors may motivate you to enjoy your workouts more. It's a safety issue.

Your workout clothes should be comfortable, breathable, and should let you move freely. Whether you prefer loose clothes or more form-fitting body wear is a matter of personal preference. Body-clinging, Lycra-based clothes provide muscles with greater support and help keep muscles warm. Apparel manufacturers provide a broad selection of moisture wicking, lightweight, easy-care fabrics. Shop around to find what feels good to you.

Both women and men will experience greater exercise comfort with supportive undergarments. As you become more active and move quickly, it's important to keep sensitive body parts well supported. In other words, women should wear exercise bras and men should wear jock straps. You're much more likely to stick with your exercise program if you feel secure when you're active and comfortable when you're finished.

When you work out, your body temperature increases. Therefore, it's important to dress in layers. Wear a lightweight, short sleeved or sleeveless top and shorts, capris, pants, or leggings. Depending on the weather, you may wear a lightweight or heavyweight sweatshirt or jacket and sweatpants over your first layer. This way, as you become warmer, you can shed excess clothes and stay comfortable. When your workout is finished and you start to cool down, you can put your sweats back on again.

If you are using equipment or training in a gym, invest in a good pair of exercise shoes. Your shoes will provide you with traction and support and play an important role in injury prevention. Depending on whether or not you participate in other activities, you may want to purchase a cross-training styled shoe.

The number one consideration when buying shoes is comfort. Shoe technology is very sophisticated. Shoe models are sport specific, tailored for particular terrain and designed for different shaped feet. If you are not familiar with the specific needs of your foot, go to a reputable athletic footwear shop.

ESSENTIALS

For advice on foot conditions and the importance of the right shoes for your feet, check out The American Podiatric Medical Association Web site *(www.apma.org)*. This site has everything you would ever want to know about feet. It can even help you find a podiatrist. Remember, workout comfort starts from the ground up.

Always Warm Up

Before you pick up any weights, you need to prepare your muscles and joints. The warm-up accomplishes several purposes and prepares you physically and mentally. Use this time to transition from your daily activities to a more physical focus of being in your body and paying attention to its responses.

The most important purpose of the warm-up is to warm your body up. Take at least five to ten minutes in a rhythmic activity that engages the large muscles of your legs and torso. You want to slowly elevate your heart rate and increase the blood flow to the working muscles. Your body's temperature will increase and the increased circulation delivers important fuel to your muscles.

Examples of good warm-up activities include walking or jogging slowly, gradually increasing your speed as you feel more at ease. You can also ride a stationary bicycle, use a stairclimber or rowing machine, or jump rope. To engage the muscles of your back, shoulders, and arms, pump your arms as you move.

Joints also need to be warmed up. Move your limbs to stimulate the flow of synovial fluid that lubricates the joints. This lubrication facilitates smooth movement and reduces the risk of injury. To warm up your joints, start out with shoulder rolls. Add backstroke arm circles. Drop your arms to your sides. Gently swing your arms forward and back as you alternately squeeze your shoulder blades together in the back and squeeze your chest muscles together in the front. Release, then add some wrist circles in both directions, open and close your hands and shake out your fingers.

Your warm-up stimulates your neuromuscular system and prepares your brain for coordinated movement activities. As you start putting more mind into your muscles, you'll increase your body awareness. This heightened body awareness reduces your risk of injury. When you finish your warm-up, you should have broken into a light sweat. You should feel a greater ease of movement. Now, your body is prepared for more vigorous activity.

ALERT

As you age, you may notice that it takes a few minutes longer for you to reach that stage where you feel like your body is moving easily. That's normal. Just give yourself a few extra minutes. It will improve your enjoyment of your workout and you're less likely to injure yourself.

When it comes to stretching as part of your warm-up, this is really a matter of personal preference. Research studies have not been able to demonstrate conclusively that stretching as part of the warm-up prevents injury. Studies, however, have shown that post-workout stretching reduces muscle soreness. If you enjoy incorporating warm-up stretches, be sure not to bounce, as you risk tearing a cold muscle. Keep your stretches shorter (eight to ten seconds), since your muscles are not warm enough yet to improve flexibility and you don't want to cool down so much that you need to repeat your warm up

Start Light

When you start lifting weights, be conservative. Take your time to build strength. Especially in the beginning, you need to condition your joints. If you attempt to lift too much, you dramatically increase your risk of injury. Play it safe. You'll be able to play again tomorrow.

Slow and Controlled Movements

When you perform a movement, move with control. People who are new to weight training often use momentum to move weights. Using momentum results from building up speed by swinging your weights. Because an object in motion tends to remain in motion unless acted on by an external force, the use of speed requires less muscle control. It also makes it easier. Weight training is one of those activities where you need to pay attention so you force yourself to keep it challenging.

Focus on your goal for weight training. You're not weight training to win a prize for the number of pounds that you lift. Weight training is more process oriented. The specific number of pounds that you lift is not important. You get stronger over time. What's important is that you are able to execute your exercises in a slow and controlled manner with good posture. This is how you will improve your strength.

When you use your muscles and not momentum, you should be able to lower the weight and lift it with control. Since many movements are assisted by gravity on the way down, slow movements challenge your muscles. If you simply drop weights on the way down, you risk hurting yourself or damaging equipment—and it's painful on the eardrums.

Fast, jerky movements mean you're not maximizing your training benefits. Every minute you spend training should count. Perfect practice leads to perfect results. Take your time. Remember why you are training. Move with control. Execute your exercises smoothly through a full range of motion. Over time, you'll notice a huge difference in your body awareness and ability to control your movements. This is exciting.

The Need to Breathe

Some of you concentrate so hard, you forget to breathe. It's great that you're bringing so much mental focus to your practice. Breathing, however, is extremely important. It's one of the few things we definitely can't live without. Holding your breath can deprive your brain of precious oxygen. This can lead to fainting, which is very dangerous, especially when weight training.

Pay attention to your breathing patterns as you exercise. As a general rule of thumb, inhale to prepare and exhale on the exertion phase of your exercises. If this is too difficult to think about, simply breathe in a natural, rhythmic pattern. People tend to forget to breathe when weights are too heavy or when they are fatigued near the end of a set.

Lifting weights causes blood pressure to elevate. If this is combined with breath holding, blood pressure increases even more. When you release the weight, blood pressure drops. This rapid change can be dangerous, especially for people with chronic medical conditions such as heart disease or diabetes.

You may hear the term, "Valsalva maneuver." This refers to a technique of intentionally holding one's breath to create pressure in the chest and abdominal cavity. This pressure prevents blood from leaving the muscles. Professional weight lifters use the Valsalva maneuver to slightly increase their strength for a competitive edge. However, it is dangerous and it is not recommended.

At the same time, too much breathing is also not good. Over breathing can cause hyperventilation. This can lead to dizziness, light-headedness, and fainting. Simply breathe naturally.

Focus on Technique

Good technique when weight lifting is critical to prevent injuries. You need to be aware of your spinal alignment, movement speed, range of motion, and breathing. You need to set up your equipment properly and use all equipment as directed. All of these elements together represent good technique. It only takes a moment to get hurt. Even if you're working with a spotter or with a personal trainer, you always need to take care.

FACTS

Dehydration is defined as a 1 percent or greater loss of body weight resulting from fluid loss. Mild dehydration is a 1 percent loss, moderate is 2 to 3 percent, and severe dehydration is a loss of 4 percent or more. Early dehydration signs include fatigue, loss of appetite, flushed skin, burning in stomach, lightheadedness, headache, dry mouth, dry cough, heat intolerance, and dark urine with a strong odor.

Drink Plenty of Water

Have you ever felt tired and wilted—the way your house plants look when you forget to water them? Maybe we'd be better off if we did wilt. At least, we'd know when we're dehydrated. According to nutritionist Susan Kleiner, Ph.D., R.D., with High Performance Nutrition in Mercer Island, "Nearly one-third of the U.S. population is walking around in a state of chronic mild dehydration." All of us know that we should be drinking eight to ten cups of water a day. This is even more important as you start to increase your regular activity.

"People don't realize that they experience a normal daily turnover of fluids throughout the day. People lose water simply by breathing. If they speak for long periods of time, they're also losing fluids," explains Kleiner. Eight to ten cups is a baseline minimum amount we should replenish on a daily basis. "If a person is dehydrated up to 2 percent, a proper fluid balance can be restored by taking in fluids within six hours. Once a person is past three percent it can take up to twenty-four hours to restore balance."

Water is essential to cellular function. Water regulates body temperature, lubricates joints, assists in elimination of wastes, and protects body tissues. Approximately 60 percent of an adult's body weight is water. Of all the nutrients, water is most essential to survival. Every system in your body depends on water to function. It makes sense that systems are affected by dehydration.

When you are training, remember to carry a water bottle with you. Take small sips in between sets or when you switch exercises. Your muscles can't perform effectively if you're dehydrated. Thirst is not a good indicator of hydration. We often become thirsty far beyond the point when we should have started to replenish fluids. And, as we age our thirst mechanism loses sensitivity.

Kleiner recommends that you design a fluid plan to make sure you get your daily eight to ten cups of water.

- Measure out eight to ten cups so you can visualize the amount.
- Carry a water bottle with you all day. Know how much it holds so you know your consumption when you empty it.
- Drink bottled water in the car.
- Drink in the morning, at your desk, lunch, mid-afternoon, and at dinner.
- Carry your water bottle with you at the gym or whenever you exercise.
- For every fifteen minutes of exercise, drink one additional cup.
- If you're a skier, walker, or long distance runner, carry a back pouch with water. Regularly wash and disinfect your water bottles and pouches.

ALERT

If you drink less than two average size cups of coffee or alcoholic beverages a day, they can count as part of your daily water. If you drink more than two cups, drink one cup of water for every additional cup of coffee or alcohol.

Stretch and Cool Down

After weight training, thoroughly stretch the areas you've challenged. This increases blood flow to the area and stimulates the muscle recovery and repair process. Research studies demonstrate that post-workout stretching helps to prevent or minimize muscle soreness after exercise. Stretching also relieves feelings of muscle tension and increases feelings of well-being.

Additional Safety Tips for Exercise on Machines

When training, keep in mind the following tips to ensure that your workout is safe and effective.

Proper fit—When you use weight machines for the first time, if you're in a gym, be sure to get an equipment orientation from weight training staff. Most machines have numerous adjustments to account for your height, limb lengths, and thickness of your chest. Take advantage of these opportunities to create the best possible fit for your body. In some cases, when people are particularly small or large, it may not be possible to achieve a good fit. Don't risk any injury to yourself by trying to adapt to a piece of equipment that is simply not designed to accommodate your body type.

Use seat belts—Many machines have seat belts to provide greater stability when performing movements. Use the seat belts if they come with the equipment. If the seat belts are not large enough, feel free to ask if they can obtain an extender. It's always better to be safe.

Using free weights—When you work out with free weights, you need to use more of your body's smaller stabilizer muscles to maintain proper form. Balance and control are particularly important. It's always a good idea to be conservative as you train. Do not attempt to work with weights that are too heavy. If you are in doubt about the proper form for any exercise, always ask or check your book.

Working with a spotter—When you work with very heavy weights or when you are brand new to weight training, it's a good idea to work with a spotter. A spotter watches you as you perform your exercise and is ready to grab the weight and provide assistance if you are unable to control it. If you work out with a personal trainer, he or she will spot you. Or, if you train with a buddy, you can spot each other.

Avoid overtraining—Take your time. Progress your program conservatively. Give your body time to adapt to new stresses.

CHAPTER 5

Measure Your Progress and Set Goals

There are as many ways to measure your progress as there are reasons for wanting to exercise. It's important that you find a method of assessment of your program that reflects both your goals and what motivates you to want to achieve those goals. Take a look at the choices that are provided and decide what works best for you.

Get a Fitness Appraisal

If you have been cleared for exercise by your health care provider, it's a good idea to have a fitness appraisal, to get some baseline information. This is the easiest way for you to gather information about where you are in your current level of conditioning. You can use this information to plan your exercise program, as well as to measure your progress. If you work with a personal trainer, your trainer can use this information to design a program for you.

You can have a fitness appraisal or assessment performed at a health and fitness facility or you can also gather and record your own data. This information may include:

- Resting heart rate
- Blood pressure
- Height and weight
- Waist measurement
- Hip to waist ratio
- Body mass index

- Body composition
- Aerobic capacity or maximum VO_2
- Muscular strength
- Muscular endurance
- Flexibility

Not all of these data points are essential. The fitness appraisal does not need to be a judgmental session, nor is it designed to demoralize you. The value it provides is that you have a baseline from which to evaluate your on-going progress. If you want to collect this information on your own, that's fine, too. You don't need to record every data point, simply some parameters that can help you monitor your progress.

If the thought of weighing and measuring yourself doesn't feel like a good idea, then by all means don't do it. You will soon enough be aware of any physical changes in your body's tone, shape, or size by how your clothes fit. Some changes that may occur physiologically as you continue your exercise program include resting heart rate, blood pressure, and blood cholesterol levels. These are real indicators of improvement in your overall health as well. If you fall into a category of people who should see their health care provider before they start an exercise program, be sure to ask your physician for a copy of this information for your own reference. After you've been training for at least two months, you can check this information again. You may already be able to see changes for the better!

Ask Yourself How You Feel

Part of the process of getting and staying in shape includes increasing your body awareness. What exactly is body awareness? Some people would define it as knowing where your body is in space. Others would consider body awareness to be the ability to use the muscles of your body by concentrating on contracting and releasing a muscle and getting your body to respond.

Body awareness is more than simply a physical experience. Body awareness is an integration of mind, body, and spirit. It comes with learning to listen to your inner voice. Your body has an innate knowledge and wisdom that wants to be acknowledged.

As you start to physically assess your body's strengths and weaknesses, it's a great time to begin this inner dialogue with your own body's wisdom. The following questions can serve as a great starting point to begin your conversation with your body.

Questions to Ask Yourself

1. What is your energy level? Have you noticed that you feel more tired than you would like to feel? If yes, what are some of the activities that you do regularly that cause you to notice that you lack energy? For example, do you need to sit down frequently? Are you able to run simple errands without feeling exhausted? Can you walk up a flight of stairs without feeling winded? How would you describe the feeling of being fit and energetic? How would that feel to you?
2. Do you want to increase your activity level? If yes, why?
3. Do you have a specific activity that you want to be able to do when you are "fit"? If yes, what is that activity and why is being able to do that important to you? If no, what are some things you can think about now that you would really enjoy being able to do and that represent fitness to you?

4. What do you think about your nutritional habits? If you think that they can be improved, are you ready to make some efforts to learn about nutrition and change your habits? If yes, why?
5. How do you feel about your current level of flexibility? If you feel tight, are you willing to make some time in your day to fit in stretching? What times of day would work best in your schedule to add some stretches?

After you complete this process, you may be surprised by some of the things that you learn. Some women discover that even though they thought what they wanted was to be a size four or six, what they really wanted was to have that feeling of energy and aliveness that they remember from their youth. Some men discover that it's time for a reality check. When you realize that what you really want is to simply feel good when you play a game of pick-up basketball with some friends, then you will know it when you get there.

Exercises to Measure Your Progress

Before you start doing any exercises, be sure to take the PAR-Q (Physical Activity Readiness Questionnaire) in Chapter 4. If you're ready to begin, the following exercises can provide a quantitative measure for you to compare your gains in strength. For best results, do not repeat these tests more frequently than once every two months. You need to give your body some time to improve.

Measure Your Endurance: Walking Test

EQUIPMENT Stop watch or watch.

GET READY Go to a local indoor or outdoor track where you can measure how far you walk. If you don't know the exact distance, that's okay. You can measure your progress in terms of laps.

ACTION Click the stop watch or note the time on your watch and begin walking. If you don't use a stop watch, it helps to start at an easily remembered point, such as on the hour, quarter hour, or half hour. Walk comfortably for ten minutes. If you are not used to walking vigorously, do not push yourself. Simply walk at a comfortable pace.

MEASUREMENTS At the end of ten minutes, notice how many laps you have walked. Note it down for future reference.

VARIATIONS If you want to increase the time of the test, that is okay. Another way to perform this measurement is to go by distance rather than time. Rather than walking for ten minutes, you can choose to walk four laps or you can walk one mile. Whatever method you choose is fine. Be cautious not to push yourself too hard if you are new to exercise.

TIPS You can also check your heart rate at the end of the walk. Keep your feet moving and take your pulse as explained in Chapter 14. After one minute has passed, repeat taking your pulse. Note down both figures. As you improve you may see reductions in your overall heart rate as well as a more rapid recovery rate after one minute.

Measure Your Upper Body Strength: Push-Ups

EQUIPMENT Exercise mat or none if done on a comfortable carpeted surface.

GET SET Kneel on all fours on the floor. Walk your hands forward until your hands are slightly wider than shoulder width apart and your torso resembles a slanted board. Engage your abdominal muscles. Maintain neutral alignment. If you prefer, you can select another variation, depending on your current level of strength.

ACTION Straighten your arms and push your body up through your palms. Keep your shoulders relaxed. Maintain neutral alignment.

MEASUREMENTS Count as you perform as many push-ups as you can with complete range of motion. When you can no longer maintain form, that repetition does not count. Record the number of push-ups, as well as the style of push-up that you did. When you repeat the test, be sure to use the same style. For example, if you did wall push-ups, repeat the test with wall push-ups.

VARIATIONS (EASIER) If it is not comfortable for you to kneel on the floor, you can perform this exercise against a wall. Stand in front of a wall. Place hands on wall slightly wider than shoulder width apart. Bend elbows and lower body towards wall. Straighten arms as you push through hands.

(EASIER) On floor, instead of working from a slanting board position, kneel on all fours. Lower your chest towards the floor by bending your elbows. Adjust the amount of load by shifting more or less weight from your knees into your hands.

(HARDER) On floor, instead of working from a slanting board position, extend your legs long and rest on the balls of your feet, so your body resembles a plank.

TIPS Inhale to prepare, exhale as you push up. Inhale, return to start. Place a towel under your palms to elevate palms and reduce pressure on your wrists.

To reduce pressure on your wrists, hold on to dumbbells that rest on the floor. Avoid dropping your head. Your push-up should not resemble a nose dive. Avoid locking your elbows when you lift. Lower as low as possible.

Measure Your Abdominal and Core Strength: Sit-Ups

EQUIPMENT Exercise mat or none if done on a comfortable carpeted surface, watch, clock, or timer.

GET READY Lie on your back on the floor with your knees bent at approximately a 90-degree angle and your feet flat on the floor. Place the palms of your hands flat on your thighs. Tuck your chin in slightly.

ACTION Set the timer for one minute. If you're not using a timer, watch a clock that you can see easily, or use a watch. Start at the beginning of a minute if you are using a second hand to measure time. Count each complete repetition as you slide your palms towards your knees as you roll your body up. Make sure that your fingertips come to the top of your knee before you go back down. It helps if you count out loud.

MEASUREMENTS At the end of one minute, notice how many sit-ups you have completed. Note it down for future reference.

TIPS Exhale on your way up, inhale on your way down. This style of sit-up is not recommended for training purposes. It is useful, however, as a general measure of endurance. This style of sit-up uses a lot of hip flexor muscles as well as abdominal muscles so it's not a true test of abdominal endurance, but rather a measure of the combination of muscles.

Measure Your Flexibility: Sit and Reach

EQUIPMENT   An exercise mat, masking tape, and a yardstick.

GET READY   Use the masking tape to tape the yardstick lengthwise in the center of the exercise mat right across the 15-inch mark. The masking tape should run over the width of the mat and secure the yardstick in place. Take off your shoes. Sit on the mat with your legs stretched out in front of you. Place your heels on the edge of the tape right at the 15-inch marking.

ACTION   Relax your shoulders. Place one hand on top of the other. Place the palm of the bottom hand on top of the yardstick. Take a nice deep breath. As you exhale, lean forward from your hips and slide the palm of your bottom hand forward along the mat along the yardstick.

MEASUREMENTS   Make three attempts. Each time, note how far the farthest tip of your finger made it on the yardstick. Record the best score out of your three attempts.

TIPS   Stay relaxed. If you feel tension on the tops of your thighs, go ahead and bend your knees slightly. If you find that you are feeling tight, start a thorough stretching program to accompany your weight training. Not only will you be stronger, but you'll also feel longer.

RECORD YOUR PROGRESS

TEST		DATE	DATE	DATE
Endurance	# of laps = in 10 minutes			
Push-Ups	# of push-ups = total, note style			
Sit-Ups	# of sit-ups = in 1 minute			
Flexibility	yardstick measure =			

Record Your Weight Loads

Some of you may not need elaborate tests to measure your progress. For you, it may be as simple as keeping track of how much weight you are lifting from week to week. The best way to monitor this is by either keeping a log or recording it right in your daily calendar or your PDA. Whatever your mode of technology or data collection and storage, the important point is to keep track of information that is meaningful to you.

ESSENTIALS

If you're the type of person who gets motivated and inspired by visibly seeing your improved physical achievements, then write down your test scores. If you would rather know exactly how much you bench press on any given week, then find a handy and convenient way to watch this information.

Setting Goals

Many people set unrealistic, unreasonable goals. Some people want to lose 30 pounds in three weeks. Others want to run a marathon in two months, when they haven't laid a proper training foundation. It would be great if after you got stronger, you trained and ran in your first marathon. But that's not the point of this book.

Here's the point. Ultimately, you don't have control over your body shape or type (barring plastic surgery, of course). You don't have control over your genetic gifts or pre-disposition. You can't stop the clock. We're all getting older each and every day. And wiser too, I hope.

What you can do, however, is to try to be the best with what you've got. Each morning when you wake up, you have a fresh opportunity to make your day work for you. Every day, you have chances to choose activity over sitting on the sofa and to select foods that will enhance your health. You can make your best efforts to incorporate exercise into your lifestyle in the best balance that you can with all your many other competing demands.

You can work each day towards healthy habits. You can drink plenty of fluids. Try to eat more fruits and vegetables. Walk as much as possible. Take stretching breaks during the day. Make an effort to manage stress in your life. Learn about fitness and health. Develop friendships and support systems with people who share your interest in a healthy and positive life.

When you set goals, think about what those goals mean to you. Next time, when you consider your goals, even as they relate to your fitness and health, think about what it really is that you want from your life. Do you really want washboard abs? What do you think your life will be like if you had them? Pretend you have a personal genie and your wish is granted. You have the washboard abs you've yearned for. What is your life like?

Are more people attracted to you? Are they attracted to you because of your physical self or do they admire the person you are, your inner self? Okay, so you want to be a sex object. That's fine. But, be clear about why you want what you want and what it is you think it will bring to you. Life as a sex object may not be the wild fantasy you've yearned for. Or, maybe it will be . . . you are ultimately the best judge of that.

Maybe it will be enough for you to do your best to incorporate at least one healthy habit into your day each day. As your energy levels increase and you start to enjoy the feeling of simply being alive, maybe that will be your reward. As you can enjoy playing with children or helping people in your community or even enjoying a hike with your spouse or friends, maybe that can feel good too.

Think about it. If you set a goal to do at least one healthful thing for yourself each day, it will make a difference. And, it may also make a meaningful difference to the people who love you and want you also to live a long and healthy life. And, it may be realistic and achievable for you today.

Okay. So you still want washboard abs.

Overcoming Excuses

"If you say you don't have enough time to exercise, you're not alone," says Jack Raglin, Ph.D., Associate Professor in the Department of

Kinesiology at Indiana University in Bloomington, Indiana, who specializes in research on exercise behavior.

FACTS

Studies show that the typical drop-out rate from a new exercise program is 50 percent, and it usually occurs in the first six to eight weeks. Most participants say they quit because of lack of time. But a study of prison inmates who were introduced to a new exercise program showed the same drop-out rate. "Since the prisoners had time to exercise, what can we learn from this?" asks Jack Raglin. "It's very difficult to make a long-term behavioral change."

The first tip on how to succeed with your exercise program is to start thinking about it. Secondly, start thinking about the benefits you will receive from exercise. Numerous research studies show that moderate activity improves health, sleep, mood, and helps fight stress. The ACSM and the CDC recommend a minimum of thirty minutes of accumulated activity on most days of the week to realize these health benefits. For example, you can add up three ten-minute walks over the course of one day to get your total of thirty minutes.

You also need to think about living an active lifestyle, instead of thinking that only a formal exercise program will make you fit and strong. That doesn't mean your workout program isn't important, because it is. What it does mean is that your workout program should fit into the larger context of your active living. Think about living actively throughout your day and you will reap many benefits.

Daily life offers lots of opportunities for increasing your activity. Take stairs instead of the elevator or escalator. Park farther away from the store and walk across the parking lot. Get up from your desk and go to a coworker's desk to deliver a message instead of sending an e-mail. Walk briskly around the office. Send your papers to a printer that's far away. Use the restrooms on the other side of the building. Essentially, take advantage of every opportunity you have to move during the day.

"It's important to make being active a part of your life, not a segregated activity that requires a big change of routine," says Raglin. "Something is always better than nothing," says Jennifer Dodge from the Cooper Institute. You can make the choice to have activity in your life—and it's easier than you think. Next time, get up from your chair to change channels. Every step makes a difference. After all, if you can bench press your spouse's weight, you can certainly change channels. Consider it.

Staying Motivated When Everything Falls Apart

Many people think that if they lose their momentum and miss workouts, they might as well quit entirely. No! That's not true. It's okay to miss your workouts. Life happens. It's important to accept that. What makes "falling off the wagon" part of your success story is taking the time to learn why.

What does that mean? It means taking the time to evaluate why your well-intentioned plans to start exercising have gone astray. What was it that got in the way of your plans? What are your personal barriers to doing what it is you want to do?

Are your plans too ambitious? Or, are you not really committed to your goal? What is it that you want to achieve from your weight training? How important is it to you to achieve your weight training goals? What are you willing to give up in order to receive those benefits?

By learning about yourself during the process of working on your weight training goals, you will define your own way to success. Everything that you learn about yourself is valuable. Each time you miss your workouts, see it as an opportunity to learn about why that schedule didn't work for you. Think about solutions that will work.

Each time you make an effort to integrate more exercise into your lifestyle, you learn. Over time, you will strike success! The secret to success is to keep trying. Don't give up. You can do it.

Don't Beat Yourself up, Get Pumped Instead

What should you do if you notice none of your plans to exercise ever seem to work? Brainstorm all the things that come up. For example, you may have to work late, or you have to watch the kids, or you need to go shopping. Note whatever it is that comes up that ends up taking over your scheduled workout time.

Evaluate whether your strength training workout plan is too cumbersome for your lifestyle. Maybe it's simply not realistic for you to go to a gym two nights a week.

Develop your "Plan B," for those times when you can't do your original "Plan A". Then go ahead and plan on doing Plan B. It's probably a more realistic match for your lifestyle.

Don't give up when your best plans don't work out. Use these experiences as precious opportunities for you to learn more about what will work for your lifestyle. By learning what realistically works for you, you increase your ultimate odds of reaching your goals successfully.

Don't beat yourself up. Pump yourself up! You simply don't have any time to waste in self-criticism. You're losing precious minutes from your workout. Get on with the program. Let go of what didn't work for you yesterday. You'll soon be finding a scheme for a stronger you, tomorrow.

Professional Coaching

If you find it challenging to take the time to evaluate how your training goals fit into your overall life plan, you may want to consult a professional coach. Today, professional lifestyle coaches work with clients to help them identify priorities and evaluate how to achieve personal and professional goals. Taking advantage of this type of resource can enhance your success in fulfilling your goals.

CHAPTER 6

Weight Training Etiquette

Weight training, like other activities, has a code of conduct. When you are new to the gym environment, you may feel awkward and not sure of what you should or shouldn't do. For the most part, basic principles of courtesy remain the same. The bottom line is that you should remember that an exercise facility is a space that you share with other participants.

Maximize Your Exercise Experience

Peak times for most exercise centers include early morning from opening until 10 A.M. Some facilities may have a busy noon crowd. The evening rush doesn't start picking up until after 4 P.M., with peak usage usually between 5:30 and 8:30 P.M. Each organization may have slightly different usage patterns depending on whether it's located in a business or residential area and whether it serves families or adults only. It's always a good idea to ask staff when are the busy and quiet times.

One way to avoid crowds is to schedule your workouts at nonpeak times. In addition, some health and fitness clubs offer reduced membership rates for people who use the club during slow times, such as between the hours of 10 A.M. and 2 P.M.

Take an Equipment Orientation if Available

Most gyms offer a weight training room orientation for beginners. Even if you have some prior experience with machines or with training, it's a good idea to take the orientation as equipment provided by various manufacturers may have some subtle differences.

Exercise clothes need to be washed after each workout. You may not be aware of your personal body odor, but others can sense it. Bacteria also collect in unwashed clothing. Practicing good personal hygiene habits is not only courteous to your fellow members, but also can help prevent skin irritation and infections.

Do Not Wear Scented Products

When you exercise, your body temperature rises. This will amplify the intensity of any scented products you are wearing, such as heavy perfumes, colognes, or aftershave. If you're accustomed to the smell, you may not notice the strength of the odor. Many people, especially those with allergies, can be very sensitive to these smells. Please be considerate and try to wear unscented products in the gym.

Bring a Towel

When you exercise on equipment, you don't want to sit in someone else's sweat. As a courtesy, place a towel on equipment before you sit or lie down to absorb sweat from your body. After you get up, wipe down equipment before you move on to your next exercise. Some facilities even provide spray cleaner and towels for this purpose.

If you forget to bring a towel, use your sweatshirt or sweatpants to absorb your perspiration. If you don't have sweats, you can ask whether or not the staff have paper towels for this purpose. Make the effort to be considerate to other users of the equipment. Treat it as you wish someone would treat it for you. Your consideration will be appreciated and hopefully will come back around for you.

Don't Carry Your Gym Bag

By now you're getting the picture that a weight training room is busy, crowded and filled with people who have a purpose. Anything that interferes with this purpose should be avoided. When you are working out in the training room, all you need to carry with you is your towel and a water bottle (and your list if you're still trying to remember your exercises). Leave your gym bag in your locker. Hopefully, you have a combination lock, so you don't even need to carry a key.

Some gyms won't allow you to even bring a gym bag into the weight room. Others provide cubbies along the wall for you to store your gym bag while you exercise. Since you don't need it, why bring it at all?

Share the Drinking Fountain

Many people may be hot, sweaty, and thirsty in the training room. A refreshing sip of water may be just the antidote. When it's your turn at the fountain, get your drink quickly and move on.

If you need to catch your breath first, wait until you're ready to drink before you go to the fountain. If your water bottle is empty and people are waiting behind you, it's not necessary to fill it to the top. And, if one of your best friends shows up just as you're about to take a sip . . . sip, then visit, away from the fountain.

If you need to spit something out, do not use the drinking fountain. One would think that this goes without saying. And, since you're already considerate enough to take time to read about weight training etiquette, you're not likely to ever do such a thing. But, it does happen, so it bears mentioning. The drinking fountain is for drinking. Everyone shares it. Remember the Golden Rule and you will be fine.

Be Efficient

If you exercise at peak times, the weight training room is likely to be busy. Many people want to use the equipment. It's important to be efficient with your time. When you get to a machine, adjust your weights, execute your reps, and move on to the next piece of equipment.

When you first start training, it's a good idea to take a list of your exercises with you to the different stations. You can annotate your list with the name of the piece of equipment, the amount of weight that you lift, and what adjustments you make for bench height or leg length. Over time, you'll memorize your personal settings. In the beginning, however, it can be almost an overwhelming amount of information. Better to carry a list with you so you can quickly adjust your machines and get in and out.

If you do more than one set at a particular exercise station, someone else may ask to "work in" with you. "Working in" involves sharing equipment between the two of you as you alternate sets and rest periods. When one of you works, the other rests, and vice versa. This works best if you both lift the same amount of weight and are approximately the same size. When you finish your set, get up. The next person "works in" and performs their set. Then, you return to complete your additional set.

This can be an efficient way to work out, especially if you have an exercise buddy who is working at approximately the same level that you work. If you are about the same size, you may not need to readjust the equipment each time for seat height and leg length. Instead, you can both use the same settings. And, you can spot each other while you rest.

If someone is waiting patiently for you to finish, remember you can always offer that they share or "work in" with you. They may decline. However, both of you are likely to feel better knowing that you were considerate enough to notice. This is an example of good gym etiquette and a way to make friends as you workout.

Watch Your Step

People can get injured in a weight training room. It's important to pay attention at all times, both to yourself and to others. Watch where you are moving. Be mindful not to bump into others or into machines when people are performing exercises. This can cause serious accidents.

If you feel that equipment is placed too closely together and you can't navigate comfortably between machines, mention it to staff immediately. When you make constructive comments to staff, a helpful approach will generally result in an appreciative response for your concern. If you "attack" the staff with critical comments, they may become defensive and not receive the benefit of hearing the true value of what you are trying to offer.

It's helpful to remember that fitness facility staff are in a customer service role at all times. Often, they enjoy people and that's why they're in that position. But, they sometimes do get bombarded with negative comments. If you also remember to share your positive observations about the good things you experience and appreciate about the facility, you're likely to cultivate a better relationship with staff over time.

ESSENTIALS

Club staff are there to help you. But, your attitude in how you approach them can also make a big difference in the kind of service that you receive. As part of being a member of a weight training community, remember that it's nice to be polite and respectful to everyone. It's likely to come back to you tenfold.

Don't Block Access to Machines

In most fitness facilities, space is at a premium. Managers are constantly evaluating more efficient uses of space and how to fit in new pieces of equipment. If you create a gathering of people who are not exercising, this disrupts the movement flow in the room.

Furthermore, if you block an aisle and someone scoots around you to get to equipment, they may move dangerously close to someone who is exercising. If they bump a machine or someone's weight, this can distract the person who is training. Even a slight loss of attention can cause a serious injury when weights are involved. Therefore, remember, it's wonderful to visit with your friends, just take it outside of the training room and out of the way of other people. Safety always needs to come first.

Keep Loud Noises to a Minimum

A weight training room can be a noisy place simply from the commotion of active bodies, moving machinery, conversation, and background music or television. Try to keep additional sounds to a minimum. Avoid dropping weight stacks with a loud clang. Not only is this lack of control dangerous, it can harm equipment, as well as distress the eardrums.

When you lower your weights, use your muscles to control the movement against gravity. Weight training is not just the lifting part, it's also the lowering segment. Exercise smooth movements and gently lower your weights.

It's acceptable to make motivational grunts as you expel air and contract your abdominal muscles in the execution phase of your movements. However, there's a difference between a strong exhalation and shouting. Please exercise discretion, as well as your muscles.

Spot Check

Before you lift a weight, make sure that you will not hit anyone around you. If you hit someone, you may injure both yourself as well as the other party. Always take a moment to look all around you before you move. Be sure to take into account the full length of your limbs as well as some safety space beyond.

Unload the Weights

When you finish your last rep on a weight machine, simply pull out the pin from your weight stack. I'll never forget the time when one petite woman got on a machine, put in a pin and announced that the machine was broken. (She couldn't make it budge.) On closer inspection, we realized a very strong man had left a pin at the very bottom of the stack. It was easy to overlook. Remember to be courteous. Simply leave the machine unloaded for the next person to set up.

This rule applies even more when you use weight plates to load up a barbell or dumbbells. This weight can be too much for the next lifter. Never make the assumption that you are the weakest person in the weight room, even if you feel that way sometimes.

Many health care providers are recommending that their frail, elderly patients start weight training programs. And, fortunately for them, many older adults are hitting the weight rooms. It's great! So, make it possible for everyone to get the workout that they need by being considerate enough to unload your weights.

"Rack" Your Weights

When you're finished with your dumbbells or have removed your weight plates, return them to their relative racks. Weight racks are usually organized with the lightest weights on top to the heaviest on the bottom. Return items you use to their appropriate place. Next time, it will be easy to find what you want.

Besides, it's extra exercise to carry them back to the weight rack and put them away. Isn't that the reason you're in the weight training room in the first place? Always look for those extra opportunities to move your body more. It all counts as exercise. Remember to get out of energy conservation mode. As an added plus, your fellow gym mates will appreciate your consideration.

Should I bring my children along on my workout?
If you are a parent and want to work out, do not bring along your child to watch. Many exercise clubs have child care centers. If this is important to you, be sure to look for this service when you select which club to join.

Locker Room Etiquette

For the uninitiated, your first locker room experiences may bring back all those insecurities that you experienced during PE classes as a kid.

Here are some basic do's and don'ts so you can navigate the locker room and not make any enemies in the process.

Don't . . .

- Hog more than one locker.
- Spread your things all over the place. Keep yourself contained in front of one locker.
- Block aisles or pathways where people need to travel. If you require ambulatory assistance such as a walker or crutches, try to travel towards one side of the space provided so that others can move around you.
- Bring food, leave food, or throw away food in the locker room if you can avoid it. It can attract ants and other pests.
- Offer your unsolicited opinions in other people's conversations.
- Watch when other people weigh themselves.
- Leave your used towels lying around wherever you feel like it.
- Shed your hair everywhere. If you have long hair, collect it and throw it away. Don't leave it to clog drains and cover counters.
- Leave empty shampoo bottles and old razors in the shower stall.
- Exercise in the locker room. Use the exercise facilities for your workout. The locker room is for changing pre- and post-workout.
- Let your children run around or talk loudly.
- Get involved in a confrontation with another gym member. If someone creates a dispute with you, get away from the situation as quickly as you can and go speak directly to management.

Do . . .

- Use one locker.
- Respect other people's need for space.
- Take a brief, efficient shower if people are waiting.
- Dry yourself off as well as you can in the shower area before you walk into the changing area. This helps keep the floors dry for everyone in the changing rooms.
- Clean up after yourself in the shower or at the counter.
- Speak softly among your friends or on the cell phone.
- Supervise your children and keep them orderly and well behaved.
- Report to management any confrontational individuals.
- Report to management any suspicious-looking people who seem to be going through other people's things or who are not actively engaged in either getting ready to work out or getting back to their daily business.
- Have social conversations away from areas such as aisles where people need to travel.

Any time after you've been in a public place, it's always a good idea to wash your hands with soap and warm water. This is even more important after you use gym equipment that is shared by many people.

Fight Germs at the Gym

Regular exercise is a great way to reduce winter colds. Research suggests that active people have fewer colds than your typical couch potato. Everyone benefits from managing exposure to germs at the gym. Here are some tips on cold prevention:

Wipe down equipment. Good gym etiquette requires that you spray down equipment before and after you use it. It's also a great way to prevent transmitting germs. Most gyms stock spray cleaners just for this purpose. Help yourself to the supplies and help prevent the spread of viruses.

Carry antibacterial wipes. You can buy great antibacterial cleansers these days at most grocery and drug stores. In case you can't find the gym supplies, carry your own handy tissue sized wipes to clean off equipment. Most colds are spread through the hands so clean all the surfaces you plan to touch.

The Well-Equipped Gym Bag

Emerging fresh and well groomed after your workout requires bringing the right items in your gym bag. Here are a few essentials, as well as some optional items depending on your personal needs.

ESSENTIALS	OPTIONAL
ID tag for your gym bag	Blow dryer
Body lotion	Anti-frizz hair cream
Shampoo	Shoe bag
Conditioner	Make up
Razor	Powder
Deodorant	Skin toner
Comb	Cotton swabs
Brush	Cotton balls or pads
Shower shoes	Nail file
Plastic bag for dirty gym clothes	Clear nail polish
Sunscreen	Bandages
Liquid soap	Antibiotic cream
Face lotion	Hair clip
Post workout snack	Athlete's foot lotion
	Hand or workout towel
	Bath towel
	Combination lock for your locker
	Feminine supplies

CHAPTER 7

Understanding Weight Training Equipment

Selecting the right tools from the variety of weight training equipment is an intimidating task. Dumbbells, barbells, machines, cables, bands, tubes, and every other type of miraculous body-altering device all compete for your attention and dollars. The purpose of this chapter is to demystify the selection process.

The Purpose of Equipment

Weight training requires that you provide enough resistance to your muscles to create overload. This stress stimulates your muscles to respond by becoming stronger. Your body responds to whatever is used to create resistance to movement. For example, your muscles don't know the difference between lifting a dumbbell, a container filled with sand or water, or a grocery bag of the same weight. Your muscles simply respond to the fact that they're being challenged. Early Greek records describe a famous strength athlete who used a growing heifer to display his weight lifting prowess. As the calf matured, it gained weight. The weight lifter continued to lift the heifer until, at four years of age, it became so heavy that it was no longer possible. This is one method of progressive resistance training. It's clearly, however, not the most convenient equipment choice, especially if you don't live on a cattle farm.

Equipment Choices

Today, you can work with a variety of equipment to achieve the same experience. The most common weight training tools include free weights, machines, and rubber props. You may also use your own body weight as resistance. Bodyweight exercises have the added benefit of complete portability. In other words, you have no excuses not to do bodyweight resistance exercises since you can do them anywhere and at any time. And, you can't beat the free price.

FACTS

Balls and balance boards not only challenge your strength, but also require you to practice your balance. Research shows that our sense of balance begins to decline after age thirty. Unless we actively practice, we can lose muscle control over our balance. Since falls represent a particularly high cause of injury among older adults, it makes sense to include balance exercises in your program.

Free Weights

Free weights are metal bars with weights on both ends. These weights are either permanently attached or can be added and adjusted. Free weights include dumbbells and barbells. Dumbbells are held in one hand and can be used singly or in pairs. A barbell is a long bar that is held with both hands.

Dumbbells and barbells are called "free" weights because your body is free to determine the movement pattern that you perform when you use the weights. Machines, on the other hand, put your body into a specific position to target particular muscles. Free weights, combined with the force of gravity, simply provide resistance. You choose the movement.

To progressively increase resistance, you can use pre-molded weights of increasing size. Or, if you are using adjustable weights, you can add plates in different weight increments. The plates are affixed with collars at the end of the bars to prevent them from falling off. Plates range in weight starting as low as 2½ pounds each up to 100 pounds. Plates are usually stored on vertical racks with the lightest weights on top and heaviest weights on the bottom. Weights of the same amount are meant to be grouped together. Depending on how courteous your gym mates are, you may or may not find them this way.

Dumbbells

In the gym, dumbbells typically come in predetermined weight increments. "Hex head" dumbbells have hexagonal ends to prevent the weights from rolling.

One of the advantages of dumbbells is that you train each arm independently. You will immediately become aware of strength imbalances between your right and left sides of your body. Ideally, you want to improve the strength of your nondominant side. Remember, your body is only as strong as its weakest link. Using dumbbells will highlight some of these muscular imbalances and help you to address them.

Another advantage with dumbbells is that you have more freedom to alter your body position. For example, when you are doing a biceps curl, you can turn your palms in if you're holding dumbbells. This is not possible with a barbell. Therefore, you can do a greater variety of exercises with dumbbells.

For home use, you may prefer to get adjustable dumbbells. A personal favorite set is chrome with a variety of weight plates. You can adjust the weight plates to change the heaviness and only have one set of bars. This is more time consuming. However, it requires less storage space and is lighter to transport, relative to a full set of barbells and molded dumbbells.

Barbells

In the gym, you may have a selection of barbells from which to choose. A bar has a collar and a lock on each end. You slide the weight plate against the collar. You secure the weight plate with the lock. The bar alone with collars and locks can weigh anywhere from 25 to 45 pounds. A typical bar with collars and locks weighs approximately 5 pounds per foot. Therefore, a 5-foot bar weighs 25 pounds, a 6-foot bar 30 pounds, and a 7-foot bar 35 pounds.

The Olympic bar, however, is an exception to this rule. An Olympic bar is 7-feet long and weighs 45 pounds without locks. You can use a variety of locks with the Olympic bar with a weight range of less than one pound to 5 pounds each. A fully loaded Olympic bar can weigh as much as 55 pounds with locks. This is before any weight plates are added. With weight plates, an Olympic bar can hold more than 700 pounds.

You may also see a wavy looking **W**-shaped bar in the gym. This is called a "cambered curl" bar or simply a "curl" bar. The purpose for the waves is not only to give you special handles to hold. By positioning your hands at an angle you can isolate certain muscle groups more effectively. In particular, you can use these barbells to strengthen your biceps and triceps more comfortably.

Similar to dumbbells, barbells come in fixed weights or allow for adjustment by adding weight plates. When you're working with adjustable weights, it's critically important that you know how to properly load your bar. Not only must the weight be even on both sides, but the weight plates must be appropriately placed. In addition, collars and locks need to be secure. If a lock is not fastened properly, plates can fall off and hurt you, others, or equipment and furnishings around you.

Although it's true that dumbbells permit more movement variety, barbells provide extra stability. With enhanced stability, you can lift heavier amounts of weight. For example, when you decide to do a bench press, which is a weightlifting classic, you can lift a heavier amount of weight with a barbell than you can with a dumbbell in each hand.

Dumbbells Versus Barbells

Dumbbells offer:

- More freedom of movement
- More exercise variety
- Independent training of each side of the body
- Great versatility for at-home workouts
- Easy storage

While barbells offer:

- Greater stability
- Ability to lift heavier weight
- Stronger side may compensate for weaker side

Machines

Weight machines position your body to target specific muscles. The machine supports your body and only permits certain movement patterns. This reduces the likelihood of improper movements that increase the risk of injury. Weight machines can provide either fixed resistance or variable resistance. Machines can use weight plates or hydraulic or air pressure, and can be manually or electronically controlled. Some machines, like the Smith machine, blend features of free weights and machines.

Note that this book concentrates on teaching you how to weight-train without machines. For proper usage of gym machines, talk to your personal trainer or weight room supervisor.

Fixed Resistance Weight Stack Machines

A weight stack machine features a stack of rectangular weight plates, generally in 10- or 20-pound increments. Sometimes you can find 5-pound plates, if a 10-pound increase is too large a jump. After you adjust the equipment, you select the weight you want to lift by placing a metal pin under the plate that represents the total amount that you want to lift. For example, you place your pin under the fourth plate if you want to lift 40 pounds.

ALERT

Some pins require that you push a button in the center to remove it. Others simply require a good tug. Some pins slide straight in between the weights. Others are inserted at an angle. Make sure you pay attention to how the pins are removed and inserted.

Pins seem to have a life of their own and wander off in search of adventure when they are bored. For years teaching my circuit weight training class, we could never figure out where they went. If you cannot find a pin, check with a staff member. It's not a good idea to take one from another piece of equipment, unless it is by the same manufacturer. It may not work. You don't want the weight stack to slam down in mid-lift to surprise you and notify everyone else in the gym.

You may notice an interesting phenomenon when you use fixed resistance weight stack machines. As you lift your weight, some aspects of the movement arc require more effort than other aspects. It's almost as if the weight changes as you move it. For example, at the beginning of lifting a 40-pound weight stack, you will be moving 40 pounds. Towards the end of the lift, however, it will feel much lighter.

What is really happening is that the weight stack moves in relationship to the pivot point, resulting in a change in the required amount of effort to move the weight. In other words, as the weight stack moves, it changes the leverage required. A fixed resistance machine, therefore, does not challenge your muscles with a consistent level of resistance through the full range of motion. Once you are past the "sticking point," you are no longer lifting maximal resistance.

A typical multi-station weight machine will feature a square center with weight plates and stations on each side of the square. All the weight stacks and pulleys are located in the center. As you exercise, you can easily move from one station to the other with minimal adjustments. This machine is produced by several different manufacturers, but is popularly known as a "universal gym."

Fixed Resistance Weight Plate Machines

These machines resemble weight stack machines. The key difference is that instead of having a weight stack, they have a peg upon which you stack round weight plates. As with the use of adjustable dumbbells and barbells, you need to exercise care when adding and removing weight plates. It's important to remember good body mechanics when you carry your weight plates as well as when you perform your exercises. You would not want to injure your back because of improper lifting form when you pick up the plates.

Cable Machines

Some weight stack machines use a cable and pulley to move the weights. A cable machine usually consists of a tower with a pulley attached. The weight stack is inside the tower. Some cable machines have two towers and you stand in the middle to perform your exercise. Cable machines provide more versatility because you can adjust the height of the pulley or you can change the handle bar.

Since you can change handles and move the cable bar in multiple directions, you can vary your hand grips and you can challenge your muscles in multiple ways. Cable attachments include a long bar, curved short bar, straight short bar, V-bar, horseshoe, rope, and ankle cuffs or collars. Experiment with different handles. Ask the weight room staff for advice. Find what feels comfortable for you. Go ahead and change it around as you progress your training.

Variable Resistance Machines

Variable resistance machines address the "sticking point" limitation of fixed resistance machines. On a variable resistance piece of equipment, the weight stack will change position to remain in the same relationship to the pivot point. A variable resistance machine provides uniform resistance throughout the full range of motion from a full stretch to a full contraction. Nautilus popularized the first variable resistance machines in the late '60s and throughout the '70s.

Some variable resistance machines do not have weight stacks. Instead, these machines use air pressure. Within the machines, air is pumped through a piston to create resistance. Other machines use a combination of weight stacks and air pressure. The advantage of these dynamic variable resistance exercises is that resistance is applied through a full range of joint motion. Training is more demanding and results come more quickly.

Another variation of the variable resistance machine uses hydraulics or the resistance of fluids. Instead of air, fluid is pumped through a piston. Depending on the size of the piston, the speed at which you lift may affect the resistance. For example, in fluid dynamics, which are discussed more thoroughly in Chapter 8, the faster you push, the greater the resistance.

Electronic Machines

In more and more gyms, high-tech electronic devices are manipulating workouts. When you sit down at a piece of equipment, you input a code that identifies you or you swipe your ID card. The machine retrieves your workout data. Some machines automatically set your resistance. Others remind you of your training program guidelines. Some machines are so personalized that the machine measures the muscular force that you apply and matches it with resistive force to maintain a certain level of resistance, as well as speed throughout the movement.

FACTS

The Gravitron is an electronic machine that allows you to perform an assisted chin up or pull up. Instead of lifting your entire body weight, you can select a percentage of your body weight. When you stand on the platform, it will help lift your body up to perform pull ups. It's almost like being a kid again and having someone pop you up and down. Fun, if you like that sort of thing. And, it's also a great conditioning exercise.

The Smith Machine

The Smith machine combines use of a bar bell free weight within a vertical track that controls movement similar to a weight machine. The track ensures that the bar travels straight up and down. To further increase safety, most Smith machines have self-spotting pins that you can use to prevent the bar from being lowered beyond a certain point. This helps protect your hip and knee joints from bending too low.

The Smith machine is best for exercises such as squats, the overhead press, lunges, and the bench press. By using the Smith machine instead of free weights, you do not need to have as much coordination, balance, and control. The machine provides guidance and security. The disadvantage is that you are limited to a vertical up and down motion.

Many Smith machines use a standard Olympic barbell. The weight of the barbell is counter balanced by springs. This negates the weight of the bar. The only weight you lift is what you've added to the bar. You still need to use correct form when using the Smith machine. The features simply add greater stability and safety.

The Great Debate: Free Weights or Machines?

For years, exercise enthusiasts and physiologists have debated the relative superiority of free weights and machines. As the debate ensues, research continues to give us new insight into the training potential of the human body. Another value judgment that affects anyone's opinion is the training perspective. What you consider to be a valuable outcome will affect what you think is the most effective method to achieve it. People train for many reasons. Some simply want to be able to get out of a chair without assistance. Others want to run a four-minute mile.

The fitness industry is moving away from a position of recommending that certain exercises be eliminated absolutely. Instead, the current thinking is that exercises should be evaluated from a perspective of "relative risk." For example, an appropriate exercise for an Olympic gymnast would not be recommended for the average person. As you consider which exercises and modes of exercise are appropriate for you,

you need to look at what the benefits of an exercise are, what the potential risk of injury is and what is the safest and most effective method for you to achieve your goals.

Keep in mind that exercises need to fit you—your body and your lifestyle—not the other way around. And, you need to find exercises that you enjoy and that you will do regularly. Again, the finest training program in the world is of absolutely no value if you do not do it. Be realistic; be practical. Try different exercises; find what suits you. Remember that as with anything in life, your tastes may change over time. Keep an open mind. Enjoy the variety of life.

Pros and Cons of Free Weights

Free weights permit greater exercise variety. You have more freedom of movement. In addition to targeting specific muscle groups, as in a biceps curl, you also need to use your smaller stabilizer muscles to keep good form throughout each movement. For example, with a standing biceps curl, you need to engage your abdominal muscles, back muscles, and shoulder stabilizers for good posture. To further challenge your balance, you can perform the exercise while standing on one leg. Free weights therefore train the entire body to support a movement, rather than specific muscle groups.

Free weights are much less expensive. They are more practical for home use and require less storage space. Free weights, however, require excellent technique and knowledge of good alignment. Since positioning your body is critical to effective exercise performance, you need to pay attention to ensure that you continue to do your exercises safely and correctly.

Dumbbells allow you to train each side of your body independently. This makes you aware of muscular imbalances in your body between your dominant and nondominant sides. You can use dumbbells to help equalize this strength differential for better overall muscular development.

Free weights are fixed resistance and use the force of gravity combined with the resistance of the weight. An advantage of this type of training is that it is very functional. When we use free weights, it resembles the typical challenges we face in daily living when we need to use strength. A disadvantage is that you are limited by your weakest links.

Bill Pearl, four-time Mr. Universe and author of *Getting Stronger* (Shelter Publications), recommends, "I believe that beginning weight lifters or bodybuilders should use free weights . . . as the best way to build a solid foundation. The exercises should be basic . . . As you enter the intermediate stage, machines will play a part, maybe an ever-increasing part. They can be used to work certain muscles specifically and this can improve proportion, balance, and symmetry."

Pros and Cons of Machines

Weight machines take many alignment questions out of the picture. When you adjust the machine to fit your body correctly, your body is supported and is only allowed to perform a specific movement pattern. Your stabilizers do not need to work as hard. You do not need as much coordination. This makes it less likely that you will injure yourself. However, you do not receive the extra training benefit of challenging your balance and coordination.

Weight machines isolate specific muscle groups. Since you are structurally supported and can only perform one range of motion, you can target a muscle in a way that is not possible with free weights. This design flexibility overcomes some of the limitations of free weights that can only use the force of gravity and body positioning. Some experts argue that this specificity of design is good, since you can fine tune your training on a particular muscle. Others argue that this is not functional and that our bodies do not move this way.

Since machines are designed to target muscle groups precisely, they do not permit much versatility. The number of possible exercises therefore is much fewer than the possible exercises with free weights. This lack of training variety may contribute to boredom. Furthermore, since you need so many different machines to perform a total body workout, it is both expensive and requires a lot of space.

Another advantage of machines is that you can perform your workout routine quickly and efficiently. Machines are usually organized in the same sequence that you would perform your exercises. You don't have to think as much about which exercise to do next. You travel from one machine to the next, adjust for fit, insert your pin and go. In gyms with electronic equipment, the machines even remind you of your routine at each station.

Many weight machines provide variable resistance. The machine ideally presents proportionately less resistance in weaker muscle positions and more resistance in stronger muscle positions. For people who are particularly weak, this can facilitate training. Without this variability, you are limited to what you can lift at your weakest point. For people seeking maximal resistance, this may permit maximal challenges.

With machines, the weight stacks or source of resistance is secure. You are much less likely to injure yourself. You need to exercise care when you are placing and removing your pin, never to put your fingers between the weight plates. Other than that, it's not likely you will drop the weights on yourself. You may not ever drop your free weights either, but the risk of it happening is greater.

Variable resistance machines train muscles to maintain tension. Tension movements require force throughout the movement. Sports such as wrestling and gymnastics use tension. Free weights train muscles to initiate a movement from rest with maximal force. Ballistic movements require an initial maximal forceful contraction. The movement continues due to momentum or less force. Free weights develop ballistic skills since you need to exert the most force at the beginning of the movement.

Equipment Odds and Ends

There are a number of other equipment options available in most gyms. Following are a few of them.

Weight Benches

The weight bench offers a number of training options with free weights. Benches are used in four positions: flat, vertical, incline, and decline. Some benches are adjustable. Others are in a fixed position. When you have an equipment orientation at the gym, be sure to take a good look at the benches so you know whether or not they are adjustable.

A flat bench allows you to perform both upper and lower body exercises. You may lie with your back on the bench or kneel with one hand and one knee on the bench. You may also use the bench for push-ups, dips, and sit-ups.

A vertical bench resembles a high backed chair. The back of the bench provides support while you perform seated exercises.

The incline bench resembles the vertical bench, except the back is inclined at an angle. Some benches allow you to adjust the angle of the back support. Others are at a fixed angle. When you sit on the incline bench, you rest your back at the angle of your choice depending on how you want to challenge your muscle fibers.

On a decline bench, your head is lower than your hips. This position is useful for certain chest exercises. Generally, by positioning your body this way, you have increased the challenge to overcome gravity.

For home use, a step aerobics bench with removable risers can be adapted successfully for use as a weight bench. For a flat bench, use an equal amount of risers on each side. For a decline or incline affect, use an unequal amount of risers. To avoid sliding off the step, I've found that it's helpful to use a specially designed step mat or a towel. The mat also adds cushioning that increases comfort when lying on the step.

The preacher bench looks like a bench with a backwards lectern attached at the end. In other words, the lectern is facing away from instead of towards the bench. This bench is known as a preacher bench. The purpose of the preacher bench is to train your biceps. As you sit on the bench, you can rest the back of your upper arms on the slanted surface for support.

The abdominal board resembles a decline bench. At the upper end, however, it has pads under which you put your feet. You anchor your body with your feet. The abdominal board permits you to train your abdominal muscles at a decline that increases the resistance from the force of gravity. This is for more advanced abdominal training.

Ankle Weights

Ankle weights are another useful tool for your home gym weight training workout. Ankle weights come in a variety of weights from as light as 1 pound each to as heavy as 5 pounds each. Some come with adjustable weight pockets so you can increase the weight as you become stronger. Ankle weights are useful for your lower body exercises.

Under no circumstances, however, should you walk around or perform any type of aerobic exercise while wearing ankle weights. If you swing your leg without control while wearing your weights, you increase your risk of injury. Play it safe and avoid injury.

Tubing and Bands

Elastic tubing and bands designed for exercise are excellent for resistance training. Tubes and bands come in a variety of weights to provide progressive levels of challenge. They are lightweight. You can easily exercise with them at home or take them with you when you travel. If you have latex allergies, some companies produce latex-free bands.

Tubes and bands are color-coded so you know the level of resistance. Unfortunately, not all manufacturers use the same color-coding system. All you need to do is use your bands once to determine the level of difficulty. When you purchase bands or tubes, it's best to select at least three different levels (light, medium, and heavy) so you can work smaller and larger muscles.

Tubes and bands come in a variety of shapes and lengths. Shapes include a long strip, a circle, double circles, and figure eights. Some tubing comes with padded handles to improve comfort. I recommend my students to wear weight training gloves if bands hurt their hands. I also recommend bands of at least four to five feet in length. You won't need this extra length for all of your exercises. However, this length greatly increases your exercise options.

Some bands come in a kit with a hook that attaches to a doorknob or doorway. The hook allows you to stabilize one end of the band to enhance effectiveness and increase your exercise options. Some manufacturers also offer detachable handles and cuffs.

Bands are subject to wear and tear so you need to check them frequently. Inspect for tiny holes, splits, or tears by holding up to a light.

If you see any flaws, discard the band. Store your bands away from direct sunlight or other sources of heat in a bag or box with a little baby powder. This keeps them fresh and dry. From time to time, you can wash them in water and allow them to drip dry.

Pay as much attention when you use bands as you would with any other type of weight training tool. If a band snaps out of position, it can hit you in the face. If a band is wrapped too tightly around your hand, it can inhibit circulation. It's important to control the movement both on the pull and the release portion. When you are releasing the move, you need to resist the temptation to be assisted by the band and move quickly. Instead, resist the movement in both directions.

The advantage of bands and tubes is that you are not limited by gravity to create the resistive force for your exercises as you are with weights. You can place the resistance where you want it.

The disadvantage to using bands is that, in contrast to free weights that require the greatest force to initiate the movement, the resistance provided by bands increases as the band stretches. A band at a full stretch is more difficult to manipulate than a slack band. The resistance, therefore, is not consistent through the movement. A heavy band may not permit a full range of motion.

Tom Purvis, PT and exercise physiologist, suggests that multiple thinner tubing permits a better range of elasticity and a greater ability to add resistance incrementally, than a single heavier tube. Instead of progressing to heavier tubing when you want to increase intensity, Purvis recommends two pieces of medium tubing. Two pieces of lighter weight tubing may provide greater resistance yet still permit a full range of motion. A heavier tube may not allow full range of motion and may cause too much stress at certain joint positions.

ESSENTIALS

Ultimately, bands can't provide as much resistance as free weights or machines. However, the resistance may be sufficient for your purposes, depending on your level of strength and training constraints. For home or on the road workouts, bands are practical, convenient, and easy to use.

Body Weight

Your body weight is one of the easiest and most convenient tools for weight training. If your goal is general conditioning, you can perform many successful exercises using your body weight and gravity for resistance. Similar to the challenge of using free weights, when you use body weight, you need to know the appropriate positioning and form for performing your exercises.

The advantage of using your body weight is that the types of movements you perform are very close to what you need to do in your daily life. The exercises, therefore, can't be beat for functionality. Furthermore, the exercises generally require using the whole body. You benefit from training balance, coordination, and smaller stabilizer muscles as well as your major muscle groups.

The disadvantages of using body weight include the limitations provided by your own size. You can use positioning to make an exercise easier or more difficult. However, ultimately, you cannot do anything about your body size and it may not provide you with the most appropriate level of resistance for your training. If you need to make an exercise more difficult, you have to use some sort of tool to increase resistance.

Furthermore, you may need a trainer to watch your movement form and to guide you through appropriate exercise selection. If you are new or returning to exercise after a long layoff, you may not have the body awareness that you need to focus stimulation on specific muscles. When you use a prop or tool, it can help focus your attention. Body weight can provide tremendous exercise variety, but more advanced exercises require a higher level of sophistication to understand the subtle nuances of body placement and muscle activation.

CHAPTER 8

Power in the Pool—Your Liquid Weight Trainer

Pools are not only for swimming anymore. If you're tired of the gym and need a change of pace, exercising in the pool may be the solution you need. From Olympic athletes to people who need a cane to walk, the pool is a friendly workout environment.

The Pool as Weight "Machine"

Weight training is based on using resistance to create overload. Here's why and how you can manipulate water's resistance to provide a great workout.

Water resists every move you make. Water is denser than air. When your body is under water, every move you make encounters resistance.

You can adjust water's resistance to suit your needs. You can increase resistance to your movements in water by adding surface area, traveling, or changing the size and speed of your moves. For example, if you run across a pool, it's harder than if you walk across a pool or if you run in place. Any action that stirs up water currents increases the resistance against your body.

Your body is buoyant in water. Archimedes' principle describes buoyancy as the upward force exerted on an immersed object at rest that is equal to the weight of fluid that is displaced. If you know how to float, you have experienced water's buoyancy.

You can use water's buoyancy to support or resist movement. How to manipulate buoyancy is one of the more difficult concepts related to exercising in water. The reason understanding how to use buoyancy in exercise is tricky is that buoyancy can make your exercises easier *or* it can make your exercises harder. It all depends on how you use it.

You can use water's buoyancy to promote balanced muscle development. The buoyancy of water provides an interesting training advantage. When you are on land, the primary resistance to movement is gravity. Gravity also assists certain movements. That's why it's more work to lift your leg than to lower it.

In the water, this principle is reversed. The force of buoyancy is an upward thrust. The force of gravity is a downward thrust. Muscles that are constantly assisted by gravity tend to be weaker than those that work against gravity. When you train in water, you reverse the forces that resist your body's movements. Instead of being helped by gravity, your weaker muscles are challenged. With consistent aquatic training, your weaker muscles become stronger and you achieve more balanced muscles.

Water Depth for Weight Training

Muscle toning and dynamic range of motion exercises can be performed in deep or shallow water. In general, when you are in shallow water, you want to submerge the working limb. For example, if you are doing a chest fly-styled exercise, your arms and shoulders should be under water. You can work in water of this depth. Or, you can bend your knees in a lunge position to lower your shoulders when you execute the specific movement.

Deep water training requires basic swimming skills. Unless you know how to float and tread water, deep water training is not recommended. Safety always comes first. If you train in deep water, you need to wear a flotation device so that you can concentrate on your exercises and not be concerned about treading to stay afloat. Deep water provides an excellent environment to fully stretch out your limbs. Deep water is especially appropriate for people who need to avoid potential impact with others.

Reps and Sets in the Water

Intensity guidelines for weight training in water are consistent with weight training on land. If you are healthy and under age fifty-five, your goal is to perform 8 to 12 repetitions of eight to ten exercises for your major muscle groups in good form before reaching muscle fatigue. If you are new to exercise, or returning after a long break, or are over fifty-five, your goal is to perform 10 to 15 reps before reaching muscle overload.

The same rules also apply regarding sets and frequency of training. The minimum amount of exercise is two times a week. If you train three times a week you will receive more benefits. You can also mix this up with your land training. For example, you may water train one time a week and land train one or two times a week. It's all about program variety and keeping your workouts fun and interesting for you.

Water Exercise Equipment

Exercising in water can bring you back to the days when you played in the pool as a kid. Check out the following essentials and extras.

Essentials:
- Athletic swimsuit (one that stays on when you exercise)
- Sports bra (for women who are well endowed)
- Protective footwear (aqua socks or water training shoes)
- One pair of water mitts or gloves
- One pair of paddles

Extras:
- Flotation belt for deep water
- Water dumbbells
- Aquatic step
- Kickboard
- Four-foot band

Water Temperature and Staying Warm

Most recreational pools are around 83 to 86 degrees Fahrenheit or 28 to 30 degrees Celsius. If you find that you are getting cold in between sets, you can jog in place for a few minutes. Another way to get a great "interval" workout is to perform a strength training set, do some stretches, and then travel vigorously back and forth across the pool in two to three minute sets. If you do ten different exercises, you will have accumulated twenty to thirty minutes of traveling.

Additional Benefits of Aquatic Training

Improves posture. Every exercise performed in a pool challenges your postural stabilizer muscles. In order to maintain good posture and movement form, your abdominal and back muscles must work constantly against the water currents. In every exercise, even when you're working another primary muscle group, you must engage your shoulder stabilizers and core stabilizers. With regular training, this additional exercise focus results in improved posture and body awareness.

Provides soothing water massage. When you are in the pool, your body is surrounded by the pressure of water. The water currents provide constant massaging strokes against the body. This pumping action of the water promotes circulation. This can speed recovery after exercise.

Beneficial exercise for people recovering from injury. Pool training can provide a comfortable alternative for people who can't exercise on land due to movement restrictions from injuries. No one should exercise when experiencing acute pain. Aquatic exercise, however, may be appropriate for those in post-rehabilitation when released for physical activity by their health care providers.

Comfortable exercise for people suffering from back pain or arthritis. People who are unable to perform land exercises due to back pain or arthritis may be able to exercise without pain in the water. The buoyancy of water unloads the spine and provides essential support for the body. The compressive effects of water decrease stress on inflamed joints and reduce local swelling.

Aquatic Exercise Guidelines for Back Pain Sufferers

- Do not perform any exercise that causes pain.
- Maintain neutral spinal alignment for the low back during exercise.
- Do not excessively repeat extremes of flattening or arching the low back.
- Avoid excessive load on the spine. For example, any jumping movements will increase spinal load.
- Wear a flotation belt in shallow water exercise to reduce impact.
- Consider conducting all exercises in deep water.
- Change activities and body positions frequently.
- Move with control. For example, uncontrolled overhead arm movements may cause excessive spinal extension.
- Wear aqua mitts or webbed gloves to increase resistance and provide stability.
- Keep leg movements smaller.
- Use shortened arm and leg movements. For example, replace high kicks with low knee lifts.
- Avoid rapid, twisting spinal movements.
- Practice movements that keep shoulders and hips aligned.

- Impact should only be increased gradually. Keep in mind that even in shallow water there is impact.
- See your health care provider if you experience a severe increase in pain, a decrease in functional activity level, or any pain, numbness, or tingling in the legs after exercise.

Before doing any exercises in the pool, you need to be water safe. Any type of exercise runs the risk of injury. In the pool, you add the risk of drowning among other water accidents. You should know how to execute an emergency plan, such as how to call 911 and how to find first aid supplies.

If you exercise in a pool that is managed by a facility, you should familiarize yourself with all of the pool rules. In addition, exercise when lifeguards are on duty. Use good common sense. Wear appropriate pool exercise attire. Do not eat right before you exercise. Do not exercise in electrical storms. Do not wear breakable glass eyewear. And, if you are exercising outdoors, be sure to protect yourself from the sun with sunscreen, a hat, and sunglasses. Make sure to drink plenty of water.

Water Weight Training Exercises

If you're a swimmer, you can fit your water weight training exercises in after your swimming workout. Your muscles will be warmed up. You can complete one set of each of your exercises. After you do your laps, your weight training will only take an extra twenty or thirty minutes.

If you're not swimming, you can do your weight training exercises in the pool after you perform a five- to ten-minute rhythmic warm up. To warm up in the pool, you can jog, walk vigorously, or swim. Your personal preferences can determine how you choose to organize your workouts.

Following are sample toning and stretching exercises. Remember when using equipment to grip gently and to exhale upon the exertion phase of the movement. The recommended sequence of exercises is to perform a muscle-conditioning exercise for a specific muscle group, followed by a stretching set, followed by a cardio-interval to keep your muscles warm. Then repeat the sequence again beginning with a muscle toning exercise for a different muscle group.

Hold each stretch for fifteen to thirty seconds (depending on the temperature of the water), and mix stretches with movement activities to stay warm.

WATER WALKING TO WARM UP

Water Weight Training Exercises

ACTION   Walk in shallow water. Swing arms freely as if walking on land. This will help your balance and loosen up your back muscles.

TIPS   Breathe naturally. Concentrate on maintaining good posture with your shoulders relaxed and above your hips-and abdominals engaged. Avoid leaning forward excessively. Make sure the opposite arm and leg are moving forward.

VARIATIONS

(HARDER) Hold hands out of the water.

(HARDER) Walk with elbows in and arms extended outward to increase resistance, while maintaining neutral spine.

(HARDER) Increase speed of walking.

Other warm-up ideas include jogging, hopping, traveling lunges, jumping jacks, knee lifts, kicks, rocking, cross-country skiing, bounding, skipping, or backwards traveling moves.

POOL SQUATS

Water Weight Training Exercises

MUSCLES   gluteals, hamstrings, quadriceps, (hips, buttocks, thighs)

GET SET   Stand in water chest deep with feet hip width apart, feet pointing straight ahead.

ACTION   Bend your knees and sit back as if you are going to sit in a chair. Push yourself back up with your weight firmly centered in your heel and mid-foot.

TIPS   Inhale as you sit back, exhale as you push up. Maintain neutral spinal alignment.

VARIATIONS

(HARDER) Perform the exercise in shallower water.

(HARDER) Lift one knee up so thigh is parallel to the floor. Sit back into a one legged squat. Push up through the heel. This is also a great balance challenge.

(HARDER) On both legs, add a jump as you push yourself back up. Land softly and bend your hips, knees, and ankles.

(HARDER) Squat on an aquatic step and push off into a jump. Land on the pool floor behind the step to cushion impact. Or, land on the step for a greater challenge in shallower water.

POOL LUNGES

Water Weight
Training
Exercises

MUSCLES   gluteals, hamstrings, quadriceps (hips, buttocks, thighs)

GET SET   Stand in chest-deep water with your feet hip width apart. Take one generous step backward. Stand on the full sole of your front foot and ball of your back foot.

ACTION   Bend your knees and lower your shoulders into the water. Lengthen your spine, relax your shoulders. Push up to starting position. If you add a jump, push up and switch forward legs. Land with other foot forward.

TIPS   Inhale as you lower, exhale as you push up. Keep tone in your abdominals. Maintain good posture with neutral spinal alignment. If you need to lean forward slightly, bend from your hips. When you add jumping moves, land softly and with control.

VARIATIONS

(HARDER) Push off and jump up slightly as you come up.

(HARDER) Increase size of jump.

(HARDER) Perform exercise in shallower water.

(HARDER) Travel forward across the pool as you lunge.

(HARDER) Perform exercise on an aquatic step. Push off with forward foot that is on the step. Switch lead legs and land with other foot on the step.

SINGLE OR DOUBLE LEG KNEE LIFTS AND KICKS

Water Weight
Training
Exercises

MUSCLES   hip flexors, quadriceps (hips, thighs)

GET SET   Stand in chest deep water with your feet hip width apart. Bend your knees slightly. Lengthen your spine, relax your shoulders. Alternate lifting your knees no higher than waist height so your thigh is parallel to the pool floor. Avoid simply letting the leg float up. Instead, energetically lift your knees up.

ACTION   Alternate extending your leg from your knee lift. Feel the top of the thigh work against the resistance of the water as you extend your leg.

TIPS   Breathe naturally. Keep tone in your abdominals. Maintain good posture with neutral spinal alignment. Stand tall and avoid slumping or slouching forward as you kick your leg. Use your arms for support.

VARIATIONS

(HARDER) Increase height of knee lift and kick.

(HARDER) Increase speed of knee lifts and kicks. Feel the resistance of water as you kick forward.

(HARDER) Add a jump to your knee lifts and kicks. Land softly and with control.

(HARDER) Lift arms overhead out of water with your jumps. Move to shallower water.

(HARDER) Use an aquatic step. Step up, lift your knee and kick. Alternate legs. Increase step up to a hop up. This is the most difficult level since the force of gravity is increased. More of the body is out of the water due to the step's elevation.

SINGLE OR DOUBLE LEG CURLS

Water Weight
Training
Exercises

MUSCLES   gluteals, hamstrings (hips, buttocks, thighs)

GET SET   Stand in chest deep water with your feet hip width apart. Bend your knees slightly. Lengthen your spine, relax your shoulders.

ACTION   Alternate lifting your heels towards your buttocks. Feel the exercise in the back of the legs. Avoid simply letting the leg float up. Instead, energetically lift your heel up.

TIPS   Breathe naturally. Keep tone in your abdominals. Maintain good posture with neutral spinal alignment. Avoid arching your back. When you add jumping moves, land softly and with control. Bend elbows and press water downward as you lift up.

VARIATIONS

(HARDER) Increase speed of single leg curls.

(HARDER) Lift both heels up and jump up.

(HARDER) Increase height and speed of jumps.

(HARDER) Lift arms overhead out of water with jumps. Move to shallower water.

(HARDER) Use an aquatic step. Start with both legs on pool floor next to step. Perform double leg curl jumps. Put one foot on step, one foot on pool floor, while performing double leg curl jumps. Focus weight of body on pool leg, continue jumps. Shift weight of body to leg on step, continue jumps. This is the most difficult level since the force of gravity is increased. More of the body is out of the water due to the step's elevation.

JUMPING JACKS POWER IN AND OUT

Water Weight
Training
Exercises

MUSCLES gluteals, adductors, abductors (hips, buttocks, inner thighs, outer thighs)

GET SET Stand in chest-deep water with your feet close together. Bend your knees slightly. Lengthen your spine, relax your shoulders.

ACTION Perform a jumping jack movement. If you are toning the outer thighs, focus on powering out as you jump, returning gently to center. If you are toning the inner thighs, focus on powering in as you jump, return gently to a wide stance.

TIPS Inhale to prepare, exhale on the power phase. Inhale on the return phase. Keep tone in your abdominals. Maintain good posture with neutral spinal alignment. Avoid arching your back. Land softly and with control. Use arms to assist your balance

VARIATIONS

(HARDER) Increase size of movement on the power phase.

(HARDER) Increase speed of movement on the power phase.

(HARDER) Increase height of jumps.

(HARDER) Perform exercise in shallower water.

(HARDER) Use an aquatic step. Start with both legs on pool floor behind step. Perform jacks with power phase. Jump up on step. If you are toning the outer thighs, focus on powering out as you jump down and straddle the step. If you are toning the inner thighs, focus on powering in as you jump up onto the step. Using the aquatic step is the most difficult level since the force of gravity is increased. More of the body is out of the water due to the step's elevation.

CHEST PRESS: SHOULDER BLADE SQUEEZE

Water Weight
Training
Exercises

MUSCLES   rhomboids, trapezius (upper and mid-back)

GET SET   Stand in chest-deep water with your feet hip width apart. Bend your knees slightly. Lengthen your spine, relax your shoulders. Roll shoulders down and back to stabilize your shoulder blades. Lengthen your arms out in front of your body with elbows slightly bent and palms facing down towards pool floor with fingers together.

ACTION   Move arms forcefully back through the water as you squeeze your shoulder blades together. Slice hands with fingers together and palms flat face-down through water as you return arms to start position.

TIPS   Inhale to prepare, exhale as you squeeze back muscles. Inhale, return to start. Keep tone in your abdominals. Maintain good posture with neutral spinal alignment. Avoid arching your back.

VARIATIONS

(HARDER) Increase size of the movement.

(HARDER) Increase speed of the movement.

(HARDER) Vary hand positions. Use cupped hands with palms facing front. To increase difficulty, open up fingers into a "webbed" hand position. Or, add aquatic gloves to maximize resistance of the hands.

(HARDER) Gently grip an aquatic paddle to increase surface area and repeat progression of moves.

(HARDER) Perform exercise while standing on one leg to challenge your core stabilizers to maintain your postural alignment and balance.

(HARDER) Travel backwards at the same time that you squeeze your shoulder blades together and move your arms backwards.

CHEST PRESS: LAT PRESS DOWN

Water Weight
Training
Exercises

MUSCLES   latissimus dorsi (back)

GET SET   Stand in chest-deep water with your feet in a split stance. Bend your knees slightly. Lengthen your spine, relax your shoulders. Roll shoulders down and back to stabilize your shoulder blades. Lengthen your arms out to the sides of your body with elbows slightly bent and palms face down towards pool floor with fingers together.

ACTION   Move arms forcefully down through the water. Slice hands with fingers together and palm flat facing front through water as you return arms to start position.

TIPS   Inhale to prepare, exhale as you work back muscles. Inhale, return to start. Keep tone in your abdominals. Maintain good posture with neutral spinal alignment. Avoid arching your back.

VARIATIONS

(HARDER) Increase speed of the movement.

(HARDER) Vary hand positions. Use cupped hands with palms facing down. To increase difficulty, open up fingers into a "webbed" hand position. Or, add aquatic gloves to maximize resistance of the hands.

(HARDER) Gently grip an aquatic paddle to increase surface area and repeat progression of moves.

(HARDER) Perform exercise while standing on one leg to challenge your core stabilizers to maintain your postural alignment and balance.

(HARDER) Travel downwards by bending both knees and lunging as you move your arms downwards.

TRICEPS PRESS DOWN

Water Weight
Training
Exercises

MUSCLES triceps (arms)

GET SET Stand in chest-deep water with your feet in a split stance. Bend your knees slightly. Lengthen your spine, relax your shoulders. Roll shoulders down and back to stabilize your shoulder blades.

Hold your forearms close to your torso. Grip a flotation dumbbell gently and bend elbows with palms facing towards you.

ACTION   Move arms forcefully downward through the water as you lengthen your arms. Maintain neutral wrist.

TIPS   Inhale to prepare, exhale as you work triceps. Inhale, return to start. Keep tone in your abdominals. Maintain good posture with neutral spinal alignment. Avoid arching your back.

VARIATIONS

(HARDER) Increase speed of the movement.

(HARDER) Perform exercise while standing on one leg to challenge your core stabilizers to maintain your postural alignment and balance.

(HARDER) Bend both knees and lunge downwards as you extend your arms. Perform with one or both arms simultaneously.

BICEPS CURL

Water Weight
Training
Exercises

MUSCLES biceps (arms)

GET SET Stand in chest-deep water with your feet in a split stance. Bend your knees slightly. Lengthen your spine, relax your shoulders. Roll shoulders down and back to stabilize your shoulder blades. Allow your arms to hang at your sides, palms facing front.

ACTION Bend elbows and move arms forcefully upward through the water. Maintain neutral wrist.

TIPS Inhale to prepare, exhale as you work biceps. Inhale, return to start. Keep tone in your abdominals. Avoid arching your back. Feel the resistance of the water as you try to lift it.

VARIATIONS

(HARDER) Increase speed of the movement.

(HARDER) Perform exercise while standing on one leg to challenge your core stabilizers to maintain your postural alignment and balance.

(HARDER) Vary hand positions. Use cupped hands with palms facing up. To increase difficulty, open up fingers into a "webbed" hand position.

(HARDER) Travel forward as you perform movement. Perform with one or both arms simultaneously.

PELVIC TILT

Water Weight Training Exercises

MUSCLES rectus abdominus, transversus (abdominals)

GET SET Begin with back against pool wall. Stand in chest-deep water with your feet hip width apart. Bend your knees slightly. Lengthen your spine, relax your shoulders. Roll shoulders down and back to stabilize your shoulder blades.

ACTION Tuck tailbone under and feel back flatten against pool wall and release.

TIPS Inhale to prepare, exhale as you squeeze abdominal muscles. Inhale, return to start. Focus attention on contraction of abdominal muscles to tilt pelvis, rather than squeezing gluteal muscles.

VARIATIONS

(HARDER) Move away from the pool wall.

(HARDER) Practice finding neutral spine and feeling the difference between neutral and a posterior tilt.

HAMSTRING STRETCH

Pool Stretches

MUSCLES   Stand in chest-deep water with your feet hip width apart.

ACTION   Bring knee to chest and extend leg forward while standing on one leg. Support leg by holding hands under thigh. Extend tailbone towards back of pool. Feel length in back of upper leg. Flex foot. Relax shoulders.

TIPS   Relax shoulders. Scull with hands for support. As you exhale, relax and release further into the stretch.

VARIATIONS

(HARDER) Place a buoyancy belt or pool noodle under the thigh to support leg.

(HARDER) Move belt or noodle under lower leg.

(HARDER) Use a step. Place heel on step, extend tailbone towards back of pool, exhale and relax into stretch. Keep leg extended without locking knee. Scull with hands for support.

HIP FLEXOR STRETCH

Pool Stretches

GET SET Stand with feet hip width apart next to pool wall for support. Step back with one leg and drop down into a lunge position.

ACTION Press pelvis forward and feel the stretch in the front of the thigh of the back leg.

TIPS Maintain a posterior pelvic tilt and engage abdominal muscles to avoid over-arching the upper back. As you exhale, relax and release further into the stretch.

VARIATIONS

(EASIER) Stand with back towards wall and one foot forward. Bend knee of one leg and place foot on the pool wall for support. Press pelvis forward to feel the stretch.

(HARDER) Hold one foot in your hand and press your hips forward.

STANDING CALF STRETCH

GET SET   Stand in a split stance with front knee bent and back heel touching the floor.

ACTION   Press heel into the pool floor. Move your arms in a biceps curl motion to assist in creating a downward movement into the heel. Feel the stretch in the back of your lower leg.

TIPS   Maintain neutral posture with a slight forward lean. As you exhale, relax and release further into the stretch.

VARIATIONS

(EASIER) Stand facing pool wall in a split stance. Lengthen back leg and push heel into the pool floor.

(HARDER) Push the ball of your foot into the pool wall while the heel rests on the pool floor. Lean into the stretch. Feel the stretch behind your heel and in the back of your lower leg.

DEEP GLUTEAL STRETCH

GET SET   Stand in mid-chest deep water next to the pool wall. Place one hand on the pool wall.

ACTION   Sit with one leg across the other by bringing one knee up and out as you place your ankle across the thigh of your other leg. Sit back and feel the stretch in the buttocks.

TIPS   Breathe fully. As you exhale, relax and release into the stretch.

VARIATIONS

(HARDER) Let go of the pool wall and pick your other foot up off the pool floor. Lift your knee up higher towards your chest and scull with your hands to stay afloat.

LOWER BACK AND GLUTEAL STRETCH

Pool Stretches

GET SET   Stand in mid-chest deep water.

ACTION   Bring one knee towards chest by holding behind the thigh. Tuck pelvis under. Feel the stretch in the low back and in the buttocks.

TIPS   Breathe fully. As you exhale, relax and release into the stretch.

VARIATIONS   Hug knee towards chest and then bring knee across the body. Feel the stretch in the low back, waist, and in the buttocks. Do not do this variation if you have a hip replacement.

LOWER BACK AND HAMSTRING STRETCH

Pool Stretches

GET SET   Place hands on pool wall. Slide shoulder blades down and back.

ACTION   Walk both legs up the pool wall. Relax your shoulders and round your back into a tuck position. Bring your chin towards your chest and tuck your tailbone under. Feel the stretch all along your back, particularly in the lower back. Gently extend legs long and feel the stretch in the back of your legs.

TIPS   Breathe fully. As you exhale, relax and release into the stretch. Maintain length in the back of your neck. Avoid hunching your shoulders.

VARIATIONS   Alternate between a tuck and lengthened legs position.

CHEST STRETCH WITH BACK STRETCH VARIATION

Pool Stretches

GET SET   Stand with neutral postural alignment. Open up chest and allow arms to stream behind body with palms open facing front.

ACTION   Walk slowly across the pool. Allow the currents of the water to gently stretch open the front of your shoulders and chest.

TIPS   Breathe fully. As you exhale, relax and release into the stretch.

VARIATIONS   Walk backwards and gently feel the stretch in your back. Alternate walking forward and backward allowing the water to assist your stretch and gently massage your body.

BACK AND BACK OF SHOULDER STRETCH

GET SET   Stand with neutral postural alignment. Stream both arms long across the front of your body to one side.

ACTION   Walk slowly in a large circle in the opposite direction of your fingertips. Feel the stretch in your back and rear shoulder muscles.

TIPS   Breathe fully. As you exhale, relax and release into the stretch.

VARIATIONS   **(HARDER)** Hold aquatic paddles in your hands to increase surface area and create more resistance to increase the feeling of stretch. First move in one direction and then move in the other.

SIDE OF TORSO STRETCH

GET SET   Stand next to the pool wall with one hand on side of pool.

ACTION   Extend hip to the outside. Feel the stretch all along the side of legs and hips. Extend outer arm out to side, palm up. Sweep arm upward. Feel stretch all along side of upper body as well.

TIPS   Breathe comfortably into the stretch. As you exhale, relax and release as you lengthen the side of your body.

VARIATIONS   Move your feet as close to the pool wall as possible to maximize the stretch in your lower body.

TORSO STRETCH WITH A PARTNER

GET SET   Partners stand one behind the other. Front partner lunges down, submerging shoulders. Back partner places hands on opposite shoulders and extends body like a plank.

ACTION   Front partner stands and walks forward as back partner lengthens body and relaxes into stretch. Partners switch.

TIPS   Relax and release your back into the stretch. Feel the length of your spine. Enjoy this wonderful stretch.

VARIATIONS   **(MORE FUN)** As front partner walks forward, back partner provides a relaxing shoulder massage while receiving full body stretch. Partners switch. Other partner receives relaxing massage.

BASIC CONDITIONING PROGRAM IN THE POOL

WARM-UP

At least 5–10 minutes of aerobic exercise such as water walking, jogging, jumping jacks, cross-country skiing, skipping, bounding, hopping, and or kicking

LOWER BODY

Buttocks, Hips, Thighs	Squats
Buttocks, Hips, Thighs	Lunges
Thighs	Jumping Jacks Power Out
Thighs	Jumping Jacks Power In
Thighs	Knee Lifts and Kicks
Thighs	Single or Double Leg Curls

UPPER BODY

Chest	Chest Press
Chest	Hugs
Back	Lat Press Down
Back	Shoulder Blade Squeeze
Shoulders	Lateral Raise
Arms	Biceps Curls
Arms	Triceps Press with Flotation Dumbbell

ABDOMINALS AND CORE

Abdominals	Pelvic Tilt
Abdominals	Crunch
Abdominals	Reverse Curls
Abdominals	Oblique Crunches
Back	Back Extension

COOL-DOWN STRETCHES

CHAPTER 9

Exercises for the Major Muscle Groups: The Lower Body

For each muscle group, two types of resistance exercises are presented: free weights or body weight, and bands or tubing. Pick and choose among the exercises depending on what you prefer. For variety, keep in mind that you can also combine your dumbbell and band or tubing exercise for a different style of resistance.

The Lower Body Muscles

Buttocks or "Glutes"

The largest muscle group in your body is the glutei: maximus, medius, and minimus. These muscles are commonly referred to as the "glutes." Your gluteus maximus is the largest. You engage this muscle when you walk, run, and jump. The gluteus medius is smaller and assists in more lateral movements such as skating, tennis, or basketball. The gluteus minimus is the smallest of the three. When you rotate your leg outward from the hip, you use your gluteus minimus. This is the muscle underneath what some people refer to as the "saddlebags" area.

Strong glutes support your back, power your walk, and help you get in and out of chairs. Since your glutes are the largest muscles in your body, strong glutes are like your calorie-burning engine. I always encourage my students to think of lunges and squats as "revving up" their engines. Without strong glutes, you will not have much leg endurance and you may have lower back pain.

Hip Flexors

The hip flexors are located opposite your glutes. They assist in lifting your leg towards the front. Every time you climb a stair you are using your hip flexors. Since many of us sit throughout the day, our hip flexors tend to be tight and short. It's equally important to stretch your hip flexors as it is to strengthen them.

Quadriceps or "Quads"

Your quadriceps, or quads, are located in the front of your thighs. The quadriceps are actually four different muscles that work together. The quadriceps include the rectus femoris, vastus medialis, vastus lateralis, and vastus intermedius. The largest of your quads is the rectus femoris. The rectus femoris attaches at the hip joint as well as at the knee joint. The rectus femoris is part of your hip flexors since it lifts your upper leg when it contracts. Your quads allow you to extend your leg from the knee.

Hamstrings or "Hams"

Your hamstrings are opposite to your quads. Your hamstring muscles are in the back of your thighs. The function of the hamstrings is to bend your knee and bring your heel towards your buttocks. Your hamstrings and glutes often work together to extend your leg behind you.

SQUATS

MUSCLES   gluteals, hamstrings, quadriceps, (hips, buttocks, thighs)

Squats
with weights

GET SET   Stand with feet hip width apart, feet pointing straight ahead. Place hands on your thighs to support your back.

ACTION   Sit back as if you are going to sit in a chair. Do not bend your knees more than 90 degrees. Push yourself back up with your weight firmly centered in your heel and mid-foot. Do not allow your knees to extend beyond your toes.

TIPS   Inhale as you sit back, exhale as you push up.

VARIATIONS

(EASIER) Use a chair or bench to spot you. Sit back until you just feel the bench without sitting down. Push up through your heels.

(EASIER) Only lower half way to bench. Push up.

(HARDER) Perform the exercise while holding dumbbells in each hand.

(HARDER) Lift one knee up so thigh is parallel to the floor. Sit back into a one legged squat. Push up through heels. This is also a great balance challenge.

Squats
with bands

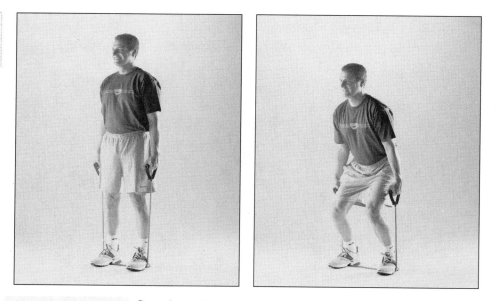

BANDS OR TUBING   Stand on the center of a band or tubing while holding an end in each hand. Perform squat as described.

LUNGES

MUSCLES   gluteals, hamstrings, quadriceps (hips, buttocks, thighs)

Lunges
with weights

GET SET   Stand next to your chair or a wall with your feet hip width apart. You can use one hand against the wall for support. Take one generous step backward with your outside leg. Stand on the full sole of your front foot and ball of your back foot.

ACTION   Bend both knees. Lengthen your spine, relax your shoulders. Your bent knee of the back leg will almost touch the floor. Make sure the bent knee of the front leg does not extend beyond your toes. Push up through the heel of your front foot.

TIPS   Inhale as you lower, exhale as you push up. Keep tone in your abdominals. Maintain good posture with neutral spinal alignment. If you need to lean forward slightly, bend from your hips.

VARIATIONS   **(HARDER)** Do not use the wall for support.

(HARDER) Hold a dumbbell in each hand.

(HARDER) Stand with feet hip width apart to begin. Step forward with one leg into the lunge. Push off to return to start.

(HARDER) Step backward with one leg into lunge. Return to start. Can do either version with alternating legs.

(HARDER) Travel forward across the room as you lunge. Keep weight over heel of forward leg.

Lunges
with bands

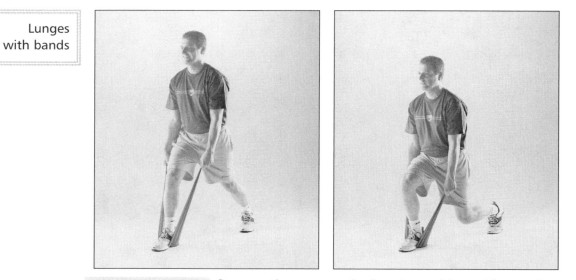

BANDS OR TUBING   Step on the center of a band or tubing with your front foot. Hold an end in each hand. Perform lunge as described.

LEG EXTENSIONS

MUSCLES   quadriceps (front of thighs)

Leg extension
with ankle
weights

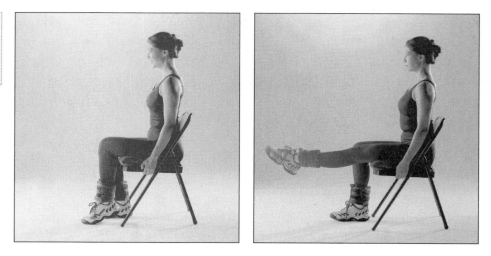

GET SET   Sit tall in chair with ankle weight on leg. Place feet hip width apart with knees above your feet. Place a towel underneath your thigh to elevate your weighted leg. Place hands on lap or hold sides of chair seat.

ACTION   Extend your leg forward without locking your knee. Lower slowly to starting position.

TIPS   Inhale to prepare, exhale as you raise your legs. Inhale as you return to start. Relax your shoulders and jaw. Maintain good posture throughout the exercise.

Leg extension with bands

BANDS OR TUBING   Sit on the floor with your legs extended in front of you. Bring knee towards your chest. Place center of band underneath sole of your foot. Hold one end of the band in each hand. Extend your leg forward pressing against band's resistance. Return slowly to start.

LEG CURLS

MUSCLES hamstrings (back of thighs)

Leg curls with
ankle weights

GET SET Kneel on all fours with an ankle weight on one leg. Place elbows on floor under shoulders. Maintain neutral spinal alignment. Avoid dropping your head.

ACTION Extend weighted leg back with heel in line with buttocks. Raise heel toward buttocks. Slowly lower.

TIPS Inhale to prepare, exhale as you raise your leg. Inhale as you return to start. Keep abdominals contracted and keep thigh parallel to the floor.

VARIATIONS After you straighten leg back to start, lower foot towards floor. Return to buttocks height and add leg curl.

Leg curls
with tubing

BANDS OR TUBING   Lie face down on the floor. Place a towel under your hips to support your back. Place a circular tube or band tied in a circle around your ankles. Keep one leg long with band or tube anchored under it. Slowly bend knee and raise other foot towards the sky against resistance. Keep hips in contact with the towel. Return slowly to start.

The Thigh Muscles

Inner Thighs

The muscles along your inner thighs are called hip adductors. Your hip adductors move your leg across the midline of your body. Your adductors assist the tracking of your knee over your foot and stabilize your knee joint. For example, when your leg travels forward and back in exercises like squats and lunges, your inner thighs are working together with your glutes, quads, and hamstrings to stabilize this action.

When it comes to functional fitness, toning your inner thigh muscles often assists in toning muscles of the pelvic floor. To gain body awareness of your pelvic floor muscles, try to stop the flow of urine when you go to the bathroom. Both men and women can discover these muscles this way. This, however, is not a method for training these muscles as it can contribute to bacteria in your urinary tract if you don't completely empty your bladder.

Remember to contract these muscles as you exhale and squeeze your inner thighs. Before long, you'll notice improvements both in bladder control and in your sex life. Here again, these are important muscles to tone to enhance the quality of your life and add life to your years.

Outer Thighs

The muscles in your outer thighs are called hip abductors. When you contract your abductors, your leg moves away from your body. Your abductors along with the tensor fasciae latae muscle stabilize your hip and knee joints. Strong inner and outer thigh muscles also protect your knees and hips when you move from side to side. If you're a skier, tennis player, or basketball player, these muscles are particularly important to prevent knee injuries.

SIDE-LYING TOP LEG LIFT

MUSCLES   hip abductors, tensor fasciae latae (outer thighs, hips)

Side-lying top leg lift with ankle weights

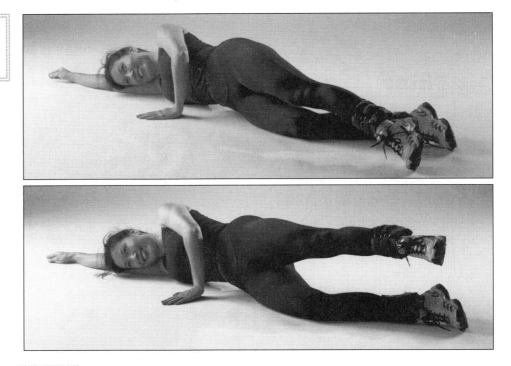

GET SET   Lie on your side, extend your lower arm on the floor. Rest your head on your lower arm. Use your upper arm like a kick-stand to support your body. Stack your hips perpendicular to the floor, engage your abdominal muscles. Lengthen your top leg from the hip through the soles of your feet with your ankle pointed towards the ceiling.

ACTION   Lift your top leg to shoulder height. Keep your hips stable. Avoid rolling forward or backwards.

TIPS   Inhale to prepare, exhale to lift, inhale as your return to start. Relax your shoulders. Engage your abdominals. Maintain neutral spinal alignment.

VARIATIONS Point your toes. Flex your feet.

(HARDER) Flex your foot and rotate your leg internally with your heel towards the ceiling. Lift.

(HARDER) Add ankle weights on your ankle, or place on your outer thighs above your knee joint if you have knee problems.

Side-lying leg
lift with bands

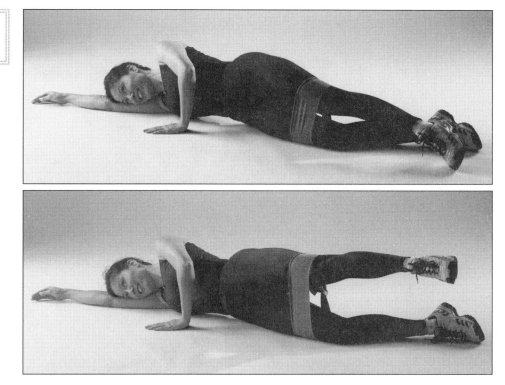

BANDS OR TUBING Tie your band in a circle or use a circular tube. Place around both thighs above the knee in side-lying position. Perform movement as described.

STANDING SINGLE LEG LIFT

MUSCLES hip abductors (outer thighs)

Standing single leg lift with ankle weights

GET SET Put on ankle weights. Stand behind your chair or facing a wall. Use hands for support.

ACTION Lift one leg out to the side. Flex foot and keep knee and toes facing forward. Keep shoulders relaxed, abdominals engaged, and maintain neutral spinal alignment. Lean torso to the side as you lift your leg to maintain alignment.

TIPS Inhale to prepare, exhale as you lift. Inhale, return to start. Avoid a tight grip if using a chair.

VARIATIONS Perform exercise without weights. Flex your foot and rotate leg internally (looks like a karate side kick).

BANDS OR TUBING Use a circle tube or a band tied in a circle. Place around your ankles. Stand hip width apart with toes pointing straight ahead. Relax your shoulders. Engage your abdominals. Lift your leg out to the side while standing tall. Return to start.

SIDE-LYING LOWER LEG LIFT

MUSCLES   hip adductors (inner thighs)

Side-lying
lower leg lift
with weights

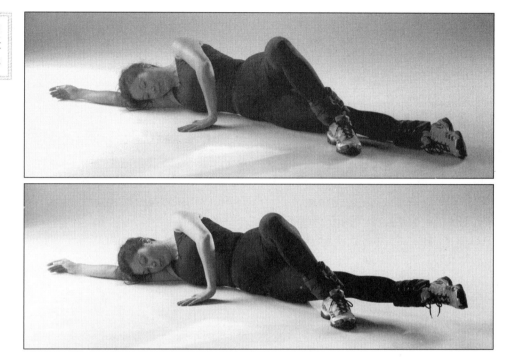

GET SET   Same initial body position as in side-lying top leg lift. Bend knee of your top leg and place your foot on the floor behind your lower leg. Lengthen your lower leg from the hip through the soles of your feet with your ankle pointed towards the ceiling.

ACTION   Lift the lower leg up as high as possible without changing your spinal alignment, then lower.

TIPS   Inhale to prepare, exhale to lift, inhale as your return to start. Relax your shoulders. Engage your abdominals. Maintain neutral spinal alignment.

VARIATIONS   Instead of placing top leg behind your lower leg, bend knee and place in front of your body. You can rest your lower leg on a towel for support.

(HARDER) Flex your foot and rotate your leg internally with your heel towards the ceiling. Lift.

(HARDER) Add ankle weights on your ankle, or place on your inner thighs above your knee joint if you have knee problems.

BANDS OR TUBING   Tie your band in a circle or use a circular tube. Anchor under foot of top leg in side-lying position. Slip lower leg through loop. Perform movement as described.

The Calf and Shin Muscles

Calves or "Gastroc" and Soleus

The muscles in the back of your lower leg make up your calves. The calf consists of two muscles, the soleus and the gastrocnemius. Every time you stand on tiptoe, you contract your calf muscles. Every time you lift your heels, you contract your calf muscles. Strengthening your calves will allow you to walk and run comfortably for longer periods of time.

A benefit of strengthening your calves is that you will increase mobility of your ankle joint. This will improve your stability and reduce the risk of wrenching your ankle or losing your balance.

Your gastrocnemius muscle is what you see first when you look at your calf muscles. It is responsible for the calf's rounded shape. The soleus muscle is underneath the gastrocnemius. The soleus assists the gastrocnemius to lift the heel when you are seated. Exercises to target the soleus muscle need to be done in a seated position.

Shins

Many people neglect the shins. Your shins are in front of your lower leg. Anterior tibialis is the name of the muscle. If you've had shin splints or other lower leg problems in the past, it may be related to a muscle imbalance between your calves and shins. If you strengthen your calves, you should also strengthen your shins. Each time you pick up the ball of your foot, you contract your shins.

STANDING CALF RAISE

MUSCLES soleus, gastrocnemius (calves)

Standing calf raises with weights

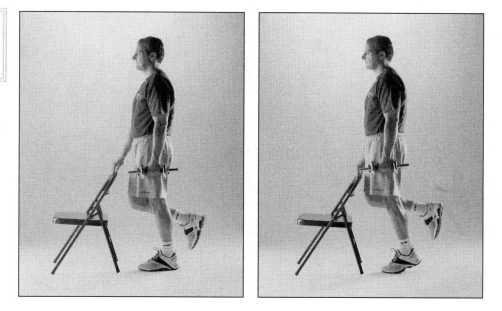

GET SET Stand behind your chair or facing a wall. Use hands for support. Balance on ball of foot of working leg.

ACTION Push up onto the ball of your foot as high as you can lift. Slowly lower down without touching the floor.

TIPS Inhale to prepare, exhale as you push up. Inhale, return to start. Avoid a tight grip if using a chair. Maintain neutral spinal alignment throughout the movement. Relax your shoulders. Keep your head level.

VARIATIONS Stand on a step so your foot is elevated from the floor. Place the ball of the foot on the step and let your heel hang off the edge. Slowly lower your heels before you begin, then push up as high as you can raise.

(EASIER) Do both legs together.

(HARDER) Do one leg at a time.

(HARDER) Hold a dumbbell in your hand to add more resistance than your body weight.

(HARDER) Use less and less hand support to challenge your balance. Progress to using one fingertip only or no support at all.

STANDING TOE RAISE

MUSCLES anterior tibialis (calves)

Standing toe raises with body weight

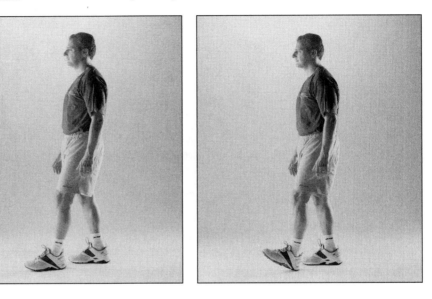

GET SET Stand on both feet behind your chair or facing a wall. Use hands for support.

ACTION Shift weight into your heels. Lift the ball of your foot as high as you can.

TIPS Inhale to prepare, exhale as you lift your toes up. Inhale, return to start. Avoid a tight grip if using a chair. Maintain neutral spinal alignment throughout the movement. Relax your shoulders. Keep your head level.

VARIATIONS

(EASIER) Sit in a chair and lift balls of your feet up.

(EASIER) Do both legs together.

(HARDER) Do one leg at a time.

(HARDER) Hold a dumbbell in your hand to add more resistance than your body weight.

(HARDER) Use less and less hand support to challenge your balance. Progress to using one fingertip only or no support at all.

CHAPTER 10

Exercises for the Major Muscle Groups: The Upper Body

As in the previous chapter, two types of resistance exercises are presented for each muscle group: free weights or body weight, and bands or tubing. The exercises you pick and choose depend on what you prefer. If you're working out at a gym, also try to include weight machines in your workout program.

The Chest Muscles or "Pecs"

When people think about strength training, visions of bodybuilders with enormous chests and arms come to mind. Around certain bodybuilding gyms, a man's entire strength-training reputation can rest on how much he can press. While we do not need to aspire to bench press the body weight of our spouses, both men and women can benefit from strong chest muscles.

Your chest muscles include the pectoralis major and the pectoralis minor, known collectively as the "pecs." The pectoralis major is a large, fan-shaped muscle that is closer to the surface. Part of the pectoralis major attaches to the middle of the collarbone and runs to the upper arm in a horizontal direction. The pectoralis major works together with your shoulder muscles to move your arms forward, upward, and across the front of your body, and to rotate your arms inward.

The other part of the pectoralis major runs from the sternum, or breastbone, in the center of your chest, across your chest and up to the top of your upper arm in a diagonal direction. When you press your arms downward and inward you contract these muscles. Training on an incline bench will enable you to most effectively challenge these muscle fibers. The pectoralis minor is underneath the pectoralis major.

DUMBBELL CHEST PRESS

MUSCLES   pectoralis major, anterior deltoids, triceps (chest, shoulders, arms)

Dumbbell
chest press

GET SET Lie on a horizontal bench or the floor, gently holding a dumbbell in each hand. Place your feet flat on the bench or on the floor. Maintain neutral spine. Bend your elbows to about 90 degrees. Hold weights with an overhand grip with your palms facing away.

ACTION Press the dumbbells up above the center of your chest (in line with the nipple line) without locking your elbows. Keep your shoulders relaxed, abdominals engaged. Maintain neutral wrist alignment.

TIPS Inhale to prepare, exhale press up. Inhale, return to start. Avoid excessive arching in your lower back. Do not let elbows fall below bench level. Lengthen arms without locking elbows.

VARIATIONS

(EASIER) If you experience any discomfort in your elbows or shoulders, do not lower weights all the way back to start. Try lowering only partially down and keep weights above shoulders.

(HARDER) Elevate your knees above your hips, knee bent at approximately 90 degrees. Make sure your lower back is supported against the bench.

Chest press with tubing

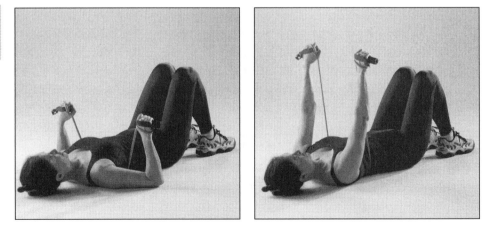

BANDS OR TUBING Lie on top of a piece of tubing behind your back. Hold one handle in each hand. Press up against resistance. Lower slowly.

DUMBBELL CHEST FLY

MUSCLES   pectoralis major, anterior deltoids, (chest, shoulders)

Dumbbell
chest fly

GET SET   Lie on a horizontal bench or the floor, gently holding
a dumbbell
in each hand. Place your feet flat on the bench or on the floor.
Maintain neutral spine. Hold weights with your palms towards each
other. Push dumbbells over chest with arms fully extended without
locking elbows.

ACTION   Slowly open arms and lower dumbbells towards floor until arms
are parallel with the bench. Do not let elbows fall below bench height.
Lift arms back to start in a big hugging motion.

TIPS   Inhale as arms open, exhale as you lift and squeeze.

VARIATIONS

(EASIER) If you experience any discomfort in the shoulder area, do
not lower as much. Keep hands above shoulder height. If you have
any discomfort in the elbows, try the exercise with your elbows bent
throughout the movement. Do not continue exercise if you
experience pain.

(HARDER) Perform exercise on an incline bench. Also known as an
Incline Chest Fly.

Chest fly
with tubing

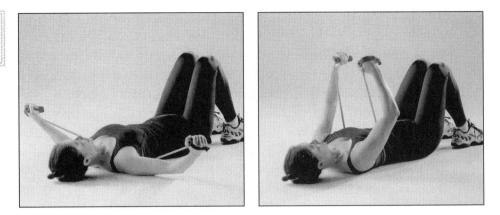

BANDS OR TUBING   Lie on top of a piece of tubing behind your back. Hold one handle in each hand. Start with both hands extended outward with elbows slightly bent. Make a big hugging motion against resistance. Lower slowly.

PUSH-UPS

MUSCLES   pectoralis major, anterior deltoid, triceps (chest, shoulder, arms)

Push-ups with
body weight

GET SET   Kneel on all fours on the floor. Walk your hands forward until your hands are slightly wider than shoulder width apart and your torso resembles a slanted board. Engage your abdominal muscles. Maintain neutral alignment.

ACTION Straighten your arms and push your body up through your palms. Keep your shoulders relaxed. Maintain neutral alignment.

TIPS Inhale to prepare, exhale as you push up. Inhale, return to start. Place a towel under your palms to elevate palms and reduce pressure on your wrists. Another option to reduce pressure on your wrists is to hold onto dumbbells that rest on the floor. Avoid dropping your head. Your push up should not resemble a nose dive. Avoid locking your elbows when you lift. Lower as low as possible.

VARIATIONS

(EASIER) Stand in front of a wall. Place hands on wall slightly wider than shoulder width apart. Bend elbows and lower body towards wall. Straighten arms as you push through hands.

(EASIER) On floor, instead of working from a slanting board position, kneel on all fours. Lower your chest towards the floor by bending your elbows. Adjust the amount of load by shifting more or less weight from your knees into your hands.

(HARDER) On floor, instead of working from a slanting board position, extend your legs long and rest on the balls of your feet, so your body resembles a plank.

BANDS OR TUBING Assume same body position. Place one end of the band under each of your hands and around your back. Push up against the increased resistance of the band. Lower with control.

The Back Muscles

Your back consists of several muscles. Your latissimus dorsi ("lats") is a large triangular shaped muscle that helps give the "V" shape to athletic backs. Your trapezius ("traps") is a large kite shaped muscle that spans the base of the neck, across your shoulders, and down through the center of your upper and mid-back. Across the upper back and in between your shoulder blades are the rhomboid muscles. The rhomboids, along with the traps, squeeze your shoulder blades together.

Functionally, strong and healthy back muscles assist whenever you pull anything towards you. They hold your torso erect and provide support when you sit so you avoid pain from muscle fatigue. Your upper and mid-back muscles stabilize your scapula and support your shoulders. Strong back muscles are critical to injury prevention. More lower back muscles are covered in the section that includes abdominal and core muscle training.

ONE ARM DUMBBELL ROW

MUSCLES   latissimus dorsi, trapezius, posterior deltoids, biceps (back, shoulders, arms)

One arm row with dumbbells

GET SET   Place the knee and hand of the same side of your body on a bench or chair like half of an "all fours" position. Maintain neutral spine. Your hips and shoulders should be level. Gently hold a dumbbell in your other hand with your arm hanging directly below your shoulder without locking your elbow. Your palm faces inward. Maintain neutral wrist.

ACTION   Bend your elbow and pull your arm up, while keeping your shoulder blade stabilized. Keep your elbow in close to your body. Slowly lower.

TIPS   Inhale to prepare, exhale to lift. Inhale, return to start. Keep your abdominals engaged, shoulders relaxed. Avoid arching or sagging through your back.

BANDS OR TUBING Stand in a generous split stance. Place one end of the band under your forward foot. Gently hold other end of the band in your opposite hand with your palm facing back. Place same hand as forward foot on mid-thigh for support. Inhale to prepare, exhale and bend your elbow as you pull your arm in toward your waist. Rotate your palm facing inward. Inhale, return to start.

SEATED BACK DUMBBELL FLY

MUSCLES trapezius, posterior deltoids (back, shoulders)

Seated back dumbbell fly

GET SET Sit on a chair or bench. Bend forward at the waist. You can place a pillow on your lap for comfort. Gently hold a dumbbell in each hand. Slide your shoulders down. Let your arms hang at your side. Maintain a neutral neck position.

ACTION Bend your elbows slightly. Squeeze your shoulder blades together. Raise your dumbbells away from your body. Keep squeezing your shoulder blades together. Lower your arms slowly. Then release shoulder blades.

TIPS Inhale to prepare, exhale, squeeze your shoulder blades and lift. Inhale, return to start. Keep your abdominals engaged.

The Shoulder Muscles or "Delts"

Your shoulder muscles are known collectively as your deltoids, or "delts," and include three muscles—your anterior, medial, and posterior deltoids. Your deltoids work together with the "rotator cuff" muscles to enable your shoulder to perform its broad variety of movements.

The rotator cuff muscles include the supraspinatus, subscapularis, infraspinatus, and teres minor. If you memorize their names you may be able to impress your friends. More important, if you strengthen them you will have stronger joints and more stable shoulders.

OVERHEAD PRESS

MUSCLES medial deltoids, triceps, trapezius (shoulders, arms, back)

Overhead press with dumbbells

GET SET Stand in a split stance. Gently hold a dumbbell in each hand. Bend your elbows, with your palms facing forward, place your hands outside of your shoulders. It's like a "stick 'em up" position.

ACTION   Press weights up as high as you can go without locking your elbows. Lower to shoulder height or slightly lower than shoulder height.

TIPS   Inhale to prepare, exhale, press up. Inhale, return to start. Maintain neutral spine. Engage your abdominal muscles and stabilize your back.

VARIATIONS

(EASIER) Face your palms in, instead of forward.
Stand in a split stance while performing exercise.

BANDS OR TUBING   Stand in a split stance. Anchor one end of band in hand held in front of center of your body. Slowly press band up with your other arm, extending your arm fully without locking your elbow. Your arm will travel slightly forward. Maintain neutral spine. Keep your abdominals engaged.

LATERAL RAISE

MUSCLES   medial deltoids (shoulders)

Lateral raise
with
dumbbells

GET SET Stand in a split stance. Gently hold a dumbbell in each hand. Hang your arms at your sides with palms facing in.

ACTION Lift your arms out to the side to approximately shoulder height. Avoid locking your elbows. Lower slowly and with control.

TIPS Inhale to prepare, exhale to lift. Inhale to return. Lift arms directly to the side. Maintain neutral spine. Keep abdominals engaged. Relax your shoulders. Keep your head level.

VARIATIONS

(EASIER) Do one arm at a time.

(EASIER) Perform while seated.

Lateral raise with bands

BANDS OR TUBING Stand in a split stance, with the middle of your band resting under your foot. Lift your arms in a lateral raise (as above).

FORWARD RAISE

MUSCLES anterior deltoid, pectoralis major (front of shoulder, chest)

Forward raise
with
dumbbells

GET SET Stand with feet hip width apart. Use the split stance. Take one step back, bend both knees slightly, and balance your body weight between both legs and in the centers of your feet. Hold a dumbbell with a gentle grip in each hand.

ACTION Slowly raise your arms in front of your body to shoulder height. Palms face toward the ground. Keep your shoulders relaxed, abdominals engaged. Slowly lower weights back to start.

TIPS Inhale to prepare, exhale to lift. Inhale, return to start. Maintain neutral posture. Keep your head level. Avoid rocking your body forward and back. Avoid excessive arching in your lower back.

VARIATIONS

(EASIER) Lift one arm at a time.

(HARDER) Stand with legs parallel. It's more difficult to maintain neutral posture.

(HARDER) Perform while seated in a chair. It's more difficult to rock your body and use momentum to lift.

(HARDER) Lying on your back on the floor

BANDS OR TUBING Stand with feet hip width apart in split stance. Hold one end of band in each hand. Place one hand on your hip. Raise other arm forward feeling the resistance of the band. Be sure to keep the opposite end stable.

The Arm Muscles

The main muscles in your arms are your biceps and triceps. Your biceps brachii actually works together with your brachialis. They are the primary muscles on the front of your upper arms.

The brachialis lies underneath your biceps. The brachialis is actually larger and stronger than your biceps, but because it is underneath, you can't really see it. Another function of these muscles is to rotate your forearms. When you bend your elbow and turn your palms up or down, you are using your biceps and brachialis.

The triceps muscle is in the back of the upper arm located directly opposite your biceps and brachialis muscles. It has three heads that all join in a shared tendon at the back of your elbow. The triceps heads include a lateral or outside of the arm head, medial or inside of the arm head, and long head.

The lateral head of the triceps runs from the back of the upper arm bone to the elbow. The medial head runs from the lower end of the arm bone to the elbow. The long head attaches on the shoulder blade, runs across the shoulder joint, and inserts at the elbow.

Always remember to train your triceps when you train your biceps. The synergistic work of the biceps and triceps is a perfect example of how our muscles work together. When your biceps contract, your elbow bends and your triceps muscles stretch. When you contract your triceps, your arm straightens out and your biceps muscles stretch. You can see how it is important to maintain balanced muscle development so one group of muscles does not overpower the other.

The muscles in your forearm control your wrist and hand actions. Strengthening these muscles is not likely to win beauty points, but you will score big in the functional fitness column. Every time you bend your wrist or make circles with your hands, you use your forearm muscles. In addition to controlling movements, our forearm muscles act as important stabilizers for our wrists. For many of us who work at computers regularly, these muscles become fatigued from supporting our working hands. When you use your arms, you often use your forearm muscles. The strength of your forearms determines your grip strength.

Strengthening your forearms will not only help you to perform activities that use your hands, but it will also help you do more exercises that require wrist stabilization. Strong wrists also help prevent injuries. Golfer's elbow or tennis elbow can be avoided by strengthening the forearm muscles. Strong wrists can prevent injuries associated with tendonitis, since strong muscles prevent excessive strain on joints.

BICEPS CURL

MUSCLES   biceps (front of upper arms)

Biceps curl
with
dumbbells

GET SET   Stand in split stance. Gently hold a dumbbell in each hand with your palms facing away from your body. Stabilize your upper arms against your body. Maintain neutral posture. Engage your abdominals. Slightly curl your wrists upwards and stabilize them.

ACTION   Bend your elbows and raise the weights toward your chest. Lower slowly.

TIPS   Inhale to prepare, exhale to lift. Inhale, return to start. Keep your upper arm stable. Do not rock your body or excessively arch your back.

VARIATIONS

(EASIER) Lift one weight at a time.

(EASIER) Perform exercise in a seated position.

(HARDER) Hold the dumbbells upright like two mugs. Lift and lower.

(HARDER) Start with palms facing in. Lift, rotate palms up. Lower, rotate weight palms down.

Bicep curl
with bands

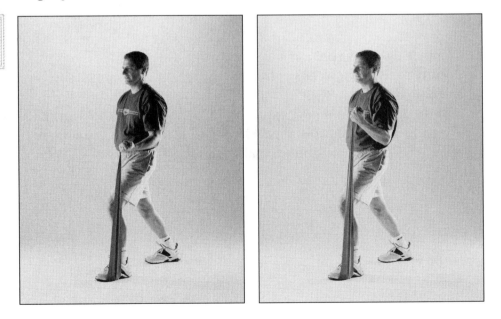

BANDS OR TUBING   Stand on a band or tube with one foot. Hold other end of band or tube with hand on same side of the body. Stabilize upper arm against the body. Begin with forearm parallel to floor. Lift palm towards body against resistance. Lower slowly.

CONCENTRATION CURL

MUSCLES biceps (front of upper arm)

Concentration curl with dumbbells

GET SET Sit on a flat bench with a wide stance. Gently hold a dumbbell in one hand. Lean forward and stabilize your upper arm against your inner thigh. Your palm is facing outward.

ACTION Bend your elbow and lift the weight to near-chin height. Lower slowly.

TIPS Inhale to prepare, exhale to lift. Inhale, return to start. Engage your abdominals. Avoid rocking your body to use momentum to lift the weight. Focus in on the working muscles.

TRICEPS PRESS

MUSCLES   triceps (back of upper arms)

Tricep press
with dumbells

GET SET   Stand in a split stance in front of chair. Bend at hip. Place same hand as your forward leg on chair for support. Lengthen the back of your neck. Maintain neutral alignment in your spine. Gently holding dumbbell in the other hand with your palm in, keep your upper arm close to torso, bend elbow and let lower arm hang straight down towards floor.

ACTION   Extend your arm and lift weight upward without locking your elbow. Slowly lower to start.

TIPS   Inhale to prepare, exhale, extend arm. Inhale, return to start. Stabilize upper arm throughout the exercise. Engage abdominals to support your back.

VARIATIONS   Stand in a lunge position. Place hand on mid-thigh of forward leg for support. Gently hold dumbbell in other hand. Perform exercise as described.

BANDS OR TUBING Stand in a lunge position. Lengthen back leg as in a calf stretch. Hold one end of band in each hand. Working arm is on same side of body as the back leg. Take hand of nonworking arm and anchor band on hip of back leg. Keep torso facing forward. Stabilize upper arm close to torso. Extend arm towards back of room and lengthen without locking elbow. Slowly return to start.

WRIST CURLS

MUSCLES forearms (bottom of lower arms)

Wrist curls

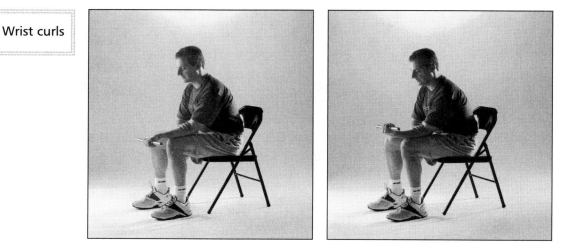

GET SET Sit comfortably on a flat bench or a chair while gently holding a dumbbell in your hand, palm up. Lean forward from your hips and rest your forearm on top of your thigh with your wrist hanging over the edge past your knee. Support your forearm by holding it with your opposite hand.

ACTION Bend your wrist and bring the weight towards you within your comfortable range of motion. Lower slowly.

TIPS Inhale to prepare, exhale and bend wrist. Inhale, return to start. Keep your forearm in contact with your leg. If wrist bothers you, try bending in a slightly smaller range of motion.

The Abdominal and Core Muscles

Core training is a popular buzz word around gyms. What does it really mean to train the core? While there isn't a universal definition for core muscles, it's generally recognized that they include muscles of the abdominal wall, the back and the pelvic floor. Collectively, these muscles provide stability and support for the body's center as you move. These muscles maintain your posture. Strong core muscles are important to prevent low back pain or back injuries. For athletes, strong core muscles are critical to access speed and power.

Everybody needs strong core muscles. Not only will you appear taller and slimmer, you will also feel more confident. Many people are motivated to train their abdominal muscles in pursuit of the elusive "six-pack" abs. It's always good when people are motivated to exercise. But what is really important about these muscles is not how they look, but what they do for you. Most people are surprised when they learn what strong abdominal muscles can do for you each and every day.

There's no guarantee that these exercises will lead to six-pack abs. However, if you do these exercises regularly you will stand taller, feel better, reduce low back pain, and improve your sports performance. Guaranteed. You can lose inches from your waist and succeed in creating a more flat belly and toned appearance. It all depends on how consistent you are with your training and whether you combine your training with healthy nutritional habits.

Abdominal Muscles

Your abdominal muscles are located in front of the torso and consist of four muscles. The muscle that people see in the "six-pack" ab photos is the rectus abdominis. It has tendonous sheaths within the muscle that create that lined appearance. It attaches under your breastbone and runs down to your pubic bone. Your rectus abdominis allows your torso to bend forward. Whether or not you can see your rectus abdominis underneath your skin depends on a number of factors. The single most important factor is genetics.

Your genetics determine the extent of muscularity that you can build and determine the location of your body fat deposits. Some people naturally store more fat under the skin on top of the rectus abdominus muscle, which makes it difficult to see the muscle development. Others tend to store more body fat in other areas of the body.

A second factor that determines whether or not you can see muscle definition under your skin is your body composition. Your body composition is the relative amount of lean body mass and fat mass that make up your body. If you have a low percentage of body fat, your muscles will be more visible under the skin. Similarly, if you have a high body fat percentage, you will not be able to see much muscle definition under the skin. The third factor is your training.

Underneath your rectus abdominus, you have two layers of oblique muscles. These muscles run at an angle down and in towards the center and up and in towards the center. The function of your obliques is to bend and twist your torso. These muscles also assist in defining your waist. The movement that most commonly leads to lower back injury is bending and twisting. This is when your spine is most vulnerable. Strong oblique muscles protect your spine in this movement and help prevent back injuries.

Last, but certainly not least, your transversus abdominus is the deepest layer of abdominal muscles. When you take a deep breath and pull your belly button towards your spine as you exhale, you are activating your transversus. This muscle is large and covers the area under your ribs, around your abdomen and above your pelvis. When the transversus contracts, it pulls in the belly in a three-dimensional fashion, like nature's girdle to support the lower back. It's primary function is to support your organs and your spine. When you cough or sneeze, you can often feel your transversus contract.

Back Muscles

Your core back muscles include the erector spinae and multifidus muscles that attach to your spine. These muscles are located along the spine in the upper, mid-, and lower back. Your erector spinae run from your neck all the way to your hips on both sides of the spine. They also branch off and attach at your ribs and spine in the mid- and upper back.

These muscles enable you to bend backwards, sideways, and to rotate your torso. Since we don't do a lot of backward bends during the day, these muscles mostly work as stabilizers to support our lower back as we sit and walk or run. These stabilizers are working isometrically in all of the exercises that require you to maintain neutral spinal alignment. Back extension exercises are the best way to challenge the erector spinae muscles to work as primary movers.

The latissimus dorsi muscles have been covered in the section related to back muscles. Because they actively play a role in stabilizing the core, they bear mentioning again in the core training section. The lats wrap around the mid to lower back. When we engage our lats, it helps to stabilize our torso and maintain good posture.

Pelvic Floor Muscles

The pelvic floor muscles span the bottom of the pelvis. These muscles support our internal organs. A fun fact to know is that one of the muscles, the coccygeus, enabled us to wag our tails, back in the ancient days when we used our tailbones. Most importantly, these muscles maintain bladder control and contribute to sexual health in both men and women.

Most women who have experienced natural childbirth become very familiar with these muscles. After the stress of pregnancy and childbirth, it's a challenge for many women to rebuild muscle tone in this area. More than 40 percent of women who've experienced natural childbirth have stress incontinence as a result of the loss of muscle tone in the pelvic floor. Stress incontinence is a loss of bladder control resulting in leaking urine triggered by sneezing, coughing, laughing, or exercising.

The most common reason for placing older adults in nursing care homes is the loss of bladder control. Caregivers find it very difficult and stressful to manage this condition. Most of us would prefer not to have to wear diapers when we age. We can prevent this by exercising our pelvic floor muscles. In addition, strong pelvic floor muscles improve a woman's sex life.

Another interesting fact about stress incontinence is that weight training, in general, seems to improve the condition. To locate these muscles, use this body awareness exercise: try to stop the flow of urine when you go to the bathroom. This works for both men and women. This, however, is not a method to exercise these muscles since it's not a good idea to prevent the complete emptying of the bladder.

To exercise and strengthen your pelvic floor muscles, you can combine the following with each of your core body exercises. As you perform your abdominal and lower back exercises, when you exhale contract your pelvic floor muscles. When you inhale, release.

PELVIC TILT

MUSCLES rectus abdominis, transversus (abdominals)

Pelvic tilt

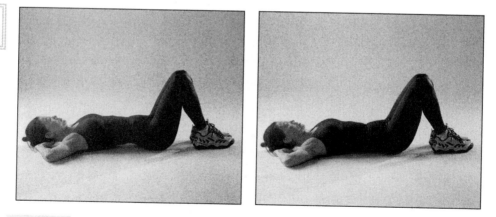

GET SET Lie on the floor with your knees bent, feet flat. Start in neutral spinal alignment with the natural curve in your lower back. Extend your arms at your sides.

ACTION Contract your abdominal muscles and feel contact of lower back against the floor. Return slowly.

TIPS   Inhale to prepare, exhale as you tilt your pelvis. Inhale, return to start. As you exhale, bring your navel towards your spine to contract your transversus. Lift pelvic floor as you exhale. Feel the stretch in your lower back. Notice if you are squeezing your buttocks to tilt your pelvis. Try to focus on using more abdominal muscles to move your hips, instead of buttocks.

VARIATIONS   Pelvic Clock—Imagine that your lower back and hips create a clock face. Behind your navel is twelve o'clock and the tip of your tailbone is six o'clock. Roll your pelvis around the clock face in both directions. Feel abdominals working.

CRUNCHES

MUSCLES   rectus abdominis, transversus (abdominals)

Crunches

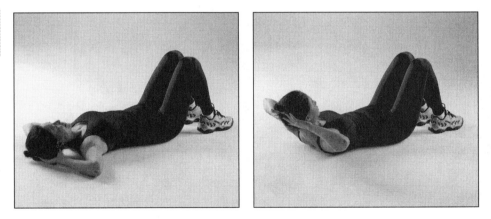

GET SET   Lie on the floor with your knees bent, feet flat. Maintain neutral spinal alignment with the natural curve in your lower back. Place your fingertips behind your head with your elbows out wide.

ACTION   Lift your head and upper back as you bring your lower ribs towards your pelvis. Contract your abdominal muscles. Lower slowly.

TIPS   Inhale to prepare, exhale as you lift up. Inhale, return to start. Avoid pulling on your head and straining your neck. As you exhale, bring your navel towards your spine to contract your transversus. Lift pelvic floor as you exhale.

VARIATIONS

(EASIER) Place your arms at your sides and lift upward as you slide your hands towards your feet.

(EASIER) Hold on to your thighs to assist you in lifting your torso forward.

(HARDER) Extend your arms long past your ears. Lift and lower as described. If you feel discomfort in lower back, try bringing your feet closer to hips.

(HARDER) Bend your knees and put your legs up on a chair or hold them in the air with your thighs perpendicular to the floor and shins parallel. When you elevate your legs, make sure your lower back is in contact with the floor for support.

(HARDER) Hold a dumbbell across your chest under folded arms.

REVERSE CURLS

MUSCLES   rectus abdominis (abdominals)

Reverse curls

GET SET   Lie on the floor, bend knees with thighs perpendicular to floor and shins parallel. Make sure your lower back is supported by the floor. Place hands at your side or across your chest.

ACTION   Contract your abdominals and lift your hips up toward the ceiling. Lower slowly.

TIPS   Relax your chest and shoulders. Avoid bouncing the body. Smoothly lift and lower. Imagine you are lifting your tailbone upward or gently tapping the ceiling. Relax your face, jaw, and neck. Lift pelvic floor as you exhale.

VARIATIONS

(HARDER) Extend legs all the way up towards the ceiling. Keep a slight bend in the knees.

(HARDER) Perform on an incline slantboard with your head higher than your hips. Place your hands above your head and gently hold on to handle. Gradually increase the incline.

BANDS OR TUBING   Start in bent knee position. Hold one end of band in each hand. Place band across top of your mid-thighs, above your knees. Keep resistance in bands. As you lift hips up, feel resistance to the movement as you work against the bands. Lower slowly.

OBLIQUE CRUNCHES

MUSCLES   obliques, rectus abdominus (abdominals)

Oblique crunches

GET SET   Lie on your back with your knees bent, feet flat on the floor. Place one hand behind your head with your elbow out. Extend other arm out to side of body, palm down. Pick up opposite foot and lay it on top of your other knee.

ACTION   Contract abs. Lift shoulder towards opposite knee, keep elbow out. Rotate the torso. Return to start.

TIPS Inhale to prepare, exhale rotate and lift. Inhale, return to start. Concentrate on lifting your shoulder towards the knee and not on bending the elbow. Keep your abdominal muscles pulled inward as you rotate. Lift pelvic floor as you exhale.

VARIATIONS

If you have discomfort in lower back, try bringing feet closer to hips.

(EASIER) Extend your arms long. Imagine you are peeling your shoulder up off the floor as you reach with both arms toward the outside of your legs. Alternate sides, or perform reps on one side, then the other.

ABDOMINAL ROLLDOWN

Abdominal
rolldown

MUSCLES rectus abdominis, transversus (abdominals)

GET SET Get on a decline bench with your knees bent. Hook your feet under the pads. Start in a lifted position with your arms extended on the outside of your thighs.

ACTION Slowly lower your torso one vertebra at a time part-way down. Curl back up to start.

TIPS Inhale to prepare, exhale as you slowly lower backwards. Keep your navel pulled in towards your spine throughout the exercise. Lift pelvic floor as you exhale.

VARIATIONS

(EASIER) Hold your thighs with your hands and use arms to assist you.

(HARDER) Place hands across chest and do not use arms at all.

BANDS OR TUBING Perform same exercise on the floor. Sit on a long band with knees bent. Hold band with hands behind head as band runs up length of your spine. Slowly lower down one vertebra at a time. Slowly roll up. If it's too difficult, only perform the lowering phase. Sit back up comfortably and repeat.

ALL FOURS ARM AND LEG EXTENSION

MUSCLES rectus abdominis, transversus, erector spinae, deltoids, gluteus, hamstrings (abdominals, back, shoulders, buttocks, hips)

All fours arm and leg extension

GET SET Kneel on all fours, hands under shoulders, knees under hips. Maintain neutral spinal alignment.

ACTION Contract your abdominals. Extend arm and opposite leg straight out in front and in behind. Maintain neutral spinal alignment, especially neutral neck. Hold for six to ten seconds. Lower slowly to start.

TIPS Inhale to prepare, exhale as you lift arm and leg. Keep your navel pulled in towards your spine throughout the exercise. Lift pelvic floor as you exhale. Avoid dropping your head and excessive arching in your back.

VARIATIONS

(EASIER) Do one arm at a time. Do one leg at a time. Concentrate on maintaining neutral alignment.

(HARDER) Repeat three to five reps on same side before doing the opposite side without placing your knee and hand fully on the floor.

BACK EXTENSION

MUSCLES erector spinae (lower back)

Back
extension

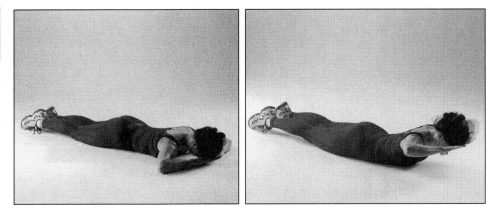

GET SET Lie facedown on your stomach. Place a towel under your hips to support your lower back. Slide your shoulder blades down your back. Place your fingertips gently on your forehead.

ACTION Contract your abdominals. Lift your chest up off the floor as you slide your shoulder blades down. Roll down to start.

TIPS Inhale, to prepare, exhale, contract your abdominals and lift through the pelvic floor. Inhale, lift your torso. Exhale, return to start. Maintain neutral neck.

VARIATIONS

If you experience any pain with this exercise, do not perform.

(EASIER) Lengthen arms along sides. Perform exercise as described.

(HARDER) Add a rotation at top of lift. Rotate shoulder back, return to center, roll down. Repeat on the other side.

MODIFIED PLANK

Modified
plank

MUSCLES   rectus abdominis, transversus, erector spinae, deltoids, gluteus maximus (abdominals, back, shoulders, buttocks)

GET SET   Kneel on all fours. Place your forearms on the floor, palms down, elbows under shoulders. Walk knees out behind hips.

ACTION   Contract your abdominals. Push up into a plank position. Maintain neutral spine. Hold ten seconds. Slowly lower down.

TIPS   Inhale, to prepare, exhale, contract your abdominals, lift through the pelvic floor and push up. Breathe naturally as you hold position. Inhale, return to start. Maintain neutral neck and avoid nose diving. Keep abdominals working, don't arch back excessively.

VARIATIONS

(HARDER) Increase length of hold to thirty seconds.

(HARDER) Lengthen legs and roll up onto toes, similar to a full push-up position.

CHAPTER 11

Your Basic Conditioning Programs

T his chapter includes sample training programs, including total body conditioning programs designed to be completed at home and at your favorite gym.

It's Your Life

Taking responsibility for your physical future, is an incredible task. Once you feel your responsibility to your physical well-being, you may never be able to ignore your energetic inner self again. What an exciting discovery to make!

The Power of Mind over Muscle

Research studies show that people who concentrate on the muscles that they are training achieve more rapid gains in strength. Keep your workouts efficient and effective. As you prepare for each and every set, mentally review not only the important elements of technique, but also how you see yourself performing the exercise. Visualize the movement, see your strong and healthy muscles, and feel the contraction as you work your exercises. When you concentrate, your workout flies by and you finish with a great sense of accomplishment.

The Power of Positive Thinking

One of my favorite research studies found that participants who communicated positive messages to their muscles were able to work harder and achieve more training gains. For example, instead of saying to yourself how tired you feel, tell your muscles how well they're performing and how proud you are of your strength.

Fill your mind with positive thoughts of everything that you can achieve. As you approach those last few reps, avoid saying, "I'm so tired. I'm never going to make it." Instead, fill your muscles with positive energy. Tell yourself, "I feel so strong. I'm doing great. I'm going to make it through one more rep." Try it, you'll be amazed by the response.

Before You Begin

Use an exercise log. When you first start out, it's a good idea to record your exercise progress. You can write down the names of the exercises, the number of sets, reps, and amount of weight that you were able to lift.

When you work out on machines, write down notes such as your seat height and any other applicable adjustments.

Perfect practice makes perfect—basic guidelines for exercise form.
For every exercise that you do, do not sacrifice quality for quantity. You will achieve superior training results in a shorter amount of time if you execute each exercise with your mind as well as your muscles.

- Always warm up for five to ten minutes before you begin your workout.
- Use full range of motion.
- Move slowly and with control. You can count up to two seconds on the lift and four seconds on the lowering phase.
- Avoid using rapid movements that move weights using momentum or your entire body weight.
- Remember to breathe. As a general rule, exhale on the exertion or effort phase of each movement.
- Maintain neutral spinal alignment. Good posture is critical and a key to avoiding injury.
- Maintain neutral neck and neutral wrist joint positions when applicable.
- Relax muscles that you don't need to use. For example, relax your jaw, neck, and shoulders, and release unnecessary tension.
- Be conservative. Err on the side of choosing lighter weights rather than heavier until you feel confident to challenge yourself with more.
- If you are feeling tired or having a low energy day, take it easy. Listen to your body and adjust accordingly.
- Make sure your equipment is properly adjusted and secured.
- Train with a spotter for any exercises that you feel may need extra assistance, such as a barbell bench press, squat, or lunge.
- Take time to stretch.

Allow your muscles forty-eight hours to repair. If you prefer to exercise every day, perform a split routine. Exercise your upper body and your lower body on alternating days and take at least one full day of rest per week.

Vary your program. Another important point to remember is that your body adapts very quickly to the challenges that you provide. On the positive side, it's great to be able to feel the difference in your body from your conditioning program in as few as four to six weeks. It's motivating and rewarding. On the negative side, you must remind yourself not to get stale. Research shows that our muscles can adapt in as few as four to five workouts.

Our minds and our muscles thrive on the stimulation of change. Even though you feel less proficient when you do something different, you challenge your neuromuscular system in a positive way. With practice, your familiar feelings of proficiency and comfort return. And, you've trained your body to respond in a new and different way to a challenge.

Sample Warm-Ups

Your warm-up should include five to ten minutes of a rhythmic activity that uses your large muscle groups. Try these activities for your warm up:

- Brisk walking
- Easy jogging
- Stationary cycling
- Indoor cross-country skiing
- Indoor rowing
- Stair climbing
- Easy jumping-rope routine

The purpose of your warm-up is to get your blood circulating to your major muscles, to raise your body temperature, to gradually elevate your heart rate, and to warm up our joints. It's also a time to make the mental transition from your daily activities to a focus on your workout. You will know that you are warmed up when your breathing rate increases slightly and you have broken out in a light sweat.

YOUR AT-HOME WORKOUTS
BASIC CONDITIONING PROGRAM—FREE WEIGHTS AND BODY WEIGHT

WARM-UP

at least 5-10 minutes of aerobic exercise

LOWER BODY

Buttocks, Hips, Thighs	Squats
Buttocks, Hips, Thighs	Lunges
Thighs	Side Lying Lower Leg Lifts
Thighs	Side Lying Top Leg Lifts
Legs	Standing Calf Raises
Legs	Standing Toe Raises

UPPER BODY

Chest, Back, Shoulders, Arms	Wall Push-Ups or Floor Push-Ups
Back	One Arm Dumbbell Row
Shoulders	Overhead Press
Arms	Concentration Curls
Arms	Triceps Press

ABDOMINALS AND CORE

Abdominals, Buttocks, Lower Back	Pelvic Tilt
Abdominals	Crunches
Abdominals	Reverse Curls
Abdominals	Oblique Crunches
Back	Back Extension

COOL-DOWN STRETCHES

YOUR AT-HOME WORKOUTS

BASIC CONDITIONING PROGRAM—BANDS/TUBING AND BODY WEIGHT

WARM-UP

at least 5–10 minutes of aerobic exercise

LOWER BODY

Buttocks, Hips, Thighs	Squats
Buttocks, Hips, Thighs	Lunges
Thighs	Side Lying Lower Leg lifts
Thighs	Side Lying Top Leg Lifts
Legs	Standing Calf Raises
Legs	Standing Toe Raises

UPPER BODY

Chest, Back, Shoulders, Arms	Wall Push-Ups or Floor Push-Ups
Back	One Arm Rows with Bands
Shoulders	Overhead Press with Bands
Arms	Biceps Curls with Bands
Arms	Triceps Press with Bands

ABDOMINALS AND CORE

Abdominals, Buttocks, Lower Back	Pelvic Tilt
Abdominals	Crunches
Abdominals	Reverse Curls
Abdominals	Oblique Crunches
Abdominals, Back	All Fours Arm and Leg Extension
Back	Back Extension

COOL-DOWN STRETCHES

YOUR AT-HOME WORKOUTS
BASIC CONDITIONING PROGRAM—BODY WEIGHT ONLY

WARM-UP

at least 5–10 minutes of aerobic exercise

LOWER BODY

Buttocks, Hips, Thighs	Squats
Buttocks, Hips, Thighs	Lunges
Thighs	Side Lying Lower Leg Lifts
Thighs	Side Lying Top Leg Lifts
Legs	Standing Calf Raises
Legs	Standing Toe Raises

UPPER BODY

Chest, Back, Shoulders, Arms	Wall Push-Ups or Floor Push-Ups

ABDOMINALS AND CORE

Abdominals, Buttocks, Lower Back	Pelvic Tilt
Abdominals	Crunches
Abdominals	Reverse Curls
Abdominals	Oblique Crunches
Abdominals, Back	All Fours Arm and Leg Extension
Back	Back Extension

COOL-DOWN STRETCHES

YOUR GYM WORKOUTS
BASIC CONDITIONING PROGRAM—MACHINES

WARM-UP

at least 5–10 minutes of aerobic exercise

LOWER BODY

Buttocks, Hips, Thighs	Leg Press
Thighs	Leg Extension
Thighs	Leg Curls

UPPER BODY

Chest, Shoulders, Arms	Chest Press
Back	Seated Row
Back	Lat Pulldown
Shoulders	Lateral Raise
Arms	Biceps Curl
Arms	Triceps Extension

ABDOMINALS AND CORE

Abdominals	Abdominal Curl
Back	Back Extension

COOL-DOWN STRETCHES

SAMPLE EXERCISE LOG FOR TWO DAY/WEEK GYM WORKOUT ON MACHINES

WEEK #1	DATE			DATE			
NAME OF EXERCISE	SETS	REPS	WEIGHT	SETS	REPS	WEIGHT	NOTES
WARM UP			5–10 minutes on treadmill				
1. Leg Press							
2. Leg Extension							
3. Leg Curls							
4. Chest Press							
5. Seated Row							
6. Lat Pulldown							
7. Lateral Raise							
8. Biceps Curl							
9. Triceps Extension							
10. Abdominal Curl							
11. Back Extension							
STRETCHES			Total body stretches, hold 15–20 seconds				

BASIC CONDITIONING PROGRAM—
FREE WEIGHTS AND MACHINES

WARM-UP

at least 5–10 minutes of aerobic exercise

LOWER BODY

Buttocks, Hips, Thighs	Squats
Thighs	Leg Extension
Thighs	Leg Curls

UPPER BODY

Chest, Back, Shoulders, Arms	Push-Ups
Back	Seated Row
Back	Lat Pulldown
Arms	Biceps Curl
Arms	Triceps Press Down

ABDOMINALS AND CORE

Abdominals	Crunch
Abdominals	Oblique Crunch
Back	Back Extension

COOL-DOWN STRETCHES

Start Out with One-Set Training

When you are new to exercise, you are filled with enthusiasm. It reminds me of the saying, "The spirit is willing, but the body is weak." Honor your willingness of spirit, that is fantastic. At the same time, respect that your body may need time to adjust.

Although it is not visible, you are accomplishing something with each and every training session. In the beginning of your weight training program, your body is working hard. You are conditioning your joints so that they can become accustomed to the challenge of extra weight. You are developing an important network of neuromuscular pathways from your brain, through your spinal column and into your muscles. It takes time to build this network!

Think of your body as an organic electronic circuit board. All of the wiring needs to be laid into place. Each time you perform an exercise movement, you are firing up the circuit board. The organic circuit board gets stronger with use over time. Respect the process. Give your body time to adjust and you will reap rewards.

Start out lifting weights that make you feel tired when you reach between the eighth to twelfth repetition. Work up to twelve repetitions. Consider one set sufficient to start. After you have worked out comfortably for a few weeks at twelve repetitions per set, go ahead and add a second set. Remember, always increase reps first, then add an additional set.

ESSENTIALS What is muscle failure? When your muscle "fails" it can no longer generate sufficient force to complete another repetition with good form. Good form relates to alignment, range of motion, speed of movement, and degree of control over the motion.

Number of Reps in Your First Program

If your goal is basic conditioning and you are training for the first time, it's generally recommended that you start out with a lower intensity. To get the best results from your training, you want to achieve muscular failure by the last rep of your set. You can safely start out a new program in a repetition range of ten to fifteen. If that does not feel like too much for you, go ahead and do as many as twelve to seventeen reps to muscle failure.

This lighter load will decrease your risk of injury. It will give your joints, ligaments, and tendons a chance to become conditioned as your muscles get stronger. You can also focus more on form initially. Add weight gradually once you feel confident with your technique.

How To Select the Right Weight Load

The weight load that you choose determines the number of reps that you can do. The best way to find a proper weight level for you is initially through trial and error. Always start out on the conservative side with a weight you think might be light for you.

If you can lift this weight easily for 15 reps, then it's too light. If you lifted between 16 to 17 reps, go ahead and add 5 pounds. If you lifted between 18 and 19 reps, try adding 10 pounds. If you easily lifted more than 20 reps, see how you do with an additional 15 pounds.

If you can successfully complete 12 to 15 reps in your first attempt, then this is your training load. You can note this on your exercise log. As you become more experienced, you will remember how much weight you lift on each of the exercises. When you're starting out, however, it can feel much more like information overload. Write it down. You will save plenty of time on your next workouts.

What if, in spite of your best efforts to select a weight on the light side, you discover that you can not even lift 12 reps? This weight level is too heavy. Save it for another day when you are stronger. If you could only lift between 10 to 11 reps, subtract 5 pounds. If you completed between 8 and 9 reps, go ahead and lower the weight by 10 pounds. If you really over-estimated your own strength and could not even lift 7 reps, don't worry. You will become stronger if you stick with your program. I guarantee it. In the meantime, drop down at least 15 pounds and be proud that you are starting out with a program.

It's always challenging to start something new. Be sure to give yourself plenty of credit. You deserve it. And, every weight that you lift, even if it's only 5 pounds to start with, is important. It is leading you on the road towards a healthier, stronger, and more active lifestyle. Keep up the great work!

CHAPTER 12

More Advanced Training Programs

Now that you've mastered the basics, you may want to add more variety to your training program. You should stick with the basic conditioning program for at least ten to twelve weeks before you switch to any more advanced variations. Then you are ready to move on to more advanced training programs, if you so choose.

How to Tell if You've Mastered the Basics

Remember to take your time to truly master your exercises before you add more resistance or try a more challenging training technique. For example, pay particularly attention to form and try to execute each repetition perfectly. Focus on maintaining tension in the working muscles throughout the full range of motion of the exercises. Really feel the working muscles contract fully during the exercise and achieve a state of fatigue at the end of your reps. When you've mastered each of these variables, then you are ready to increase the difficulty of your exercise.

If you've faithfully been pursuing your program and feel that you have achieved that level of accomplishment, then you're ready for more of a challenge. You're in the right chapter. You can continue to improve your strength levels and explore a variety of training techniques.

After you've established a basic level of conditioning, your program design will depend largely on your training objectives. If you want to focus on developing strength, you can create a program that emphasizes strength. Alternatively, you can focus on endurance or power. Or, you can train to enhance your sports performance in a particular activity that you love. The following information describes your training variables and sets forth some popular training methods. As you become more sophisticated, you will want to continue to grow and supplement your knowledge.

What Are Your Training Variables?

Designing an exercise program is as much art as it is science. That's why there are great coaches and trainers. Some individuals are particularly gifted at program design. Every coach in the world has access to these same variables.

You can use the following variables to design your exercise program:

- Frequency or length of rest between workouts
- Choice of exercise
- Number of exercises per muscle group
- Sequence of exercise

- Number of reps per set
- Number of sets
- Progression or how you increase intensity

Frequency is how often you choose to train. You can train two days a week up to six days a week. What's important is that you do not train the same muscles two days in a row. In other words you need to rest your muscles at least forty-eight hours before training again. You can, however, increase your frequency of training by starting out with a two-day-a-week program and progressing to three days a week. You will achieve more rapid strength gains if you increase frequency in this manner.

Choice of exercise refers to which exercise you decide to perform. For example, if you want to train the hamstrings and the quadriceps, do you choose squats, the leg press, the leg extension and curl, or all three? All of these exercises challenge the same muscles but in slightly different ways.

Number of exercises per muscle group means that you can decide to do as few as one exercise per major muscle group or you can perform several exercises to fatigue those muscles. The number of exercises you can do for any particular muscle group will also depend on your base level of conditioning. Most beginners can't do more than one or two exercises for a major muscle group. They simply lack the strength and endurance.

Sequence of exercise relates to how you choose to order the exercises in order to achieve the best result. The basic rule of thumb is that you always exercise your larger muscles before you exercise your smaller muscles. The reason for this is that you are only as strong as your weakest link. If you pre-fatigue the smaller muscles before you work your larger muscles, you will not be able to maximally push your larger muscles.

Another rule of sequencing is that you generally work opposing muscle groups in pairs. For example, after you work the chest then you should work the back or vice versa. Similarly, after you train your biceps, you should train your triceps. Your opposing muscle groups are as follows:

- Top of thighs and bottom of thighs
- Inner thighs and outer thighs

- Calves and shins
- Abdominals and back
- Buttocks and hip flexors
- Triceps and biceps
- Top of forearm and bottom of forearm
- Chest and back
- Front of shoulders and rear of shoulders

One of the benefits of a split routine when you train the upper body on one day and the lower body on another day is that you can afford to spend more time exploring these muscle relationships. You can devote more exercises to your smaller and deeper muscles to achieve better balance in your muscle development.

The number of reps per set is indicative of the level of intensity. If you look at the following chart, you can see that a rep range of 8 to 12 reps to fatigue is approximately 70 to 80 percent of maximum. Working in the 1- to 5-rep range would be 90 to 100 percent of maximum. Clearly, such few repetitions represent high intensity training, whereas the 8- to 12-rep range represents a more moderate level. When you start out at a new resistance level, you want to begin at the lower end of the rep range and work your way up by increasing the number of the reps before you increase the weight level. This is a more conservative approach that reduces your risk of injury.

How Hard Are You Working?

According to *ACSM Current Comment*, "Resistance Training in the Older Adult," if one repetition represents the maximum amount of weight that you can lift for an exercise, how hard are you working when you do additional reps to fatigue?

- 1 rep = 100 percent
- 2–3 reps = 95 percent
- 4–5 reps = 90 percent

- 6–7 reps = 85 percent
- 8–9 reps = 80 percent
- 10–11 reps = 75 percent
- 12–13 reps = 70 percent
- 14–15 reps = 65 percent
- 16–20 reps = 60 percent

You can see that when you work in a range of 8 to 12 reps, you are working at 70 to 80 percent. It's more difficult to work at a higher level of intensity. To achieve results, your efforts need to be at least 65 percent.

The number of sets is another measure of your strength. Initially, you can start out with one set of each of your exercises, but three sets is standard. As you get stronger, you can not only push yourself harder in each of those sets by increasing the weight, but you can also add more sets.

Progression or how you increase intensity over time is one of the most tricky aspects of your weight training program. You don't want to increase your weight levels too much too soon or you risk injury. A conservative approach would be to start a brand new program at a lower level of intensity, such as 10 to 15 reps to fatigue. Once you've mastered 15 reps to fatigue, you can then progress to two sets at that level. After you've mastered two sets at the 15 rep level, then you can progress to one set at a heavier weight level (no more than 5 percent) in the 8- to 12- rep range. If that's too much, then increase the weight level but continue to work in the 10- to 15-rep range. In this way, you can gradually and progressively build strength.

Split Routines

One of the most popular methods of manipulating your training variables is to perform a split routine. What this means is that instead of training your whole body on one day, you train part of your body on one training day and another part of your body on the next training day so that you will cover your whole body in the course of one week. By splitting your routine, you can shorten your workouts on each specific day but work out more frequently during the week. Alternatively, you can maintain the length of your workout session but devote more time to individual muscle groups.

Split routines typically rotate between the upper body and lower body or between a push and pull program. A push and pull program emphasizes the "pushing" muscles of the body on one day and the "pulling" muscles on the next. Your pushing muscles include your chest and arms such as in a push-up or bench press. Your pulling muscles include your back such as in a seated row.

UPPER BODY/LOWER BODY SPLIT ROUTINE
DAYS ONE AND FOUR—UPPER BODY
FREE WEIGHTS AND MACHINES

WARM-UP

at least 5–10 minutes of aerobic exercise

UPPER BODY

Chest	Push-Ups
Chest	Dumbbell Incline Chest Fly
Back	Seated Row
Back	Lat Pulldown
Back	Seated Back Dumbbell Fly
Shoulders	Overhead Press
Shoulders	Lateral Raise
Arms	Triceps Press Down
Arms	Triceps Extension
Arms	Biceps Curl
Arms	Concentration Curl

ABDOMINALS AND CORE

Abdominals	Crunches
Abdominals	Oblique Crunches
Back	Back Extension

COOL-DOWN STRETCHES

UPPER BODY/LOWER BODY SPLIT ROUTINE
DAYS 2 AND 5—LOWER BODY
FREE WEIGHTS AND MACHINES

WARM-UP

at least 5–10 minutes of aerobic exercise

LOWER BODY

Buttocks, Hips, Thighs	Squats
Buttocks, Hips, Thighs	Step Back Lunges
Buttocks, Hips, Thighs	Leg Press
Thighs	Leg Extension
Thighs	Leg Curls
Inner Thighs	Inner/ Outer Thigh Machine
Outer Thighs	Inner/ Outer Thigh Machine
Calves	Standing Calf Raises
Shins	Standing Toe Raises

COOL-DOWN STRETCHES

DAYS THREE, SIX, AND SEVEN ARE REST.

PUSH/PULL SPLIT ROUTINE
DAY ONE AND FOUR—PUSH CHEST, TRICEPS, AND SHOULDERS
FREE WEIGHTS AND MACHINES

WARM-UP

at least 5–10 minutes of aerobic exercise

UPPER BODY

Chest, Shoulders, Arms	Bench Press
Chest	Dumbbell Incline Chest Fly
Chest	Push-Ups
Shoulders	Dumbbell Overhead Press
Shoulders	Forward Raise
Shoulders	Lateral Raise

Shoulders	Seated Back Dumbbell Fly
Triceps	Triceps Press Down
Triceps	Triceps Extension

COOL-DOWN STRETCHES

PUSH/PULL SPLIT ROUTINE
DAYS 2 AND 5—PULL
FREE WEIGHTS AND MACHINES

WARM-UP

at least 5–10 minutes of aerobic exercise

LOWER BODY

Buttocks, Hips, Thighs	Squats
Buttocks, Hips, Thighs	Lunges
Buttocks, Hips, Thighs	Leg Press
Thighs	Leg Curls
Thighs	Leg Extension
Thighs	Inner/ Outer Thigh Machine
Thighs	Inner/ Outer Thigh Machine
Calves	Standing Calf Raise

UPPER BODY

Back	Lat Pull Down
Back	Machine Row
Arms	Biceps Curl
Arms	Concentration Curl

ABDOMINALS AND CORE

Abdominals	Crunches
Abdominals	Oblique Crunches
Back	Back Extension

COOL-DOWN STRETCHES

DAYS THREE, SIX, AND SEVEN ARE REST.

Split routines are lots of fun and provide plenty of room for training variety. With split routines, you can really get in and work a particular muscle group very thoroughly.

While split routines offer fun and variety, remember, you should not use this training approach until you have established a solid base level of total body conditioning.

Super Sets

You can enhance your training effect not only by increasing the number of days that you train but also by organizing your sets in such a way as to minimize the rest in between.

When you do super sets, you string two sets of exercises right after each other without resting. You can super set the same muscle groups or you can super set opposing muscle groups. If you perform a super set for the same muscle groups, the muscles are pre-fatigued when you begin your second set. By selecting a different exercise that challenges the same muscles, you provide a variety of stimulus to the working muscles.

Try doing super sets for opposing muscle groups. This way you rest opposing muscle groups at the same time that you work the other muscle group. It's time efficient and provides a great workout. You also really look forward to working the other body part.

SAME MUSCLE SUPER SET ROUTINE

WARM-UP

5 minutes of aerobic exercise

LOWER BODY

Buttocks, Hips, Thighs	Squats, Lunges
Thighs	Leg Curls, Leg Press

UPPER BODY

Chest, Shoulders, Arms	Dumbbell Chest Press, Dumbbell Chest Fly

Back	Lat Pulldown, One Arm Dumbbell Row
Shoulders	Overhead Press, Lateral Raise
Arms	Biceps Curl, Concentration Curl
Arms	Triceps Press Down, Triceps Extension

ABDOMINALS AND CORE

| Abdominals | Crunches, Reverse Curls |
| Back | Back Extension, Modified Plank |

COOL-DOWN STRETCHES

OPPOSING MUSCLE SUPER SET ROUTINE

WARM-UP

5 minutes of aerobic exercise

LOWER BODY

Buttocks, Hips, Thighs	Leg Press, Leg Curls
Thighs	Side-Lying Top Leg Lift, Side-Lying Lower Leg Lift
Calves, Shins	Standing Calf Raise, Toe Raise

UPPER BODY

Chest, Back	Dumbbell Chest Press, Machine Row
Chest, Back	Push-Ups, Seated Row with Bands
Shoulders	Internal Rotators, External Rotators
Arms	Biceps Curl, Triceps Extension
Arms	Concentration Curl, Triceps Dip

ABDOMINALS AND CORE

| Abdominals, Back | Crunches, Back Extension |

COOL-DOWN STRETCHES

Giant Sets

Giant sets are super sets plus one. Instead of stringing two exercises together without rest, you sequence three exercises in a row. Similar to super sets, you can put exercises for the same muscle group together or you can do an exercise for a different muscle group in each set.

SAME MUSCLE GIANT SET ROUTINES

LOWER BODY

Buttocks, Hips, Thighs	Squats, Lunges, Leg Press
Thighs	Leg Curl, Leg Extension, Leg Press

UPPER BODY

Chest, Shoulders, Arms	Chest Press, Dumbbell Chest Fly, Push-Ups
Back	Assisted Pull Up, One Arm Dumbbell Row, Seated Row
Shoulders	Dumbbell Overhead Press, Lateral Raise, Seated Back Dumbbell Fly
Arms	Biceps Curl, Concentration Curl, Barbell Curl
Arms	Triceps Press Down, Triceps Dip, Triceps Extension

ABDOMINALS AND CORE

Abdominals	Crunches, Reverse Curls, Oblique Crunches
Back	Back Extension, Plank, All Fours Arm and Leg Extension

COOL-DOWN STRETCHES

UPPER AND LOWER BODY

Buttocks, Chest, Hamstrings	Squats, Push-Ups, Leg Curls
Chest, Thighs, Shins	Dumbbell Chest Press, Lunges, Standing Toe Raise
Back, Thighs, Calves	Seated Row, Leg Extensions, Standing Calf Raise
Chest, Thighs	Dumbbell Chest Fly, Inner Thigh, Outer Thigh Machine
Back, Arms	Lat Pull Down, Biceps Curl
Chest, Shoulders	Incline Dumbbell Chest Fly, External Rotators, Internal Rotators

ABDOMINALS AND CORE

Abdominals, Back	Crunches, Back Extension, Plank

COOL-DOWN STRETCHES

Negatives

A training approach that manipulates the repetition is called a "negative." When you perform a negative, it means that you are performing only half of the exercise. You can "cheat" with negatives by receiving assistance on the way up and performing the exercise alone on the way down. Instead of both lifting and lowering the weight, you are only lowering the rep. The lowering phase of a movement is known as an eccentric contraction. Eccentric contractions occur when you contract a muscle at the same time that it is lengthening. A concentric contraction is a contraction that occurs when a muscle is shortening.

Eccentric contractions are believed to cause greater muscle tearing and consequently more post-exercise soreness. You should not perform a lot of eccentric exercise in order to avoid excessive soreness. It is considered, however an excellent way to increase strength. An example of performing a "negative" would be using one hand to assist lifting your dumbbell up for a concentration curl and using your single arm to lower the weight. You can also use the assistance of a spotter.

How to Continue Learning

You can now see that there are many different types of weight training approaches. As you continue on your journey of inner and outer strength, you will learn many things about your body. You will start to gain an inner understanding of what works for you and what does not.

Research in weight training today is very exciting and dynamic. If you want to stay informed, read books and magazines. Check scientific Web sites such as PubMed or MEDLINE. Subscribe to evidence based publications such as the American College of Sports Medicine's *Health and Fitness Journal.* Although it's directed to health and fitness professionals, it's packed with information on how to put current exercise science research into practice.

Another good source of strength training information is the National Strength and Conditioning Association. For general information on exercise that includes weight training, check out the American Council on Exercise and IDEA, The Health and Fitness Source. Both of these organizations offer information created specifically for consumers, as well as information for fitness professionals.

CHAPTER 13

Sports-Specific Training Programs

In addition to your basic conditioning program, you can add sports-specific exercises. What this means is that if you are a golf enthusiast, there are weight training exercises that may enhance your game or prevent you from injuring yourself when you play.

Conditioning To Improve Performance

The sports-specific conditioning programs that follow vary for different sports in that they emphasize strengthening different muscle groups. This variation in emphasis is based on the fact that different sports challenge different muscles. Due to the repetitive actions of some sports, muscle imbalances can result. For example, a runner can have very strong legs, but lack good upper body development. In a long run, such as a marathon, upper body endurance is very important since a strong arm swing helps drive the rhythm of the legs. A good strength-conditioning program can improve balanced muscle development to enhance overall sports performance.

Historically, many elite endurance athletes have stayed away from excessive strength training because of the fear that they would develop bulky muscles. To a certain extent this is true, because muscles can't specialize in both endurance and strength. If you're a competitive endurance athlete, you may want to reserve your more serious strength training for your off-peak season.

For forty-two-year-old Danny, weight training made all the difference. This former professional soccer player noted, "I've been an athlete all of my life, relying up to college on my 'natural' fitness. After college, I became a professional soccer player for the Buffalo Stallions and then the New Jersey Rockets, Major Indoor Soccer League. Later for the Edmonton Drillers of the North American Soccer League and Georgia Generals, American Soccer League. In the pros, I discovered weight training. My strength, speed, and endurance improved; I didn't get injured as easily even though the wear and tear at that level was intense.

"I retired from professional sports in my mid twenties, and stopped weight training. I continued playing at the club level, and joined the Greek-American Athletic Club, one of the most competitive club teams in the nation. At the club level, players usually were paid a per diem, and only practiced a couple of times a week. Extra fitness was really up to the individual.

"In my mid thirties, I noticed I had 'lost' some of my edge in terms of quickness, fight on the ball, and durability (I pulled more muscles). I had become only a spot starter. I was competing for a regular position with much younger men—most of our players were in their mid to late twenties, and several used our team as a launching pad for their professional careers (their sunrise was my sunset!).

"I wasn't ready to give up. At that point of reckoning I went back into the weight room and complemented my soccer training with weight training. After a couple of months, I noticed everything about my physical preparedness had improved, the most significant being the ability to run harder and faster for the entire duration of the game. That physical improvement allowed my soccer skills to flourish because I wasn't as tired.

"I became a consistent starter and that year the club won the first of three national titles. On our way to the title we beat college and minor league professional teams and scrimmaged the national teams of Brazil and Russia. I was the second oldest player on the side but opponents didn't know that from how I measured up. Coincidentally, the oldest player also lifted weights. We both played at this high level into our early forties.

"Weight training is only part of a complete training regime, but undoubtedly it contributes to competitive longevity. I recommend it for every athlete, young or old."

Most people, however, are not involved in such rigorous and serious sports competition. For the general active person or typical recreational enthusiast, general conditioning and sports-specific conditioning will improve performance. And, it will play an important role in injury prevention.

The following weight training programs are designed to enhance your golf or tennis game or improve your recreational hiking, running, or cycling. These programs include a selection of free weight and body weight exercises.

SSENTIALS Stretching exercises should also be included in your regular sports conditioning program and are best performed at the end of your workouts when your muscles are warm and pliable. This will not only feel good, but will enhance your recovery. Improved range of motion can also lead to better performance.

Golf

Many golfers begin their seasons with trips to the physical therapist because they have somehow managed to hurt their back. When a golfer swings his or her club, momentum is added to an already powerful rotational force. Strong core muscles are essential to protect the back from injury. Strong wrists are also important to control the swing.

Exercises that can improve a golf game and prevent injury focus on the core, forearms, arms, shoulder, and back. In addition to core training and other strength-conditioning exercises, a regular program of stretching will enhance performance on the course.

Golfers, like any other sports enthusiasts, benefit from an overall basic conditioning program. In addition to basic fitness, golfing movements use specific muscles. In particular, the wrist extensors and flexors or muscles of the forearm are important to provide good grip strength. Stabilizer muscles of the shoulder support the swing, and core stabilizers provide control through the torso. Power comes from the lower body as the hips rotate while the arms swing the club.

Here are some great conditioning exercises to supplement your playing time.

To improve your cardiovascular conditioning, try to walk instead of using a cart when you play. Carrying your clubs can also be great exercise. Be sure to carry them in a balanced manner so you do not stress your shoulder or back with an uneven weight load.

GOLF CONDITIONING PROGRAM
FREE WEIGHTS AND MACHINES

LOWER BODY

Buttocks, Hips, Thighs	Leg Press
Buttocks, Hips, Thighs	Lunges

UPPER BODY

Chest, Back, Shoulders, Arms	Push-Ups
Back	Lat Pulldown
Shoulders	Overhead Press
Arms	Biceps Curl
Arms	Triceps Extension
Arms	Wrist Curls
Arms	Reverse Wrist Curl

ABDOMINALS AND CORE

Abdominals	Crunches
Abdominals	Oblique Crunches
Abdominals	Reverse Curls
Back	Back Extension

Tennis

Tennis is a great social and international sport. Technology has improved racquets so much that the game is more about speed and power than ever before. Powerful serves and strokes require solid core strength to facilitate the rotation of the torso. Strong shoulder, especially rotator cuff muscles, and back muscles are essential to serves and powerful overhead shots. Strength and endurance in the forearm and wrist are important to stabilize the racquet. Balanced muscle development on both sides of the body is essential. Weight training can definitely enhance performance by strengthening all of these muscles and by preventing injuries.

In the lower body, agility and leg strength is essential to quickly travel across the court. The knees of tennis players are particularly vulnerable from rapid side to side traveling movements. Strong legs are also necessary for the quick push offs and stops involved in a fast-paced and hard fought game. To prevent knee injuries, players should strengthen the leg muscles that support the knee joint.

The famous tennis elbow is in fact an inflammation of the tendons in the elbows from the repetitive shock of hitting balls. Strengthening the wrists and arms can provide better support to the joint and relieve stress on the tendons. In addition to the following weight training exercises, tennis players may also consider sports specific training in a pool with an old racquet. Not only will the water provide resistance that is specific to the sports moves, but it will help reveal any weaknesses in the swing.

TENNIS CONDITIONING PROGRAM
FREE WEIGHTS AND MACHINES

LOWER BODY

Buttocks, Hips, Thighs	Squats
Buttocks, Hips, Thighs	Lunges
Outer Thighs	Seated Outer Thigh Machine
Inner Thighs	Seated Inner Thigh Machine
Calves	Standing Calf Raise
Shins	Standing Toe Raise

UPPER BODY

Chest, Back, Shoulders, Arms	Push-Ups
Back	Lat Pulldown
Back	One Arm Dumbbell Row
Shoulders	Overhead Press
Shoulders	Internal Rotators
Shoulders	External Rotators
Arms	Biceps Curl

Arms	Wrist Curls
Arms	Reverse Wrist Curl
ABDOMINALS AND CORE	
Abdominals	Crunches
Abdominals	Oblique Crunches
Abdominals	Reverse Curls
Back	Back Extension

Hiking

Hiking is a fantastic recreational activity for outdoor enthusiasts that can be enjoyed by people of all ages. If you are a nature lover, there's nothing like enjoying a great hike in the beautiful outdoors. Because hiking can be so pleasurable, it may not seem like the type of exercise that you can condition for. Anyone who goes for long backpacking treks definitely knows the benefits of great conditioning. Even if your hikes consist of short half-day walks through local parks, a cross-conditioning weight training program can enhance your endurance and prevent injuries.

Hiking primarily challenges the muscles of the lower body. A good arm swing, however, can keep your energy up, particularly as your legs start to fatigue. You also need strong core muscles to support your back. This can be even more important if you are carrying any supplies—or, in the event that it is a family hike, if you are carrying any young children.

The most frequent areas of fatigue among hikers are the muscles of the shins and of the back. Unless you walk regularly, your lower legs are not used to the repetitive motion of picking up your foot for hours on end. Furthermore, if you wear heavy hiking boots or are traveling through rocky paths, ankle strength and endurance are also important.

These exercises will keep you in tip-top hiking shape, so when you take those outdoor trips you can focus on the beauty of the natural surroundings rather than the various aches and pains in your body.

HIKING CONDITIONING PROGRAM
FREE WEIGHTS AND MACHINES

LOWER BODY

Buttocks, Hips, Thighs	Squats
Buttocks, Hips, Thighs	Lunges
Thighs	Leg Extensions
Thighs	Leg Curls
Calves	Standing Calf Raise
Shins	Standing Toe Raise

UPPER BODY

Chest, Back, Shoulders, Arms	Push-Ups
Back	Lat Pulldown
Back	Machine Row
Shoulders	Overhead Press
Arms	Biceps Curl

ABDOMINALS AND CORE

Abdominals	Crunches
Abdominals	Oblique Crunches
Back	Back Extension

Running

Running still persists in its popularity. For those who love running, nothing can replace the meditative fix of feeling at one with your body and spirit, breathing steadily, and enjoying the rhythmic movement of your muscles. And, you often hear that nothing can replace that wonderful feeling runners love from their sport. Many running enthusiasts become sidelined with injuries, however. So, to keep your body healthy for running, it's a good idea to include some weight training to prevent injuries.

Some of the more common running injuries include shin splints, knee or hip pain, and lower backaches. As you now well know, strong muscles can alleviate stress placed on joints. When your muscles can provide more support to your joints, the ligaments and tendons experience less stress and strain. Strengthening the muscles that support your joints will not reduce the impact from running, but it will ease the amount of stress placed on the joints with each stride.

In longer distance running, a strong arm swing is highly desirable to continue to power the legs forward. Strong shoulder stabilizer and back muscles will give your arms the support they need to keep on swinging. Runners also need to strengthen the core muscles of the abdominal and back area to provide support for the lower back and to maintain good posture. Strengthening these muscles is critical to avoid lower back pain.

ALERT

Runners should check their shoes frequently and make sure they are providing optimal support. Shop at reputable running shoe stores and tell the salesperson what type of terrain you run on, how many miles you run per week, and your preference in cushioning and weight.

Running enthusiasts can avoid excessive impact by including some deep water running in their overall training program. Research studies have shown that deep water training will not reduce conditioning for on land performance and can successfully be incorporated into a training program. Runners can strap on a buoyancy belt and perform valuable interval training to improve conditioning or easy endurance training days for active recovery.

One more important point to note about running is that if you train for distance running a muscle imbalance can develop between the hamstrings and the quadriceps. Remember, the hamstrings are in the back of the thighs. The quadriceps are in the front of the thighs. When runners propel themselves forward, they rely heavily on hamstrings in the push off phase. Over time, the hamstrings can become relatively stronger than the quadriceps which can lead to injuries.

Overly tight and strong hamstrings can pull the pelvis out of alignment and affect neutral spinal alignment. When posture is affected, back pain can result. Weight training can contribute to maintaining balanced muscle development that contributes to proper body alignment.

Here are some great weight training exercises to complement your running program.

RUNNING CONDITIONING PROGRAM
FREE WEIGHTS AND MACHINES

LOWER BODY

Buttocks, Hips, Thighs	Leg Press
Buttocks, Hips, Thighs	Lunges
Thighs	Leg Extensions
Thighs	Leg Curls
Thighs	Inner Thigh Machine
Thighs	Outer Thigh Machine
Calves	Standing Calf Raise
Shins	Standing Toe Raise

UPPER BODY

Chest, Back, Shoulders, Arms	Push-Ups
Back	Lat Pulldown
Back	One Arm Dumbbell Row
Shoulders	Overhead Press
Arms	Biceps Curl

ABDOMINALS AND CORE

Abdominals	Crunches
Abdominals	Oblique Crunches
Back	Back Extension

Cycling

Cycling is enjoying a resurgence in popularity in America. Cycling, like many other recreational activities, can be enjoyed by people of all ages.

From world class Tour de France champions like Lance Armstrong to neighborhood children with training wheels, riding a bike can be a tremendous source of pleasure. The training needs of professional athletes, are, of course, much different from the needs of mere mortals who simply want to enjoy a nice day in the sunshine. Every bike enthusiast, however, can prevent injuries and improve performance with a weight training program.

A wonderful aspect of cycling is that it is a nonimpact activity and therefore can be very joint friendly. Similar to runners, however, cyclists can experience injuries as a result of the repetitive nature of the cycling motion. Over time, a cyclist's quadriceps can become much stronger than the hamstrings, resulting in a muscle imbalance that can contribute to injury. Good muscle endurance in the inner and outer thighs is important to maintaining good alignment and tracking of the knee over the foot when the cyclist pushes the pedal. Balanced muscle development in all of these muscles that support the knee is important to prevent knee pain and injuries.

The posture of cyclists can also contribute to back and neck aches. The bent over position places a lot of strain on the muscles that support the spine. It's important to incorporate a good core conditioning program in your exercise regimen to help avoid back pain. Core conditioning also contributes to pelvic stabilization. The ability to stabilize the pelvis is important to fully develop your potential for speed.

Although riding a bicycle appears to be very easy and a relative "no-brainer" for most people, the sport of cycling actually requires a lot of technique. While conditioning programs are essential to provide you with the base level of fitness necessary to participate in a sport, much more than fitness is required to be at a competitive level.

Since cycling involves the heavy use of a piece of equipment, the bicycle, it is essential to get a bike that suits your cycling needs and to obtain experienced assistance in getting a good bike fit. Many recreational injuries from cycling are a result, not of poor conditioning, but rather of poor technique. Make sure you consult a good neighborhood bike shop. Most cycling enthusiasts are more than happy to share their knowledge with people who are new to the sport.

If you discover that you love cycling and want to include more cycling in your schedule, there are many local, national, and international groups that you can join. These groups often have beginner clinics and opportunities for new people to get access to the expertise that they need. Cycling is so much fun, once you start getting in shape from your program, you may decide you want to try many of the cycling travel opportunities that are available.

CYCLING CONDITIONING PROGRAM
FREE WEIGHTS AND MACHINES

LOWER BODY

Buttocks, Hips, Thighs	Leg Press
Buttocks, Hips, Thighs	Lunges
Thighs	Leg Extensions
Thighs	Leg Curls
Thighs	Inner Thigh Machine
Thighs	Outer Thigh Machine
Calves	Standing Calf Raise
Shins	Standing Toe Raise

UPPER BODY

Chest, Back, Shoulders, Arms	Push-Ups
Back	Lat Pulldown
Back	One Arm Dumbbell Row
Shoulders	Overhead Press
Arms	Biceps Curl

ABDOMINALS AND CORE

Abdominals	Crunches
Abdominals	Reverse Curls
Abdominals	Oblique Crunches
Back	Back Extension

CHAPTER 14

Keep the Beat— "Cardio" Still Counts

By now you're reaping rewards from your weight training routine. Conditioning your muscles is one of the best ways to begin your overall training program. As your muscles get stronger, you feel more energetic. You're even thinking about what else you can do to get moving. It may be time to step up your aerobics program.

What Is Cardio Fitness?

Cardiovascular endurance, or the ability of your heart to effectively pump oxygen-rich blood to your hard working muscles, is referred to by many terms, including stamina, endurance, aerobic fitness, and aerobic capacity. Your ability to exercise continuously for a period of time depends on the efficiency of your heart and circulatory system and your lungs and respiratory system to deliver nutrient rich blood to your working muscles, and to remove waste products that result from the energy production process. The more fit you are, the more efficient your heart and lungs work together. The aerobic conditioning process includes building up your cardiovascular endurance. Once you've developed a healthy level of aerobic fitness, you need to maintain it with regular physical activity.

QUESTIONS?

Who needs aerobic fitness?
Everybody needs a certain level of aerobic fitness. Similar to strength training and flexibility training, if you don't challenge your heart and lungs to work for you, you will lose your endurance. When you are aerobically fit, not only will you live longer, you'll also enjoy those years of life more fully.

Aerobic Versus Anaerobic

Have you ever noticed that when you start walking more quickly, at a certain point, you start to become breathless? Or, do you notice that your breathing rate increases? This is an example of approaching your "anaerobic threshold." Anaerobic literally means without oxygen.

When you engage in an aerobic activity, like walking, you heart is pumping oxygen-rich blood to your muscles. When your muscles use up that oxygen to get moving, they produce a waste product called lactic acid. As this lactic acid builds up in your bloodstream, you get that feeling of "Can I stop now?" You start to breathe heavily. You have a tremendous, irresistible desire to stop or slow down. This level of exercise is called anaerobic, since your muscles are briefly trying to work without oxygen, which makes them very tired, very quickly.

FACTS

Some fitness enthusiasts and athletes intentionally train at their anaerobic threshold to improve their level of conditioning. This type of training, however, is intense and is a matter of personal choice. Only more advanced exercisers who want to improve their cardiovascular conditioning should pursue anaerobic threshold training. You don't have to work that hard if you don't enjoy it.

Benefits of Aerobic Fitness

Aerobic exercise is good for your body, your mind, and your spirit. The key is finding activities that you enjoy. Variety is also important, so you don't become bored and so you challenge your body in different ways. Once you become accustomed to the feeling of working your body, you really can enjoy the sensation of working up a good sweat. Or, if you're the type of person who really doesn't enjoy sweating, you can always be active at a slightly lower level of intensity.

Research studies have confirmed that regular, moderate physical activity can help you to:

- Lose or manage weight
- Improve body composition by reducing body fat
- Strengthen your heart and lungs
- Tone your muscles
- Build and maintain healthy joints
- Reduce and manage stress
- Improve your balance
- Sleep better at night
- Improve feelings of well-being and self-esteem
- Reduce or manage high blood pressure
- Reduce or manage cholesterol
- Reduce risk of heart attacks and diabetes

Even if you already have heart disease or diabetes or both, regular, moderate physical activity lowers your risk of death from heart-related causes. If you have any specific medical conditions, you need to work together with your doctor to find the right exercise program for you. Be sure to always check with your health care provider if you're new or returning to exercise after a long break.

When to Start

The best news about aerobic exercise is that it really is never too late or too early to start. As long as you're ready, it's the right time. Young or old, regular physical activity benefits us all. And, it's something you can do together with your family and friends.

Your aerobic activity program complements your weight training program perfectly. As your muscles get strong and toned, you're much less likely to injure yourself in endurance oriented activities. You'll feel energetic and ready to handle anything that comes your way.

What Kinds of Activities Are Aerobic?

Many activities are aerobic. You probably didn't realize that you could get a perfectly fine daily workout simply by cleaning the house vigorously or washing your car and cleaning the yard. All you need to do is add a little elbow grease to your activities. Everything counts. It's not necessary to go to a gym. You can get all the aerobic exercise you need right in your own home and neighborhood.

Getting Results

To improve cardiovascular fitness, the American College of Sports Medicine recommends that you should include twenty to sixty minutes of aerobic activities a minimum of three to five days a week in an overall fitness program. You can do more, but this is a minimum amount to gain benefits. The lower amount is recommended for people who are new to exercise and the higher range is for more experienced exercisers.

How Long Do You Have To Do Aerobics?

The great news is that more research studies show that you can even accumulate your total exercise minutes in ten-minute bouts. Everybody can find ten minutes to walk around briskly. Any amount is always better than nothing.

The guidelines for ten-minute bouts of aerobic activities is to accumulate at least thirty minutes of activity on most days of the week. If you're serious about adding more movement to your day, take a moment to sit down and write a short list of all the ways that you can add activity in your day.

How Hard Do You Have To Work?

For so long, so many of us have absorbed the motto of, "No pain, no gain," that we have a hard time believing that exercise can actually be fun, pleasant, and effective. You really don't have to kill yourself to get in shape. In fact, you shouldn't. The whole point about exercise is that it should make you feel good and be fun. Moderate regular exercise, such as brisk walking, is sufficient to improve your health. You really don't need to run marathons. If you love marathons, that's great. But, you don't have to train for one to be healthy. It's more important to exercise regularly than it is to exercise hard.

As a rule of thumb, an effective exercise intensity of 55 to 65 percent of your maximum heart rate up to a maximum of 90 percent is recommended by the ACSM. This is a broad range, because what is an effective intensity for me, may not be effective for you. The right intensity for you depends on your current level of conditioning and your age.

ESSENTIALS

10,000 steps per day is a good measure to determine if you're getting the minimum amount of activity to benefit your health. Research studies at the Cooper Institute of Aerobics Research have found that if you wear a pedometer and take 10,000 steps per day, you're likely to have met the minimum physical activity requirements.

What Is a Moderate Amount of Physical Activity?

According to a report by the U.S. Surgeon General, the following activities exemplify moderate activity. A moderate amount of physical activity is roughly equivalent to physical activity that uses approximately 150 calories of energy per day, or 1,000 calories per week. As the examples show, you can achieve a moderate amount of physical activity in a variety of ways.

Select activities from the list that you enjoy and that you can easily fit into your daily life. We're all busy. If it's not convenient, you're not likely to do it regularly. Find what is realistic for your lifestyle. Keep in mind that a minimum amount of activity to provide health benefits is related to how long, how hard, and how often you do it.

Examples of moderate amounts of activity:

- Washing and waxing a car for forty-five to sixty minutes
- Washing windows or floors for forty-five to sixty minutes
- Playing volleyball for forty-five minutes
- Playing touch football for thirty to forty-five minutes
- Gardening for thirty to forty-five minutes
- Wheeling self in wheelchair for thirty to forty minutes
- Walking $1^3/_4$ miles in thirty-five minutes (twenty min/mile)
- Basketball (shooting baskets) for thirty minutes
- Bicycling 5 miles in thirty minutes
- Dancing fast (social) for thirty minutes
- Pushing a stroller $1^1/_2$ miles in thirty minutes
- Raking leaves for thirty minutes
- Walking 2 miles in thirty minutes (fifteen min/mile)
- Water aerobics for thirty minutes
- Swimming laps for twenty minutes
- Wheelchair basketball for twenty minutes
- Basketball (playing a game) for fifteen to twenty minutes
- Bicycling 4 miles in fifteen minutes
- Jumping rope for fifteen minutes
- Running $1^1/_2$ miles in fifteen minutes (ten min/mile)
- Shoveling snow for fifteen minutes
- Stairwalking for fifteen minutes

Source: U.S. Department of Health and Human Services. *Physical Activity and Health: A Report of the Surgeon General.* Atlanta, GA: U.S. Department of Health and Human Services, Centers for Disease Control and Prevention, National Center for Chronic Disease Prevention and Health Promotion, 1996.

Get Active with Your Kids

Young people need to be physically active too. You can start healthy habits early with children and put more activity into your day too. Here are some ideas on activities you can do as a family together:

- Play games like tag or hide and seek instead of watching television.
- Do chores like cleaning the house or the yard, going grocery shopping, or walking the dog.
- Shoot hoops in the back yard or go to a neighborhood school or park.
- Go bicycle riding, in-line skating, or hiking.

Not only will the whole family get in shape together, but you'll also enjoy more family time doing group activities.

How Hard Are You Working?

To measure how hard you're working, you need to know how to calculate your target heart rate. Your target heart rate is the training zone that is safe and effective for you to improve your cardio respiratory fitness. Heart rate is an accurate measure of exercise intensity as long as you're a healthy adult.

It's easy to estimate your target heart rate.

1. Subtract your age from 220. This is your predicted maximum heart rate.
2. Multiply your maximum heart rate number by 55 percent or 65 percent depending on whether you are a new or experienced exerciser. New exercisers should use the lower rate.

3. Multiply your maximum heart rate number by 85 percent or 90 percent. Only very experienced and fit exercisers should use the 90 percent upper limit. This would be considered high intensity training and should only be part of a very specific training program.
4. These two figures provide you with a range of heart rate intensity that represents your target heart rate zone.

ALERT

If you're taking any medications that affect your heart rate, for example beta-blockers to control high blood pressure, your heart rate will not accurately reflect your exercise intensity. Pregnancy also affects your heart rate. If you have any medical conditions, please consult your health care provider concerning an appropriate exercise intensity for your specific needs.

Let's say you are a forty-year-old woman who is just getting back into shape. Your maximum heart rate would be 220 minus 40, which equals 180. Fifty-five percent of 180 equals 99. Sixty-five percent of 180 equals 117. Eighty-five percent of 180 equals 153. The estimated minimum target heart rate for you would be 99 beats per minute. For starters, it would be a good idea for you to exercise at this rate. You should notice whether or not you start to break a light sweat and feel like you're working somewhat hard. If the answer is yes, this is a great place to begin. As your conditioning improves and this rate of exercise doesn't feel like any effort, you'll want to work up to a minimum of 117 beats per minute. You'll not want to exercise so hard that your heart rate exceeds 153 beats per minute.

When you use age to determine target heart rate, it may not be suitable for all people. This is particularly true if you have a history of lots of exercise conditioning. Lucky for you, your physiological age may be younger than your biological age. If you think you fall into that category, you may want to use the Karvonen formula to calculate your target heart rate zone.

The Karvonen Formula

The Karvonen Formula provides a more personalized estimate of your target heart rate zone.

1. Subtract your age from 220. This is your maximum heart rate.
2. Subtract your resting heart rate from your maximum heart rate. This number is referred to as your heart rate reserve.
3. Multiply your heart rate reserve by 60 percent.
4. Take this number and add your resting heart rate. This number is the lower end of your target training zone.
5. Take your heart rate reserve and multiply by 80 percent.
6. Take this number and add your resting heart rate. This number is the upper end of your target training zone.

In general, the Karvonen Formula is more appropriate for people who have a history of exercise. Another name for the Karvonen method is the heart rate reserve method.

How to Take Your Pulse

Taking your pulse is easier than you may think. To measure your exercise heart rate, the preferred locations are either at your neck (the carotid pulse) or at your wrist (the radial pulse). Choose the location that works best for you.

Here's a handy method to locate your carotid pulse at your neck. Take your first two fingertips and place them outside of your eye on your temple. Slide your fingertips down from the middle of your temple to the side of your neck. You should start to feel the pulse. Be sure not to press on your pulse or to massage your neck. Use a gentle touch.

To find your radial pulse at your wrist, place your wrist palm facing up in the palm of your other hand. Wrap your fingers around your wrist. You should feel the pulse in the area between the bone and the tendons.

Once you locate your pulse, follow these simple steps to count. Start counting immediately. For your exercise pulse, take a ten-second count. Multiply that number by six for your one-minute heart rate. If you're taking your resting heart rate first thing in the morning, count for a full one minute. A one-minute count isn't recommended for your exercise heart rate as your pulse will slow down from the time you start taking the count to when you finish. Be sure to keep your legs moving while taking your exercise heart rate. You can either walk or march in place.

FACTS

A heart rate monitor is very handy to check your resting heart rate and your training heart rate. With regular use, you can learn when your body is in its aerobic zone and how it feels to be working aerobically. When you are excessively fatigued or ill, your heart rate is likely to be elevated. Monitoring your heart rate on a regular basis can give you insight into your level of conditioning.

Rate of Perceived Exertion (RPE)

Another method to determine the intensity of your exercise is known as the rate of perceived exertion or RPE. Dr. Gunnar Borg invented this scale, which is also known as the Borg Scale. Rate of perceived exertion is based on your subjective interpretation of how hard you feel that you are working on a scale of six to twenty. Research studies show that your subjective impressions closely match particular heart rate training levels. This scale is most accurate for activities that you are already familiar with because any new activity may feel more difficult the first few times that you do it, until it becomes familiar.

Ratings of Perceived Exertion

RPE

6

7   Very, very light

8

9   Very light

10

11   Fairly Light

12

13   Somewhat hard

14	
15	Hard
16	
17	Very hard
18	
19	Very, very hard
20	

In his research, Dr. Borg found that a perceived exertion level of twelve to thirteen or "somewhat hard" corresponded to a heart rate of 60 to 70 percent of maximum heart rate. An RPE of sixteen corresponded to about 90 percent of maximum heart rate. For people who want to exercise in their training zone, however, they would want to work at a rate of somewhere between twelve and sixteen, which would be perceived as "somewhat hard" to "hard."

Weights or Cardio First?

This question comes up all the time. Exercise physiologists research it while exercisers puzzle over it. Studies show that it really boils down to six of one or a half dozen of another. In other words, do what you prefer and what meets your needs. If you enjoy weight training first and your primary goal is to build lean body mass, do your weight training first as your muscles will be fresh. If you prefer to warm up thoroughly with a good aerobics workout and you really want to increase your endurance, then do your aerobics first. You will be pre-fatigued for your weight training workout.

Alternatively, you can focus on different goals on different days. For example, on Monday you can do a great aerobics workout. On Tuesday, you can weight train. On Wednesday, you can do another aerobics workout. On Thursday, you can weight train. Or you can blend your weight training and aerobics on the same day depending on whether your workout focuses on upper body or lower body muscles. For example, if you go cycling, which uses lots of lower body muscles, you might want to include an upper body weight training workout on the same day.

Keeping Aerobics Safe and Effective

In your enthusiasm for your exercise program, be sure not to overdo it. If you feel any of the following while you are exercising aerobically, slow down and take it a little easier:

- Breathlessness
- Bright red or very pale face
- Excessive sweating
- Feelings of distress
- Dizziness or light-headedness

- Confusion
- Nausea or vomiting
- Pain or tightness in chest
- Racing heart rate
- Feelings of muscle weakness

Any signs or symptoms of a heart attack should be immediately checked out with your physician. These include chest discomfort such as aching, pressure, burning, or tightness. Anyone at risk for heart disease should check with his or her health care provider before participating in any vigorous exercise.

Heat Stress

Heat stroke is another risk of aerobic exercise in a hot, humid environment. If you travel to a hot environment for a vacation, please be sure to allow at least ten days to two weeks time for your body to acclimatize to the new weather conditions. Here are some tips to avoid heat stress:

- Stay hydrated. Drink eight ounces of water at least twenty minutes before exercise. Replenish fluids every fifteen minutes during exercise. Drink plenty after exercise.
- Wear loose fitting, breathable fabrics that permit the evaporation of sweat.
- Monitor your heart rate during exercise and take it easier if you find that your heart rate is excessively high.

- Weigh yourself. If you have lost more than 3 percent of your body weight, this is due to water loss. Be sure to drink plenty of fluids to replenish this water loss.
- If it is excessively hot, defer your aerobic exercise to another day. It's better to be safe, rather than risk heat stroke. Err on the side of caution and conservatism to ensure a positive exercise experience on the next day.

Exercising after Meals

In general, it's not a good idea to engage in aerobic exercise after a heavy meal. The reason for this is that your digestive organs need blood flow to effectively digest your food. Aerobic exercise is characterized by large, rhythmic movements of your major muscles. As these muscles move, they require increased blood flow to deliver oxygen and nutrients and to carry away the by-products of energy metabolism. If your body diverts blood from your digestive organs to your working muscles, it can cause cramping and abdominal distress. It's best to wait at least ninety minutes after a meal before you start any aerobic exercise.

Under the Influence

It may seem like common sense, but it's worthwhile to mention that it's not a good idea to engage in aerobic exercise if you are under certain medications, alcohol, or other over-the-counter drugs. Check with your health care provider if you are taking any prescription medications. Be sure to read the labels on any over-the-counter drugs that you may take.

ALERT

If you have any back discomfort, you want to avoid impact and avoid rapid twisting movements. Aerobic exercises to consider include walking, cycling, aqua aerobics, or swimming. If you want to exercise indoors, you can try stationary cycling, treadmill walking, cross-country skiing on a Nordic track machine, or using an elliptical trainer.

Unusual Symptoms

Pay attention to your body for any other signs or symptoms of excessive pain or discomfort. It is never a good idea to "push" through something that causes you to feel concerned. There is a certain level of discomfort that may be experienced when you first start an exercise program but this should not exceed feelings of minor soreness or generalized fatigue. Any acute feelings of pain are a sign to stop. Listen to your body and stay in a comfortable range of challenge for yourself.

Before you know it, your conditioning will improve and you will look forward to your aerobic activities. You will enjoy that overall tired feeling at the end of the day. You will sleep better and wake up feeling more refreshed. You will have more energy for your daily activities. Your aerobic exercise program should be fun and enhance your lifestyle. Enjoy it.

CHAPTER 15

Staying Limber— Stretch and Feel Good

I f you're not performing your exercises through a full range of motion when you train, you may develop feelings of muscular tightness. Since freedom of movement is critical to your comfort, it's important to stretch. To maximize the benefits of your strength training, it's best to combine it with stretching.

The Feel-Good Exercise for Every Body

You are never too old or too stiff to stretch. It does not require specific athletic training, nor does it require a lot of fancy, expensive equipment. All you need is your willingness to take the time to learn and do the stretches. Whether you are twenty years old or ninety years old, your body will benefit from these stretches. And, isn't one of the main characteristics of youthfulness, a limber, agile body ready to tackle anything? You, too, can feel that way. You simply have to get started.

As long as you're healthy and do not have any specific joint problems or other physical issues, you can begin stretching. For those individuals with conditions that require medical attention, please check first with your health care provider before you do these exercises. In general, if you can weight train, you can stretch. Pregnant women and older adults have some additional considerations.

Not all stretch positions work for every body type. It's not important that you do all the stretches that are included. Your goal is to find a stretch that matches the muscles you've worked. When you try the stretches, remember the ones that feel good for your body. Those will be your stretches. Don't worry about the others.

Regular stretching improves your body awareness, especially when combined with your weight training. Consistent stretching helps you tune in to your body's needs and respond appropriately. And, you'll get results. You will feel better and move with greater ease. Consistent stretching can even reduce or prevent lower back pain. You will see and feel your progress as you increase your range of motion.

Why don't recreational athletes take more time to stretch? Somehow it's been given less importance among the more "hard" modes of exercise such as aerobics or strength training. Exercises need to be both "hard" and "soft." As with many things in life, balance is key. Your muscles need to be both strong and flexible. In fact, strong healthy muscles are not rock hard, but are toned and pliable. A healthy muscle keeps its ability to move fully.

Any elite athlete will tell you that flexibility training is essential to achieve peak performance. Champions like Michael Jordan include stretching consistently as part of a regular training program. The ability to move freely and fully through a full range of motion is necessary to access maximum power and to move at peak efficiency. So, regardless of where you fall on the spectrum from couch potato to world class competitor, stretching can and should be part of your regular exercise routine.

Lisa, age thirty-eight, remembers, "I began strength training to complement step aerobics. Even after a short time, strength training improved my stamina and form when doing other types of exercise. The emphasis on proper technique and breathing has made me so much more aware of my posture during the work day. As an extra bonus, strength training is a great way to relax after a harried day."

Sebastian, age twenty-three, notes, "The reason I train is not primarily for strength or endurance, like it used to be when I was doing sports regularly. Those are tremendously nice side effects. I enjoy lifting weights and stretching, basically anything that isolates muscle groups, to get that 'burn' or alive feeling you feel when your muscles begin working.

"Sometimes there's a certain high associated with it, but for me it really boils down to body awareness. Only when I'm isolating a muscle group do I feel every muscle fiber. It's like using a new body part for the first time and then trying to coordinate it with the rest of your body. Once it's developed, it's coordinated, and you gain that satisfaction and a certain aesthetic satisfaction as well, hopefully.

"In the end, I feel accomplished that I've had time to focus and attain a certain disciplined awareness that not everyone else has. It's more of a philosophical inner body experience."

How Often Can You Stretch?

The American College of Sports Medicine recommends that you should include flexibility exercises a minimum of two to three days a week in an overall fitness program sufficient to develop and maintain range of motion. These exercises should stretch the major muscle groups. There is no reason, however, not to stretch on a daily basis or even multiple times in one day. The bottom line is that you should stretch when you feel like it and when you can fit it into your day. Stretched muscles are relaxed and feel good.

When compared to other areas of exercise such as strength training or cardiovascular exercise, there is not a lot of scientific research on stretching. Experts agree that stretching should be part of an overall exercise program to improve health. Experts do not agree, however, on which method or combination of methods of stretching is the most effective form of flexibility training. It's generally accepted that the safest approach for most people is the "static" stretch. Static stretching involves holding a muscle in a lengthened position.

Feel Good Stretching Versus Flexibility Training

You can stretch your body at any time of the day when you feel like it. In fact, most people naturally stretch after being seated for long periods of time or when just waking up. We see cats and dogs stretching after they get up from a nap, just as we do. This type of stretching is great and helps you to feel good.

Stretching a muscle without first warming it up, however, will not result in significant long-term improvements in flexibility. If you really want to increase your flexibility, you'll need to stretch when your muscles are warm and elastic. And, if you want to target specific areas for improvement in flexibility, you will need to develop a flexibility training program.

Flexibility training is easy to integrate into a weight training program. In fact, to improve your overall flexibility, the ideal time to stretch a muscle is after you've exercised and raised your body's temperature. When you're weight training, this would be right after you've performed your strength-training set for that particular muscle group. Your muscles are warm and primed. Some people prefer to save their stretching for their final cool down after they're finished with their entire exercise program. That's fine too, if you prefer it or if you're short on time.

Try stretching throughout a workout after each muscle group has been challenged. At the end of your complete program, take about ten to fifteen additional minutes for a full body stretch. This is a great time to simply relax, tune into your body, and reap the rewards of your gym efforts. Whichever way you prefer is great. The bottom line is that stretching is good for you and should be incorporated into your workout.

Why Stretch?

Stretching makes you feel good, physically and mentally.

For physical benefits, regular stretching:
- Increases your ability to move fully and freely
- Improves your balance and proprioception, which is awareness of where your body is in space
- Encourages balanced muscle development, which increases joint stability
- Reduces your risk of injury and muscle soreness
- Improves your posture
- Prevents low back pain
- Alleviates muscle cramps
- Improves joint health by lubricating joints when moved through a full range of motion
- Improves athletic performance
- Enhances weight training by preventing feelings of tightness or stiffness
- Feels great to release muscle tension and relax

For mental benefits, regular stretching:
- Relieves muscle pain
- Increases feelings of well-being
- Increases mind-body awareness so you're more able to detect muscle tension
- Helps you feel great by releasing muscle tension

Static Stretching Technique

Safe technique is essential when stretching. Pay attention to your alignment. Avoid excessive arching of the back. Keep your abdominal muscles active with a feeling of tone. This will provide support for your lower back.

Your stretching movements should be slow and controlled. Do not use force. When you execute the movement, proceed gently to the extent of your active range of motion. This is the largest possible movement you can achieve without feelings of strain. As you hold the stretch and breathe, your muscles will relax and lengthen. Allow the muscle to release into the stretch and increase the size of your stretch as your muscles permit. Always let your muscles lead the stretch. Never force your muscles into a longer position.

Avoid forced or rapid movements. This can trigger the stretch reflex. The stretch reflex is your body's natural way of protecting you from overly lengthening a muscle and harming the integrity of a joint. If you suddenly force a muscle to lengthen, the stretch reflex will trigger a contraction.

Hold your stretches for fifteen to thirty seconds. According to some research studies, it's more beneficial to stretch multiple times rather than to hold one long stretch for an excessive period of time. For example, in one study, three twenty-second stretches and two thirty-second stretches achieved greater changes in hamstring flexibility than one sixty-second stretch. Across studies, stretches of longer than thirty seconds in duration have not been shown to be more effective in increasing flexibility.

Experts agree that flexibility is complex and affected by joint mechanics, muscle and connective tissue, and neuromuscular factors. We will need to stay tuned for future research findings. In the meantime, we know that stretching is beneficial. And, researchers agree that static stretching is effective with the least amount of risk. You may hear about other methods of stretching such as dynamic range of motion, PNF, ballistic, active assisted, active isolated, and manual resistance. To complement your weight training, however, static stretching will provide you with great results.

Rules for static stretches:
- Move slowly to the edge of your active range of motion.
- Concentrate on the muscle being stretched.
- Exhale, relax, allow your muscle to release gradually.

- Inhale, check your alignment.
- Exhale, relax, continue to lengthen.
- Start with a fifteen second stretch, work up to twenty or thirty seconds.
- Always move deliberately, with control.
- Increase the stretch as the muscle releases, always working the edge of tension.
- Always feel the stretch in the belly or the central area of the muscle.
- If you feel any pain or tightness in your joint, ease up on the stretch. Pain in your joints means you are stretching too hard.
- Stretch during and at the end of every weight training session.
- Do NOT bounce.
- Do NOT move quickly.
- NEVER apply force.
- Do NOT lock your joints.
- Do NOT go beyond a joint's natural range of motion or hyperextend your joints.
- Do NOT stretch an injured joint.
- Do NOT stretch a torn muscle.
- NO pain equals NO pain.

Relaxation—The Added Bonus

Stretching also releases muscle tension. As they let go of physical tension, most people also feel mentally and emotionally more relaxed. As you stretch, always remember to take nice, long, slow breaths and consciously let go of tension as you exhale. Concentrate not only on the specific muscle that you're stretching, but also on areas where you tend to store tension.

For example, take a long, full, deep breath. Exhale completely. Feel your tensions drain away from your body. Continue to breathe with a focus on long, slow exhalations. As you exhale, relax around your hairline, soften your eyes, release your jaw, let your mouth open slightly and relax your throat. Continue to let go of tension and soften your chest. As you inhale, fill your chest with feelings of peace and serenity. Allow your shoulder blades to slide down your back as you lengthen your neck. Let all the tension drain away from your body, out onto the floor and into the earth. Release and let it go.

Isn't that a great feeling? For many of us, the daily stress of life leads to chronic physical tension. It's universal for many people to hold tension in the neck and shoulder area. People also tend to clench their jaws and tighten their throats. Some individuals store tension in their lower back or deep buttock muscles. Always think about releasing all of your physical tension throughout your body when you stretch. You will feel refreshed, more mobile, and more relaxed. It will be the new, relaxed you.

Ouch! Things to Avoid

Although static stretching is very safe and feels great, there are certain necessary precautions. You should not stretch under the following circumstances:

- Muscular or joint pain
- Muscular or joint injury
- Infection
- Joint instability
- Degenerative disc disease

As with any physical activity, if you have special medical considerations, you should consult first with your health care provider.

Certain movements and body positions should be avoided. Do not stretch beyond the natural range of motion of a joint. Do not lock joints when you stretch. In particular, it's important to avoid unsupported forward bending or inverted positions that may use body weight and gravity to increase the stretch. The concern is that if a person's muscles are overly tight, too much force can be applied with the addition of gravity. This can lead to tension in tendons and ligaments and possible tearing or injury. It's best to keep the body in positions where the application of force can be completely controlled.

If you are an older adult, or you are very stiff, proceed slowly and gently. If you have arthritis or osteoporosis, you should exercise under the direction of your physician.

Older adults, in particular, need to remember to drink plenty of water. As we age, the ability of our cells to retain water declines. In addition, our thirst mechanism becomes less sensitive. Not only do we retain water less efficiently, but we also don't feel the need to drink as much. Since dehydration can affect flexibility, it's another important reason to remember to drink eight to ten cups of fluids a day.

Women who are pregnant or who are in the post-partum phase after delivery should also exercise care with stretching. When a woman is pregnant, her body releases a hormone called relaxin into the bloodstream. This hormone facilitates lengthening of ligaments in the pelvis to accommodate the needs of the growing fetus, as well as to assist in childbirth.

Since the hormone is circulating in the bloodstream, it can affect all the body's ligaments. It is not desirable to stretch ligaments. Connective tissues are more fibrous, possess less blood flow, and are responsible for joint integrity. If ligaments become overly loose, the result is unstable joints. Pregnant and post-partum women, therefore, need to stretch conservatively. Always be sure to feel stretches in the belly of the muscle and not the joints. Exercise extreme caution not to stretch in your joints.

People who are larger sized can equally enjoy the benefits of stretching, as well as weight training. What is important is to find appropriate stretches that take into account body mass. If your arms or legs are not the size of toothpicks, it may be difficult to access certain physical positions. The following stretches include choices appropriate for body types that are large, medium, or small. Find the positions that feel most comfortable for you and use those. It's not necessary to do all the stretches, just make sure you stretch the muscles you have worked.

Similarly, people with disabilities should also combine stretching with their weight training. Due to mobility challenges, however, stretches should be designed for maximal effectiveness to the muscles that have been worked. It's important to target the stretches to muscles that are being trained and used in activities of daily living.

Factors that affect flexibility:

- Age
- Gender
- Muscle temperature
- Activity level
- Genetics
- Body type

Stretches for Each Major Muscle Group

Following are stretches that target the body's major muscle groups. A comprehensive stretching routine can reap countless benefits, so try them all.

CHEST AND FRONT OF SHOULDERS

Seated chest stretch

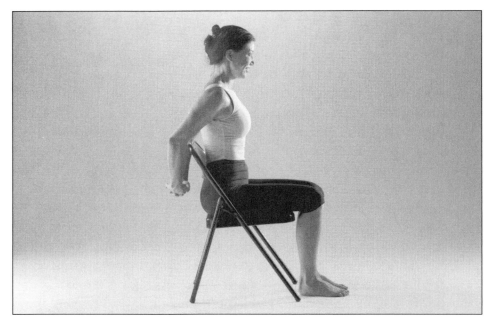

1. GET SET   Sit or stand with arms clasped gently behind your back. Support lower back by engaging abdominals.

ACTION   Squeeze shoulder blades towards each other. Open chest.

TIPS   Avoid arching the lower back.

All fours
prayer stretch

2. GET SET   Kneel on hands and knees.

ACTION   Slide hands forward as you lower hips towards your heels.
Walk fingertips forward as you tuck tailbone under.

TIPS   Avoid sitting back on legs.

3. GET SET   Kneel on hands and knees.

ACTION   Extend one arm out to side, palm down. Turn torso away from
the extended arm. Ear towards ground. Walk fingertips out.

TIPS   Keep abdominals engaged to support lower back.

LOWER BACK

Standing lower back stretch

GET SET   Stand and gently squat in a semi-seated position. Place your hands on your mid-thighs. Make sure your knees do not go beyond your toes.

ACTION   Round and release your back. Inhale as you release. Exhale as you round and engage your abdominals inward.

TIPS   As you round your back, imagine you are pulling your belly button towards your spine and tucking your tailbone under. Really try to feel the length in your lower back.

UPPER BACK

GET SET   Standing or seated, clasp your hands in front of your chest with your palms facing inward.

ACTION   Relax your shoulders and imagine sliding your shoulder blades out to the sides, widening through your upper back.

TIPS   Breathe fully into your rib cage. Imagine you are expanding the ribs like a big barrel outward with the inhalation. When you exhale, relax your ribcage.

TRICEPS (BACK OF UPPER ARMS) AND UPPER BACK (LATS)

Seated triceps stretch

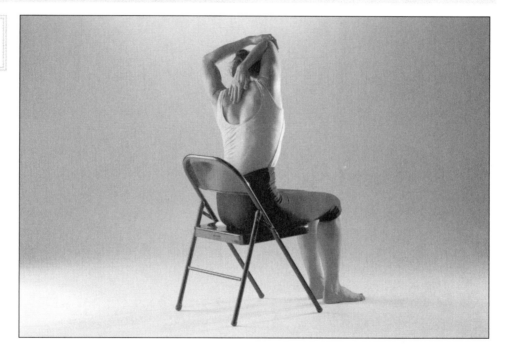

GET SET   Standing or seated, extend your elbow up towards the sky, slide the palm of the hand behind your neck. Place the opposite hand on the elbow.

ACTION   Relax your shoulders and engage your abdominals. Gently rotate at the waist and pull upward and over with your hand on your elbow. Feel the stretch in the back of your arm and in your upper back and along the side of your torso.

TIPS   Keep abdominals engaged to support your lower back. Focus on lifting upward and lengthening.

FOREARMS

GET SET Standing or seated, extend one arm straight ahead parallel to the ground. Bend the wrist and point your fingertips downward. Place your other hand on the back of the palm.

ACTION Apply gentle pressure to the back of the hand. Feel the stretch on the top of the forearm.

TIPS Relax shoulders. Keep abdominals engaged to support back.
To stretch the bottom of the forearm, repeat the same stretch except bend at the wrist and point the fingertips upward. Place the other hand on the palm and apply gentle pressure. Feel the stretch on the bottom of the forearm. Shake out the wrist and fingers when you finish this stretch to relax the forearms and wrists. This is also an excellent stretch for when you spend long hours at the computer keyboard.

SHOULDER ROLLS

GET SET Seated or standing.

ACTION Roll shoulders around, lifting up to ears, back and down and around. Repeat five or six times. Reverse directions.

TIPS Move as fully and largely as you can. Try to expand your range of motion.

BACK OF SHOULDERS

GET SET Seated or standing, extend one arm forward at shoulder height.

ACTION Take your other arm underneath the extended arm and apply gentle force to push your arm across your chest. Feel the stretch in your upper back and back of shoulders.

TIPS Keep abdominals engaged and shoulders relaxed.

CALF STRETCH (BACK OF LOWER LEG)

Standing calf stretch with a chair

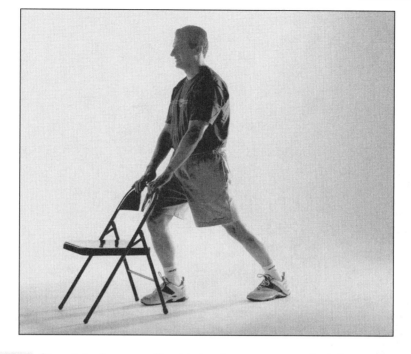

GET SET   Stand facing a wall with both arms extended. Lean forward and place hands against wall.

ACTION   Take one step back. Keep hips parallel to wall. Press heel of back leg down. Lengthen back of leg and spine.

TIPS   Keep abdominals engaged, shoulders relaxed. Keep feet pointing forward, not rotating outward. Feel stretch in back of lower leg from base of heel upward. To increase stretch, focus on one leg at a time. Take one large step back with one leg. Press back heel into ground as you bend your front leg and lengthen your spine. Feel stretch from base of your heel, behind your ankle, and along the back of your leg Straighten the knee of your back leg gently without locking it and feel the stretch behind your knee.

HIP FLEXOR AND QUAD STRETCH (FRONT OF THIGH)

Standing quad stretch in lunge position

GET SET   Stand next to wall about an arm's length away. Place arm against wall for support.

ACTION   Step back with outside leg. Come up on ball of foot of back leg. Bend both knees. Thigh of back leg is perpendicular to the floor. Press hips forward. Feel stretch in the front of thigh of back leg.

TIPS   Keep abdominals engaged, shoulders relaxed. Knee of front leg should not go beyond front toes. A slight forward lean is fine to keep your back long.

HAMSTRING STRETCH (BACK OF UPPER LEG)

GET SET   Lie on your back with both knees bent and your feet flat on the floor. Bring one knee up towards your chest. Extend leg towards ceiling.

ACTION   Inhale, clasp both hands behind upper thigh. Exhale, extend stretch, allow leg to fall towards your chest.

TIPS   Flex foot to increase stretch in lower leg. Lengthen behind the knee without locking your joint. Use a towel or stretch strap underneath your foot to help increase stretch. Feel length from your sitz bone on the base of your pelvis through the sole of your heel.

BUTTOCKS

All fours side glute stretch

1. GET SET   Kneel on all fours.

ACTION   Lower your hips towards your heels. Extend your fingertips out long with the palms of your hands on the floor. Slide your hips over to the side of your legs as you walk your fingertips out. Feel the stretch in the side of the buttocks and hips. Repeat on the other side.

TIPS   When you first slide your hips towards your heels, tuck your tailbone under for a lower back stretch. Do not sit on your heels but distribute your weight between your hands and your knees. If your knees are sensitive, place a towel underneath for cushioning.

Lying on back, cross leg glute stretch

2. GET SET Lie on your back, legs extended long. Hug one knee towards your chest and open leg out towards the side. Your ankle comes towards the midline of your body as your knee rolls outward. Slide the opposite leg up. Place your ankle on top of your other thigh.

ACTION Bring the knee of the lower leg towards you. Feel the stretch in your hips and buttocks.

TIPS Keep your shoulders, chest, throat and jaw relaxed. Exhale into the stretch. Continue to increase the stretch as you feel the muscle relax.

3. GET SET Lie on your back and slide your knee up towards your shoulder. Place your hand behind your thigh. Slide your other leg up towards your other shoulder and place your hand behind the thigh.

ACTION Hug your legs directing your knees towards your shoulders. Feel the stretch in your lower back and in your buttocks.

TIPS Engage your abdominal muscles and round your lower back. Imagine tucking your tailbone between your legs as you round and lengthen your lower back.

THE SPHINX

Sphinx
stretch

GET SET   Lie prone on your stomach with arms at sides, elbows bent, and palms flat on the ground above and wider than your shoulders (the "sphinx" position). Extend legs long, knees down.

ACTION   Press yourself up with your arms as far as is comfortable and roll back down with your face towards the floor. Feel the stretch in your abdominal muscles in the front of your torso. Lengthen your spine from the crown of your head down through your tailbone.

TIPS   Do not experience pain. Keep the movement flowing. Do not hold an extended position.

SIDELYING STRETCH

GET SET   Lying on your side, extend bottom arm under your ear past the crown of your head.

ACTION   With top arm, reach towards your toes then lift upward towards the sky and over past your ears in a large semi-circle. Feel the stretch in the side of your body.

TIPS   Inhale as you open the side of your torso. Exhale as you return to the starting position.

CAT STRETCH

Cat stretch

GET SET   Kneel on all fours, keeping your back long.

ACTION   Round your spine like a cat as you exhale. Release as you inhale and return to starting position with a neutral spine.

TIPS   If your wrists bother you, roll up a towel and place it under the palms of your hands while your fingers rest on the floor. Your wrists do not need to be at a 90-degree angle. If your knees are sensitive, place a towel underneath. If this is not enough cushioning, then do not do this stretch.

FULL BODY STRETCH

GET SET   Lie on your back, extend your legs long, reach your arms past your ears.

ACTION   On one side of your body, lengthen your arms and legs away from each other. Then, stretch the other side of your body. Then, lengthen your entire body, stretch both arms and both legs as long as possible.

TIPS   I recommend a big yawn after this stretch to relax your face and stretch out your jaw. When you get up, you'll feel like a new person!

CHAPTER 16

Eat for a Healthy Life— Good Nutrition

Your weight training program helps you to feel and look good. Consistent exercise combined with good nutrition will help you to feel and look fantastic. Studies show that regular physical activity combined with good nutrition is the single most effective method to ensure long-term weight management. If you want results, basic, sensible eating habits deliver.

Back To Basics—What Is Good Nutrition?

Trainers, nutritionists, and exercise professionals tell stories of how their clients have tried everything from eating nothing but cabbage and broth to surviving solely on meat, cheese, and eggs. They're asked about the latest fad diets and dietary supplements. Every time scientists release nutritional research findings, the food industry widely publicizes the claims. As a consumer, you're constantly bombarded with news of something being good for you one day and causing cancer the next. In the meantime, millions of concerned people struggle with determining what is a healthy weight for them and how to manage it.

Instead of going through all the crazy claims, it's more important to get back to and learn the basics. What are the fundamentals of a healthy, nutritious diet? Why does good nutrition matter? Does everyone need to pay attention to what they eat? When you exercise, should you change your nutritional habits? How do you deal with all those supplements, sports bars, and energy drinks? Where do they fit, if at all, into a training plan?

Most important, what about the fun foods that you love? Does getting in shape mean that you have to give up everything you enjoy? No, it doesn't, because, like in your exercise program, your eating plan needs to fit your lifestyle. All the guidelines in the world are irrelevant if you don't follow them. It's important to make adjustments that are realistic for you and find dietary solutions that are workable. What you eat and what you do each day makes a difference. You can make positive changes and still fully enjoy your life.

The government recognizes that good nutrition is essential to good health. In order to provide people with guidelines for healthful eating, the government has created the Food Guide Pyramid. This is a very handy tool. The information is also based on research studies.

The Food Guide Pyramid

The Food Guide Pyramid illustrates the research-based food guidance system developed by the U.S. Department of Agriculture (USDA) and supported by the Department of Health and Human Services (HHS).

Different foods contain different nutrients and other healthful substances. No single food can supply all the nutrients in the amounts you need. For example, oranges provide vitamin C and folate but no vitamin B_{12}; cheese provides calcium and vitamin B_{12} but no vitamin C. To make sure you get all the nutrients and other substances you need for health, build a healthy base by using the Food Guide Pyramid as a starting point. Choose the recommended number of daily servings from each of the five major food groups. If you avoid all foods from any of the five food groups, seek guidance to help ensure that you get all the nutrients you need.

The Food Guide Pyramid is an outline of what to eat each day based on the dietary guidelines. It's not a rigid prescription but a general guide that lets you choose a healthful diet that's right for you. The Pyramid calls for eating a variety of foods to get the nutrients you need and at the same time the right amount of calories to maintain healthy weight.

Use the Pyramid to help you eat better every day—the Dietary Guidelines way. Start with plenty of breads, cereals, rice, pasta, vegetables, and fruits. Add two to three servings from the milk group and two to three servings from the meat group. Remember to go easy on fats, oils, and sweets, the foods in the small tip of the Pyramid.

What Counts As One Serving?

The amount of food that counts as one serving is listed as follows. If you eat a larger portion, count it as more than one serving. For example, a dinner portion of spaghetti would count as two or three servings of pasta.

Be sure to eat at least the lowest number of servings from the five major food groups listed. You need them for the vitamins, minerals, carbohydrates, and protein they provide. Just try to pick the lowest fat choices from the food groups. No specific serving size is given for the fats, oils, and sweets group because the message is *use sparingly.*

Milk, Yogurt, and Cheese
- 1 cup of milk or yogurt
- 1½ ounces of natural cheese
- 2 ounces of processed cheese

Meat, Poultry, Fish, Dry Beans, Eggs, and Nuts

- 2-3 ounces of cooked lean meat, poultry, or fish
- ½ cup of cooked dry beans, 1 egg, or 2 tablespoons of peanut butter count as 1 ounce of lean meat

Vegetables

- 1 cup of raw leafy vegetables
- ½ cup of other vegetables, cooked or chopped raw
- ¾ cup of vegetable juice

Fruit

- 1 medium apple, banana, orange
- ½ cup of chopped, cooked, or canned fruit
- ¾ cup of fruit juice

Bread, Cereal, Rice, and Pasta

- 1 slice of bread
- 1 ounce of ready-to-eat cereal
- ½ cup of cooked cereal, rice, or pasta

The American Dietetic Association surveyed American eating habits in 1991. Only 28 percent of those surveyed rated themselves knowledgeable of basic food guidelines. Before we review what to eat, let's consider the building blocks of nutrition—the essential nutrients.

ESSENTIALS

If you think you need a nutritional overhaul, but are not sure, keep a food log for a few days. Record everything that you put in your mouth. Everything counts, even those extra bites of candy or fruit. Many people don't even realize what they are eating.

The Six Essential Nutrients

What follows is a very basic survey of nutrition fundamentals. As you start understanding more and more about how the body functions, you can see why what you use to fuel it is critically important. It all comes back to the saying, "You are what you eat." This is essentially true.

If you think you can benefit from professional evaluation, consult a registered dietician. Your dietician can evaluate your current eating habits, consider your goals, and help you along through a transition to healthier eating habits. Be sure to tell your dietician about your exercise program as that can be an important consideration in determining a healthy eating plan that suits your lifestyle.

Expert advice varies, but, the general rule of thumb is that 55 to 65 percent of the calories that you eat should come from carbohydrates, 20 to 30 percent should come from fat and about 15 percent should come from protein. If you have a medical condition such as diabetes, it's important to establish your nutritional guidelines with your health care provider.

Carbohydrates

In the gym, people often refer to carbohydrates as "carbs." You'll also hear the expression "carbo loading." Lately, carbohydrates have been receiving some negative press. What are they? Among athletes, carbohydrates are considered the most important nutrient. In the body, carbohydrates from foods are converted into blood sugar or glucose. Whatever is not burned up immediately, is stored in your muscles and liver as glycogen. When you exercise, your muscles draw on their reserves of glycogen to create energy. When an athlete refers to "hitting the wall" or "bonking" they mean that they have depleted the glycogen reserves in their muscles.

FACTS

Carbohydrates are either simple or complex. Simple carbohydrates are sugars that are quickly converted into energy. Soda pop, juice, or plain sugar are examples of simple carbohydrates. Complex carbohydrates are sugars that are found in pasta, bread, grains, and cereals. These need to be broken down first in the digestive system before the sugar is available as energy. The caloric value of carbohydrates is four calories per gram.

Protein

Protein is the elusive gym substance that bodybuilders crave. Protein is the building block of muscle tissue. Protein supplies the body with amino acids. Amino acids rebuild body proteins in hair, skin, muscle, cartilage, hemoglobin, enzymes, and hormones. Excess protein that is not used by the body is stored as body fat. Waste products from converting protein into fat are eliminated in urine and place additional stress on the kidneys.

Protein rich foods include meat, poultry, fish, beans, eggs, and nuts. Protein quality varies from animal and plant sources. Animal sources include all the amino acids. Plant based sources usually do not have all the amino acids. Soy is the only complete vegetable protein. In general, the American diet is protein rich and most people consume enough quantities in the foods they eat. The caloric value of proteins is four calories per gram.

Fat

Fat is not a bad word. We need sufficient fat for proper hormonal functioning. In addition, fats help the body absorb fat based nutrients such as vitamins A, D, E, and K. Fats are essentially concentrated fuel. Primary sources of fat are animal foods such as meat, poultry, and dairy products. Saturated fats are solid at room temperature and are the fats that contribute to clogging of the arteries. Unsaturated fats are better for your health and come from vegetable or fish sources.

Fats are calorie dense and provide more than twice as much energy as carbohydrates or protein. The caloric value of fats is nine calories per gram.

Fats supply energy and essential fatty acids. You need some fat in the food you eat, but choose wisely. Saturated fats increase your cholesterol and your risk for heart disease. Limit your total fat intake to 20 to 30 percent of calories. Cut back on saturated fats that are found in red meats and dairy products and trans-fats such as those used in stick margarines.

It has been suggested that the iron-overload induced cardiac deaths of three athletes may have been precipitated by megadose supplements of vitamin C. Accordingly, if some individuals are genetically prone to develop iron overload, they should limit their daily vitamin C ingestion to 500 milligrams or less.

Vitamins

Vitamins assist in the growth of body tissues and help the body release energy for fuel. Vitamin deficiencies can affect physical performance, since vitamins regulate carbohydrate, protein, and fat metabolism. However, mega-dosing with vitamins can be equally harmful to your health and is not recommended. In particular, fat-soluble vitamins such as A and D can be stored in your body and, if taken in excess, can result in permanent damage to internal organs. Water-soluble vitamins such as C pass through the body and result in expensive urine. If Vitamin C is taken in excess, it can cause gastrointestinal distress and diarrhea. If your body needs fuel, taking vitamins alone will not substitute for food.

The government is in the process of revising its dietary recommendations. Instead of the Recommended Daily Allowance or RDAs, the government is issuing new Recommended Dietary Intake guidelines or RDIs of specific nutrients.

Current nutritional research is focusing on the role of antioxidants and health. Some research shows that Vitamin E may enhance physical performance because it plays a role in exercise recovery. More research is necessary before conclusive findings can be established. Keep an eye out for future reports on research related to Vitamin C, E, and beta-carotene.

Foods high in vitamins A, C, and E include:

- Carrots
- Milk, skim
- Peanuts
- Orange juice
- Broccoli
- Spinach
- Strawberries

Minerals

Minerals are chemicals that are essential to your health. Four significant minerals are calcium, iron, magnesium, and potassium. Minerals are not in and of themselves sources of energy; however, minerals influence energy metabolism. If you are mineral deficient, it can affect your energy level. This is particularly true of iron deficiencies.

Calcium deficiencies have also received a lot of attention by nutritional scientists because of the increase in osteoporosis and osteopenia. Calcium is essential for strong teeth and bones. Calcium also affects cellular function since it assists in cell function, muscle contraction, blood clotting, and transmission of nerve impulses from nerve endings to muscle fibers. Scientists theorize that calcium deficiencies may be related to muscle cramping. Here again, however, scientists lack conclusive evidence and we need to wait to read the results of future research. Dietary calcium is important to everyone.

Iron is essential to create hemoglobin and myoglobin. People with diets low in iron may suffer from anemia, which is characterized by a low hemoglobin content in the blood. Women who are menstruating are particularly susceptible to anemia due to the loss of blood. A person who is anemic is generally tired and lacks an appetite. Athletes who suffer from iron deficiency generally experience improved performance after iron supplementation brings iron stores back up to normal. Healthy athletes that are not iron deficient do not benefit from additional iron supplementation.

Magnesium, similar to calcium, is a mineral that is important to teeth and bones. Magnesium affects muscle contraction, transmission of nerve impulses, and activates many enzymes.

Potassium is an electrolytic mineral that regulates the beating of the heart with sodium and calcium. Potassium also regulates the body's water balance, helps in muscle contraction, and conducts nerve impulses.

Foods high in minerals include lean beef and pork, skinless chicken, skim milk, and kidney beans.

Water

Water is the last, but not least, essential nutrient. No cellular process in the body can occur without water. Be sure to drink at least eight to ten eight-ounce glasses of water per day. Add an additional six to eight ounces of water for every fifteen minutes that you exercise. Adequate water intake is critical to people who are exercising since the body loses water when exercising.

The Importance of Good Nutrition

Yes! Regardless of whether you are young, old, or in between, every body needs good nutrition. When you are young, you are growing. What you eat helps to build strong bones and lay the foundation for your health in years to come. As a young adult, you are likely to be active. If you're a woman, you may become pregnant. What you eat will profoundly affect your health, not only today, but also in your older age. Studies show that the cholesterol level of a twenty-two-year-old can be a predictor of risk for a heart attack over the next forty years.

As an older adult, even if you may not be as active as you were when you were younger, it's even more important that your foods be nutrient rich. If you are consuming less food, what you eat needs to contribute more value. If you're serious about your exercise program, you will want to fuel your body with premium, not the low octane stuff. Besides, you deserve to enjoy life and enjoy good, healthful foods.

The Benefits of Good Nutrition

Since what you eat provides your body with the fuel it needs to get through each and every moment of every day, improving your nutrition can make a big difference in your daily life.

Good nutrition plays an important role in maintaining health and reducing the risks of diseases such as cancer, diabetes, and heart disease. Nutritional research is showing the relationship between various forms of cancer and the foods we eat. More and more it appears that fruits and vegetables are critical to maintain health and to prevent cancer.

Diabetes seems to also be related to nutrition and weight, among other factors. What you eat affects your cholesterol levels. Blood cholesterol is one of the main risk factors for heart disease. Your diet also affects the health of your arteries. Clearly, good health seems to be rooted in good nutrition.

You will also be able to most effectively manage your weight. If you eat healthy foods in moderate portion sizes and you combine your healthy eating habits with exercise, your weight will settle at a healthy weight for your body. If you have gained a number of pounds over the years, this will not happen over night. However, if you stick with it, you will get results.

FACTS

Research confirms that a weight loss of as little as ten percent of your total body weight provides significant health benefits. The most effective way to achieve this and make it stick is to combine healthy nutrition with regular exercise. You can do it if you just take one step at a time. Work on small, simple, realistic changes in your habits. Gradually, your new habits become a natural part of your lifestyle. Before you know it, you're fit and active.

The Risks of Poor Nutrition

One of the most prevalent risks of poor nutrition seems to be gaining excess weight. Not only are people eating nutrient poor diets, they are also consuming too much food. Getting back in shape can't be accomplished simply by cutting calories. It's possibly to eat a low calorie diet of junk food. This is not nutrient rich or healthful meal planning.

Research scientists have documented many adverse health consequences of dehydration. In one study, subjects with recurring kidney stones increased their daily water intake to eight to ten cups a day and made no other dietary changes. After five years, 88 percent of the participants were stone-free compared to 73 percent in the control group. So you can see how even such a simple change in your habits as drinking enough fluids can have a profound impact on your health and feelings of well-being.

And, that's just water. Consider what the long-term affects on your body are of not getting adequate fiber that comes largely from fresh fruits, vegetables, and grains? Dietary fiber not only helps you to feel more full, it also helps to reduce cholesterol and keep your colon healthy. Consuming more foods that are high in fiber and high in complex carbohydrates can satisfy the appetite. Scientists are also discovering beneficial effects of chemicals found in plants. These chemicals are referred to as phytochemicals and include substances like flavinoids that serve as antioxidants and contribute to a healthy heart.

Another interesting fact relates to high-fat diets. Studies show that a high-fat diet of more than 30 percent of calories from fat contributes to feelings of early fatigue during exercise.

ESSENTIALS

If you feel fatigue more quickly during your workout, it's likely that your workouts will be shorter. This will result in less activity and fewer calories burned. So, to have lots of energy for your exercise sessions, try to consume fewer than 30 percent of your calories from fat.

Why Start Eating Well Today?

Good nutrition, like physical activity, is something you need to do consistently. That's why crash diets seldom work. People are successful at losing weight on these restrictive or structured regimes but the meal plans are not realistic for the long term. As soon as the dieter goes off the diet, all of the weight and sometimes more comes right back. Healthy eating habits, therefore, need to become part of your lifestyle.

And your body reflects what you do fairly quickly. For example, by simply increasing your exercise and improving your nutrition, you can see changes in your blood cholesterol in as few as two to four weeks. Your cholesterol changes as your eating and exercise habits change. You can get great results quickly. Similarly, if you discontinue your exercise and healthy nutrition, your levels are likely to return just as quickly to where they were before you started your new healthy habits.

Start Eating Healthier Foods Now

The most meaningful changes most people can make in their diet are to include more vegetables, fruits, and plant-based foods and to reduce intake of dietary fat and refined sugar. Similarly, increase your intake of vegetables by considering how you can add vegetables throughout your day.

Here are some good foods to eat:

- Fresh fruits
- Canned fruits
- Dried fruits
- Fruit or vegetable juices
- Fresh vegetables
- Canned or frozen vegetables
- Dried or canned beans

- Whole grains
- Whole grain breads
- Bagels
- Crackers
- Pasta
- Nonfat dairy foods

Enjoy your favorite treats, but if they are rich and sugary try to enjoy them in moderation. Don't eliminate foods you love. Enjoy everything in moderation and keep a healthy balance of food types in your daily diet.

Try to reduce saturated fats in your diet. Choose fat free or low fat dairy products. These include milk, yogurt, sour cream, cottage cheese, and cheese. If you crave a particular favorite cheese, keep it in moderation as a treat and avoid eating it in excess. Use low fat or nonfat mayonnaise. Whenever possible, choose vegetable fats over meat and dairy fats or those from palm or coconut oil.

ALERT

When you start making dietary changes, your taste buds may go into a state of shock. Introduce changes gradually. Try to modify your favorite foods, rather than eliminate them from your diet completely. Remember, dietary changes are only valuable if you stick with them, so allow your taste buds time to adjust.

Here are ten guidelines for healthy eating from the U.S. Department of Agriculture and the U.S. Department of Health and Human Services:

1. Aim for a healthy weight.
2. Be physically active each day.
3. Let the Pyramid guide your food choices.
4. Choose a variety of grains daily, especially whole grains.
5. Choose a variety of fruits and vegetables daily.
6. Keep food safe to eat.
7. Choose a diet that is low in saturated fat and cholesterol and moderate in total fat.
8. Choose beverages and foods that limit your intake of sugars.
9. Choose and prepare foods with less salt.
10. If you drink alcoholic beverages, do so in moderation.

What about Extra Protein When You Weight Train?

For the person who is interested in improving general conditioning, a healthy balanced diet will provide all the essential nutrients necessary to improve body composition and build lean body mass. It is true that protein is the building block for muscle tissue. If you follow the Food Guide Pyramid guidelines, however, you will consume enough protein to meet these needs. Most Americans consume more than sufficient protein.

Athletes in heavy training do need additional protein because of the excess stress placed on the musculo-skeletal system. Most of us, however, are not in heavy training. Any excess protein calories, like excess calories from fats or carbohydrates, will be converted and stored in the body as fat, or stored energy, for the day when we need to tap our energy reserves.

Chocolate: Good for Your Heart and Your Soul

Aztec cultures considered cocoa to be a food of the gods. The news that cocoa, the basis for chocolate, may also be a heart healthy food seems too good to be true. Cocoa comes from cocoa beans, seeds from the fruit of cacao trees. Research studies show that these seeds, like red grapes, are rich in flavinoids that can help prevent the oxidizing of LDL cholesterol. This may reduce the risk of hardened arteries and cardiovascular disease.

Note: the health benefits are in the cocoa. Not all chocolates contain high concentrations of cocoa. Many are loaded with sugar and fats. Dark chocolate is the richest source of cocoa. White chocolate contains none. No one food is a magical cure all. But savoring cocoa-rich chocolate in small, occasional portions can be a pleasurable treat for your taste buds and heart.

Supplements

Food supplements are a huge business. More of a good thing, particularly in the case of supplements, is not necessarily better. Christopher Gardner, Ph.D., Nutrition Studies Director at the Stanford Center for Research in Disease Prevention, reminds us it's important to eat whole foods and not to take pills or supplements. "Focusing on foods to include rather than nutrients gets us away from taking recommendations too literally. For example, some people might think, 'If I'm supposed to get antioxidants in my diet, I'll take this 2,000 mg/day vitamin C tablet, rather than go to the trouble of eating citrus, broccoli, tomatoes, or kiwi.' The downside of taking pills is that foods that contain a particular good nutrient or phytochemical, often contain many other good nutrients and phytochemicals that you won't get if you just take the food extract or a synthetic pill."

In addition, excessive doses or megadoses of certain supplements can cause harm. For example, megadoses of vitamin C can cause gastrointestinal upset, renal stone formation, and decreased blood coagulation time. And vitamin C is a water soluble vitamin. Other vitamins such as A, E, and K are fat soluble and are stored in the body. Excess amounts of vitamin A have been linked to birth defects.

Only people who are deficient in a particular vitamin or mineral will benefit from supplements. People who eat a well-balanced diet are not likely to have these deficiencies. Also, just because something is natural, doesn't mean that it can't be harmful. Many herbs have pharmacological effects. It is just as dangerous to overdose on these herbals as it would be to take an excessive amount of any drug.

The following list includes a number of currently discussed supplements and what research studies to date tell us about them.

Androstenedione

"Andro," as it is popularly referenced, is a precursor to testosterone. When you supplement with this product, you increase testosterone levels in the body. Studies suggest that taking andro can increase breast size in men and reduce testicular size. It also may increase the risk of certain cancers. Further studies need to be done to substantiate whether or not taking this product can have a beneficial effect that outweighs its risks. In general, tampering with natural hormones is risky business.

Chromium

Chromium is a trace mineral that is essential to life. It's found primarily in unrefined foods such as whole grains. Chromium facilitates the action of insulin which is important to transport sugar, amino acids, and fats in the bloodstream to cells. If you eat a well-balanced diet, you will receive all the chromium that you need.

It's better to spend your money on fresh baked, delicious whole grain breads than on fancy and expensive supplements. Not only will you benefit from the chromium in your foods, you will also enjoy a healthy dose of B vitamins and fiber.

Creatine

Creatine is a relatively expensive supplement that promotes building muscles. Creatine is produced naturally in your own body by the liver, kidneys, and pancreas. It's found in meat, poultry, and fish. Creatine enhances the ability of your muscles to work longer and harder.

Creatine does work. The key, however, is that it only enhances your ability to work harder. You still have to do the hard work to build the muscle mass. If you don't do the work, you will not receive any benefits.

In addition, creatine is only effective as long as you take it. And, you must take it on a daily basis. Creatine, therefore, is an expensive habit.

Another important fact to note is that while creatine has not been shown to be harmful, it has also not been around for a very long time. Therefore, we do not know what the long-term effects may be.

DHEA

DHEA stands for "dehydroepiandrosterone" and is a hormone naturally produced by the adrenal glands. It's also a precursor to testosterone. Levels of DHEA peak in the body during the twenties. After age thirty, natural DHEA levels decline. Research has yet to substantiate the benefits of supplementation with DHEA after natural levels have lowered. Since it can affect your hormonal balance, you may want to wait for further research before self-treating with this supplement.

Steroids

Anabolic steroids represent the darker side of bodybuilding and other competitive sports since it is the primary drug that is used illegally to enhance physique and performance. Steroids are synthetic testosterone, a masculine hormone responsible for muscle growth. Steroids can be taken either orally or by injection. Steroid use is illegal under both state and federal laws.

More important than the fact that steroids are both illegal and banned from athletics, is the fact that they are very harmful. Steroid use can contribute to liver and heart disease. It's known to increase aggression and enhance masculine characteristics. When women take steroids it can have particularly devastating effects, including cessation of menstruation and the development of male sexual characteristics.

Steroid abuse among adolescents is dangerous since it can stunt growth and impair natural development. It can also have harmful effects when its use is discontinued. Abusing steroids can be emotionally and physically devastating and destructive.

Sports and Energy Bars

Are "health bars" commercial hype or valuable nutritional foods? State of the art food technology enables manufacturers to offer nutrient rich products. The nutrition bar trend started with sports bars packaged for athletes. These bars provide sports enthusiasts with convenient fuel for training or races and quick sugar for energy.

Today, manufacturers design bars for practically every purpose under the sun, including preventing cancer, osteoporosis, and heart disease, as well as lowering cholesterol. Fortified with calcium, herbs, antioxidants, and soy protein, among other ingredients, these bars seem to be essential to a healthy lifestyle.

Nutrition bar manufactures are targeting health conscious baby boomers and women in particular. And, why not? Bars are convenient, portable sources of nutrition when you don't have time to eat whole foods. Baby boomers in general tend to be very busy people who also want to enjoy health and longevity.

So, What Should You Buy?

Read labels carefully. Many bars are high in calories and fat, including saturated fat that contributes to higher levels of HDL or "bad" cholesterol. They're also expensive compared to whole foods, costing as much as two to three times foods with equivalent nutritional value.

Bars are also very dry to keep them compact in size. Many sports bars need to be consumed with at least one eight-ounce glass of water. In contrast, eating a fresh fruit meets some of your body's need for water and provides vitamins, minerals, phytochemicals, and fiber.

Bars or Whole Food?

Regardless of the sophistication of food technology, whole foods still are a superior source of nutrition. Nature's technology is miraculous indeed. Bananas even come in their own handy package. Next time you're looking for an easy-to-eat, portable food, consider checking out the produce department. Food manufactures now package individual servings of sliced carrots, celery, and fruit.

Caffeine

Caffeine is a true proven ergogenic or performance-enhancing aid. The reasons for its benefits are not completely clear. Researchers believe that the performance benefits are due to the fact that caffeine stimulates the release of free fatty acids into the blood stream. As a result, precious muscle glycogen reserves are spared for later use by the body. Using caffeine, therefore, enhances both longer endurance activities and short intense exercise.

The International Olympic Committee bans the use of caffeine above a urinary level of 12 ug/ml. The NCAA bans the use above a level of 15 ug/ml of urine. These levels are quite high and would not be reached by normal drinking of caffeinated beverages. The illegal levels mostly eliminate the use of supplementary caffeine tablets.

Many of the performance benefits noted in studies have been obtained from doses much lower than these sporting limits. The optimal amount of caffeine to ingest seems to be about two cups of coffee. In order to meet the illegal limits, an average-sized person would need to drink five to six cups of coffee one hour before the event. It's important to keep in mind that caffeine is a diuretic and can give some people jitters or an upset stomach.

If you're a coffee lover, here's good news for you. A moderate amount of caffeine may not be hazardous to your health. Over 50 percent of adults in the United States drink coffee every day, and another 25 percent drink coffee occasionally.

Caffeine only takes fifteen to twenty minutes to get into your bloodstream. Its effects can last for three hours or more. If you feel restless, nervous, or unable to fall asleep, you might want to gradually cut back.

Think about limiting your caffeine intake if you are pregnant or have high blood pressure or digestive problems. Pay attention to how you react to caffeine. You know your body better than anyone else.

CHAPTER 17

Select the Perfect Gym for You

These days you can find state-of-the-art equipment and well-qualified trainers who offer strength training in a variety of settings. Today's gym environment is as diverse as the clientele that they serve. Whether you want to work out with young adults, older adults, women only, body builders, or families, it's your choice.

Why Do People Join Health and Sportsclubs?

According to the International Health, Racquet, and Sportsclub Association (IHRSA), people join health and sports clubs for the following reasons:

1. To exercise regularly in a motivating and energizing environment
2. To get the support they need to stay with an exercise program
3. To learn a new sport—or continue playing a favorite sport—such as tennis, racquetball, basketball, swimming, etc.
4. To work out on a variety of user-friendly cardiovascular and resistance equipment
5. To receive one-on-one guidance and support from qualified fitness professionals
6. To exercise in a safe environment where CPR, emergency response, and other safeguards are available
7. To have a place to exercise when it is too hot, too cold, or weather conditions are hazardous
8. To improve their health and well-being through health promotion programs such as stress management, weight management, and smoking cessation
9. To maintain strength, mobility, and functionality throughout life
10. To improve physical mobility through physical therapy, and programs designed for people with special challenges, such as arthritis
11. To encourage their children to develop the life-long practice of exercising regularly
12. To take advantage of child care programs, summer camps, and special activities geared towards children
13. To meet old friends and make new friends through organized, off-site club activities such as hiking and skiing trips
14. To take advantage of social activities such as dances, parties, and picnics
15. To make new friends of all ages—from two to ninety-two

Location, Location, Location

Your first step in finding a facility that is right for you is to find a place that is conveniently located. Most people end up not going to a gym because it's not easily accessible. Location is among the most important factors. If it's not easy, you're not likely to go often. And, if you don't go, you're not going to benefit.

Think about when it's most convenient for you to slip in a workout. Is it in the morning, during the lunch hour, or at the end of the day? Would you like to use a facility mostly on the weekdays or on the weekends, too? Do you commute to work or take children to and from school? Can you stop by the gym before you go to the office or after you drop off the kids? Think about your travel logistics and where a gym would be best located to suit your schedule.

Check with your place of employment. Some organizations offer on-site programs and have internal facilities. Other organizations have negotiated corporate discounts at nearby gyms. Find out what resources may be available to you through your employer.

ALERT

Word of mouth usually provides the best referrals. Ask your friends, neighbors, co-workers, and family members. Find out if any belong to local facilities. Ask if they have any horror stories or good news they'd like to share about their experiences at any local gyms. Ask your health care providers if they have any good recommendations.

Types of Facilities

When it comes to workout facilities, the types of facilities are as diverse as types of people. The primary distinction between options is whether or not an organization is a nonprofit community center or whether it is a for-profit commercial enterprise. The fact that a place is for-profit or not-for-profit, alone, does not distinguish the type of service you will receive. It does, however, affect the type of atmosphere.

Not-for-Profit Facilities

In general, most community centers such as the YMCA, YWCA, or JCC, are nonprofit organizations. Your local city or county may sponsor fitness, recreation, or adult education programs in your area. Your City Parks and Recreation Department may even maintain a recreational facility where they run a variety of classes.

Check the Blue Pages in your telephone book under City Government or County Government. Contact Community Centers or the Department of Parks and Recreation. Tell them you want to get started with a weight training program. Ask whether or not the city or county has any strength training facilities. If not, ask if the person you're speaking with can recommend any local gyms or suggest where you can continue to search.

For-Profit Commercial Facilities

The easiest way to find for-profit facilities is to check the phone book. Look in the Yellow Pages under Exercise and Physical Fitness Programs. This will include both for-profit and nonprofit facilities. You can also check under Health Clubs.

Take the time to read the facility ads. Look at the photos and see if the type of person they are presenting appeals to you. Notice the age group, as well as the dress style. If this image does not match what you feel comfortable with, then it's likely that the facility will not be a good match for you.

You will be happiest in a facility that has people like you. In today's market, clubs serve diverse populations. Some cater to young adults, others to families, some to serious bodybuilders and athletes, others to women only. Find a place that makes it a priority to include and serve someone like you in their community.

Many international organizations have national locator services. Contact the YMCA (*www.ymca.net* in the United States or *www.ymca.ca* in Canada) or YWCA (*www.ywca.org* in the United States or *www.ywcacanada.ca* in Canada) to find facilities near you. IHRSA (*www.healthclubs.com*) is an international trade association for health, racquet, and sports clubs. IHRSA also has a nationwide locator service for all of its member facilities.

The Internet is a great source of information. See Appendix B for the URLs of sites with national locator services. These days, many townships also have community Web pages that list local events, merchants, and facilities. To find your local Web pages, go to a search engine and list the name of your town.

Choosing the Right Facility

Depending on where you live, you may or may not have a number of choices. Your next step is to tour the premises. Plan to visit at the same time of day that you intend to use it. If you visit at an off-peak hour, you may receive quite a different impression than if you come at a prime time. During peak hours, a facility may be very crowded. You should measure your comfort level in the gym at the same time that you plan to be there.

Before you drop by, call first. Find out if it's necessary to make an appointment for a tour. You can start gathering information about the facility from this first point of contact. Stay objective. How helpful is the person who responded to your call? You can learn a lot about a facility's emphasis on customer service by paying attention to staff telephone manners.

Through your own observations and by questioning your guide and current members, Healthclubs.com recommends you use the following checklist to determine if the club will be able to meet your fitness, social, and safety needs:

- Are staff members friendly and helpful?
- Is the club clean and well maintained?
- Do fitness staff members have appropriate educational backgrounds and/or certification from nationally recognized certifying agencies?
- Are new members provided with a club orientation and instruction on how to use equipment?
- Does the club have the cardiovascular resistance equipment you want and need to achieve your fitness goals?

- Does the club offer a sufficient number and variety of programs for you to achieve your fitness goals (aerobic, racquet sports, basketball, and so on)?
- Does the club offer instruction in a sport or activity that you might want to learn (tennis, squash, swimming, and so on)?
- Does the club offer a sufficient number and variety of programs for you to achieve other goals (stress management, weight management, smoking cessation, social activities, and so on)?
- Are there long lines at the equipment, or crowded aerobics classes, at the time that you would be using the club?
- Is child care available if you need it?
- Is there adequate parking available if you need it?

Taking the Tour

When you arrive, notice the staff at the front desk. Do they represent a diverse group of people, or are they all young and athletic? Collect the marketing materials available for you. Be sure to get a program guide that describes what the facility offers and who they serve. Take a moment to soak up the atmosphere. Is this a place that you feel you would come regularly? Are there people around that seem to be like you in terms of age, level of ability, and dress style? If they have a pro shop, take a look around. Are they selling products that you might want to buy and use? Or, is everything irrelevant and unappealing?

ESSENTIALS   Remember, you can't benefit from a club membership if you don't go. You won't go unless you feel comfortable. And, you won't go unless you find resources that meet your needs. Know what you want before you visit. Check in with your own personal comfort level.

When you take your tour, engage your guide in conversation. Ask questions about what kinds of programs the facility offers. Ask about the age groups of the members. Ask about the fitness levels of the members.

If you're a beginner, do they have services to meet your needs? If you're an athlete, do they have programs and facilities to meet your needs? If you're a mom and want to bring your children, do they have childcare and kids' programming? Your needs are important. Happiness lies in finding a good fit.

Schedule an appointment to tour the facility and use the following checklist:

• Does the fitness facility have certified instructors in their group fitness programs?

• Do they have certified personal trainers available?

• Do they have First Aid and CPR requirements for their employees?

• Does the facility have a safety plan?

• Remember—if the fitness facility representative does not seem interested in your questions, they may not be interested in your progress after you join.

• While touring the facility, does it seem clean to you? Pay particular attention to the locker and shower facilities. Inspect the pool area, if there is one.

• Does the equipment look like it's in good condition and has been well maintained?

• Make sure that the floor in the group exercise area is either floated wood, or has a shock absorbent padding.

• Ask if they will allow you to experience one of their classes to assess the quality of programming. Most good fitness facilities are not afraid to let you walk in or observe.

• Make sure that you enjoy the atmosphere of the fitness facility, and that you feel comfortable. If you don't feel like you fit in, you'll have a harder time making it part of your routine. Every fitness facility is different. Each has its own culture and atmosphere.

• Make sure that the fitness facility is within reasonable distance from your home or job. A long drive could prove inconvenient in the long run.

• If you have young children, you'll want to find a facility that has child care available, or some type of kids' programming that will provide you with more freedom to attend.

- Make sure that the fitness facility is affordable and that the payment plan meets your budget. Be wary of long-term contracts.
- Make sure that the facility schedule matches yours. Again, convenience is key to your success.

Review the checklist before you go and remember to ask questions. Or, bring it with you to remind you of what to check out. Since you want to find a place that is safe and well-maintained for your weight training workouts, you will want to be sure to see the following:

1. Visit the weight training room. Look at the machines and the free weight area. Meet the training floor staff.
2. Ask about personal training. If they have a personal trainer on the floor, see if you can meet him or her and talk about supervised programs and fees. Even if you're not initially interested in working with a personal trainer, it's good to know what types of services the facility offers.
3. Ask about the qualifications of the training staff.
4. Visit the locker room.
5. Ask about group muscle conditioning classes. If a group class is in session, take a few moments to observe. Listen to the instructor's cues. Notice who is in the class. Check out the age group, fitness level, dress style. Try to get a sense of the class atmosphere and consider if that is a place where you can see yourself.
6. Try to meet any instructors or program directors. If you have a chance, also try to meet some members and ask them how long they've been a member and whether or not they enjoy the facility.
7. Last, but certainly not least, collect all the membership details. Ask lots of questions about different membership options. It's usually to your advantage if you can train at off-peak hours.

Avoid signing up under any feelings of pressure. You can always come back again. It's best to go home and evaluate your impressions. Some contracts have steep penalties for early cancellation. Take your time before you make a commitment. Shop around for the best match for you.

Evaluating the Quality of a Facility

The American College of Sports Medicine (ACSM) has identified six fundamental standards for all health and fitness facilities, outlined in the next section. These standards ensure that physical activities and programs offered by facilities are held in a relatively safe environment and are conducted in an appropriate manner.

Industry research reveals that not all facilities meet these standards. In one survey, more than a quarter of health clubs and fitness centers that participated didn't provide adequate pre-screening to new members to identify potential heart problems. Half the facilities did not have written emergency plans in case a member has a heart attack or other cardiovascular emergency, and less than ten percent performed quarterly emergency drills to prepare for the occasion.

When it comes to making sure that you join a healthy and safe fitness facility, it pays to ask about these points up front.

Emergency Plans and Qualified Personnel

A facility must be able to respond in a timely manner to any reasonably foreseeable emergency event that threatens the health and safety of facility users. Towards this end, a facility must have an appropriate emergency plan that can be executed by qualified personnel in a timely manner.

Before you join a gym, ask about what type of emergency preparedness plan is in place. You can even ask staffers about how certain incidents were handled. Has anyone ever had a heart attack on the premises? If so, what happened? Heart disease is the number one killer of Americans. Therefore, heart attacks are likely to happen anywhere, including your local gym. What is important is not that this incident happened but how it was handled.

Each second is precious in a life threatening emergency. In one gym I worked for, when a gentleman had a heart attack while playing basketball, the facility staff responded immediately. A lifeguard came to the scene and immediately administered CPR, while another staff person called 911. Fortunately, the gentleman got to the hospital and survived.

If this facility did not know how to initiate its emergency plan so effectively, the result may not have been so positive. Don't be afraid to ask about emergency plans and CPR training policies. Your life may be affected.

FACTS

A member is an individual who has entered into an agreement with a fitness facility that allows her access to the facility for a fee. The definition of adult may vary from state to state but at the least would describe an individual who is capable of making an educated decision about his readiness for physical activity based on the results of a pre-activity screening.

A facility should offer each adult member a pre-activity screening that is appropriate to the physical activities to be performed by the member.

This pre-activity screening can be similar to the "PAR-Q and You" found in Chapter 4.

The Professional Competence of Supervisory Staff

Each person who has supervisory responsibility for a physical activity program or area at a facility must have demonstrable professional competence in that physical activity program or area.

Ask about the types of training standards the facility requires its staff to meet. Do all of the leadership staff either have college degrees in the field or recognized certifications? Internationally recognized certifying organizations include the American College of Sports Medicine, the American Council on Exercise, the Aerobics and Fitness Association of America, the National Strength and Conditioning Association, and the YMCA of the USA.

Signs Should Warn of Risks

A facility must post appropriate signage alerting users to the risks involved in their use of those areas of a facility that present potential increased risk(s). Users are individuals of any age who have access to a facility, either on an individual or a group basis. Users may or may not be under a fee-based agreement to use the facility.

As you walk about the facility, scan for signage.

Appropriate Supervision in Youth Programs

A facility that offers youth programs must provide appropriate supervision.

If you are looking for a family facility that includes programs for both you and your children, ask about the qualifications of staff that manage youth programs. You can inquire about the standards used to screen for qualified personnel.

A facility must also conform to all relevant laws, regulations, and published standards.

Taking the Plunge

You've found a facility that feels comfortable to you, is in the right location, provides the programs you need, has all the equipment you want and has a great safety record. You're ready to sign on the dotted line. Should you just go for it?

If possible, try it out before you sign. Find out if the staff will give you some guest passes. If not, visit on a few more occasions at the times you plan to use the facility and see if you still feel positively about it. If yes, you're probably ready to make a commitment.

Read the Fine Print

Before you sign, be sure to ask about all the membership rates. Many facilities provide different arrangements. Know what you plan to use. Purchase the membership that will give you access to what you want. For example, if taking group exercise classes requires an additional fee and there's no possibility in the world that you will be in a class, don't sign up for it.

In some facilities, everything is included in one rate. In others, you can pay for only the services and facilities that you intend to use. If you sign a long-term contract, make sure you determine the exact length of the term and what the cancellation penalties may be for early termination. Pay attention to what is refundable and what is not. It will save you aggravation in the long run.

Make sure that everything you discuss with your membership sales person is included in writing in your agreement. For example, if you have agreed upon a trial membership for a certain number of days during which there will be no penalty for cancellation, make sure it is written down. Do not sign any agreement until you are sure it represents exactly what you think it does. Keep a copy of your contract with your home files.

If you have any lingering doubts, postpone signing your membership agreement. Go home and cool off for a few days. Call the Better Business Bureau and check to see if the facility has had any complaints filed against it. Once you have conquered all of your doubts, then sign with confidence.

If you take the time to carefully select your facility before you join, you are likely to make a good match. Since access to facilities is an important predictor of your long term success in maintaining your exercise habit, you want to choose well. You may also find your needs will change over time. Continue to evaluate your satisfaction with your facility. Do not hesitate to shop around if you find it is no longer meeting your needs.

CHAPTER 18

Working with a Personal Trainer

A recent study showed that people who trained under a personal trainer's supervision had greater strength gains than people who trained on their own for the same twelve-week period. Does this mean you must have a trainer? No. But, working with a trainer can be just the thing you need to start your program or revitalize your existing routine.

The Personal Training Industry

In the United States, you're not required to have a license to be a personal trainer. For now, it's a self-regulating industry. A number of internationally recognized organizations provide training and certification for personal trainers. These organizations uphold professional standards and guidelines. Not all certifications have the same rigorous standards or degree of credibility.

Most certifications require that the trainer demonstrate proficiency in a number of competency areas in order to qualify. The certification exam consists of either a written test or a combination of a written and practical exam.

Internationally recognized certifying organizations include the following:

- The American College of Sports Medicine
- The American Council on Exercise
- The National Strength and Conditioning Association
- The Aerobics and Fitness Association of America
- The Cooper Institute for Aerobics Research
- The National Academy of Sports Medicine
- The YMCA of the USA

A number of regional certifying organizations have emerged. These may or may not possess the same high standards as those named previously.

Certification alone, however, does not indicate a trainer's competency. When you are selecting a trainer, you should also review references.

Why Work with a Trainer?

Working with a personal trainer provides many benefits. A good personal trainer can:

- Conduct a health history screening
- Conduct a fitness assessment
- Answer your training questions

- Help you set realistic goals
- Design a program for your specific needs
- Keep your program safe and effective
- Teach you how to use a variety of equipment
- Teach you correct exercise technique
- Watch your form
- Reduce your risk of injury
- Motivate you to do your exercises
- Help you establish a regular workout schedule
- Monitor your progress towards your goals
- Update your program as your goals and needs change

Locating a Personal Trainer

All of the certifying organizations previously listed have locator services that will help you find trainers in your area. See Appendix B for contact information.

You can also find personal trainers in the same way that you searched for your gym. Look in the Yellow Pages under Personal Development and Fitness Training or Physical Fitness Consultants and Trainers. Some personal training studios may also be listed under Health Clubs or Exercise and Physical Fitness Programs. Also check your local newspapers for classified ads.

If you use the Internet, you can look up personal trainers under your local city or town Web site. Alternatively, you can go to Web sites of fitness organizations to access certified trainers.

Many gyms offer personal training services and have staff on site. If you think this is something you may be interested in, ask at your club to be introduced to some trainers. Ask if you can meet clients who have worked with these trainers. Often, you can receive a personal testimonial right on the spot.

Many trainers specialize in working with men or women, kids, teens, or people of specific ability levels. Some trainers work with recreational or semi-professional athletes. Others work primarily with beginners. Some trainers have relationships with physical therapists and work with people in post-rehabilitation.

Before You Meet Your Trainer

Since there are as many trainers as types of people, you need to spend some time evaluating your needs before you start interviewing trainers. You do not need to know what exercises you want to do. That's the trainer's job. What you do need to know are answers to the following:

- Why do you want to work with a trainer?
- How often and for how long do you want to meet with a trainer?
- Where do you want to work out with your trainer?
- What fee amount are you willing to pay?

Your Training Goal

Before you meet with a trainer, consider what you want from your sessions. Do you want someone to help you start a basic conditioning program? Do you feel you've been exercising for awhile but not getting any results? Do you want to prepare for a specific event such as a college reunion (don't be embarrassed, reunions motivate lots of people)? Or, do you need to get fit for a hiking trip across Europe?

Whatever your reasons, it helps to identify what you want before you begin meeting trainers. This narrows your search. You can match your goals with a trainer who works with people like you. Just as you would see a podiatrist for foot problems, you will benefit most from seeing a trainer who specializes in your area. For example, if you want to train for your first marathon, look for a trainer who specializes in sports conditioning.

Working with a Trainer

Are you looking for someone to conduct an assessment and design a program for you, but not take you through it on a weekly basis? Or, are you looking for someone to guide you through the process for a number of weeks or months? Some trainers provide a one-time consultation. Others require that you follow an initial consultation with a minimum number of sessions.

Other trainers supplement weekly one-on-one training sessions with phone or e-mail updates. Know what type of arrangements work best for you. Do you need to have physical support twice a week to get you through your workouts? Or, do you understand the workout sufficiently that you can do it on your own and simply report back to your trainer until your next joint session? Be prepared to discuss different types of arrangements.

Location

Do you want your trainer to come to your home? Or, will you meet your trainer at a facility? To accommodate a trainer in your home, you need to have space for a workout. Depending on your trainer, he or she may bring equipment, or you may have your own home equipment.

Of course, if the trainer comes to you, this requires the least amount of effort on your behalf. All you need to do is be prepared for your workout when he or she arrives.

Having your trainer travel to your home requires more prep time and is likely to be more expensive than meeting at a facility. Furthermore, you need to be sure you can prevent other interruptions during your home training sessions.

Alternatively, you can meet your trainer at your gym, a personal training studio, or a mutually agreed upon location. If you work with a trainer at their place of business, they can see clients back to back and not have to worry about additional travel time. These factors affect fees. It may be easier for you to concentrate on your workout in the gym environment. This is a personal factor. You need to decide what works best for you.

Dollars and Sense

Finally, consider what you are willing to pay. Fees charged by personal trainers vary depending on your local market. For example, in Los Angeles, New York City, Chicago, or the San Francisco Bay area, trainers may charge as much as $150 per hour. In other parts of the country, trainers may charge $20 per hour. Familiarize yourself with the going rates in your neighborhood and also the range of fees. Typically, as in any profession, a trainer who is just starting out will be less expensive than a master trainer with many years of experience.

This is true of any professional service. Know your comfort level and decide accordingly. Remember that the hourly rate does not represent the full amount of time that the trainer gives on your behalf. If trainers come to your home, they also have travel time. All trainers prepare for sessions, regardless of whether or not they incur travel time.

Generally, trainers do not charge additional fees for travel, prep, and administration. All of that time is rolled up into one hourly rate. It can be a bargain when you think how much prep time goes into that one hour together.

Trainers typically offer reduced rates for multiple sessions. Some trainers give discounts for client referrals. Others offer discounts for payment of all sessions in advance. Find out what types of discounts your trainer offers.

Another method of training that is growing in popularity is the small group. This can be as few as two or as many as five or six clients. In small group training, you do not receive as much individualized attention. However, you do receive more personalization than you would in a group exercise class. It's a way of making the training worth the trainer's time and making the personal session more affordable for a number of people. Small group personal training is a nice alternative for both trainers and clients.

Do you tip a personal trainer?
Personal trainers pride themselves on being experts. While it's customary to tip a waiter or hair stylist, it's not customary to tip your accountant or doctor. All professionals enjoy expressions of satisfaction. A card and bonus check or gift certificate is always appreciated. It's not, however, customary or expected to receive a tip.

Interviewing Trainers

IDEA, The Health and Fitness Source, is the largest international trade association of fitness professionals with over 24,000 members worldwide. IDEA recommends that you interview at least three trainers before making your final decision regarding the personal trainer that is right for you. IDEA maintains a database of professional trainers that is available to consumers free of charge and is accessible on their Web site (✍ *www.ideafit.com*).

Even though you've never worked with a trainer before, you can successfully interview potential candidates. Even if a good friend provides you with a personal reference, it's a good idea to take time for an interview. Your personality may be different from your friend's. Or, your training needs may be different. In addition to having varying qualifications, each trainer has a unique training style.

For example, some trainers use a "boot camp" military style. Others have a high-energy cheerleader type style. Some trainers use lots of humor. Others are much more serious. They can all be talented trainers with excellent technical expertise. You need to find what style motivates you.

When you are interviewing trainers, let them know that you are new to working with a trainer and want to find a good match. Let the trainer know that you are talking to a couple of different trainers before making a final decision.

Here's a list of questions:

What are your qualifications as a professional trainer?

Ask about certification, education, and years of experience. It's perfectly acceptable to ask a trainer to show you a copy of their certification to make sure it is up to date. Just as most professionals hang their professional certificates on their office walls, certified professional trainers will have copies of their certification available for you to review.

Are you certified in CPR and First Aid and how do you handle injuries and emergencies?

Physical activities always carry a certain amount of risk. Injuries can occur even under the safest of circumstances. It's important that your trainer have an emergency preparedness plan. This is often the best preventative measure your trainer can take.

Will you provide references?

Any professional trainer will have satisfied clients that you can contact for a reference. They may also have other health and fitness professionals who will confirm their expertise.

Do you take a health history screening or require a medical release?

Competent professionals want to know your background. This is a standard procedure for any qualified professional trainer.

Do you have written payment and cancellation policies?

Professional trainers want your relationship to be successful. Easy to understand written policies avoid future misunderstandings. Make sure you know how the trainer runs the business side as well as the training side.

Do you carry liability insurance?

Professional trainers carry professional liability insurance to protect both them and their clients. If you get injured as a result of negligent training, this insurance will cover your expenses. Protect yourself up front. Ask to see a copy of the policy.

What training rates do you charge, and do you offer discount pricing?

Many trainers have a variety of compensation arrangements. Do your homework first so you know what type of training arrangement you're after. Find out if the trainer offers any discount package pricing.

Where do you offer training and what hours are you available?
It doesn't matter how fabulous the trainer is, if your schedules don't match, it won't work. Know what you need. Then, find a good fit.

Do you provide written handouts?
If you're the type of person that needs notes for references, ask if the trainer typically provides this to clients.

Are you available in between sessions for questions? Is there a fee for this service?
Some trainers provide e-mail or phone follow up for an additional fee. Some may allow you to ask casual questions in between sessions free of charge. Some trainers have Web sites with Frequently Asked Questions (FAQs). Find out in what ways the trainer may or may not be available to you in between sessions.

While you're conducting the interview, notice how you feel when the trainer responds to your questions. Does this person make you feel comfortable? Is their personality and communication style a good fit for you? Finding a good personality match is critically important to your success.

ESSENTIALS
After you meet a few trainers, you'll have a feel for the styles of different trainers. When you make your decision, you'll be much more likely to choose a good fit. Then, you'll be on your way to a mutually positive and successful relationship.

Getting the Most from Your Training

You've hired your trainer. You're excited to get started. How do you get the most from your training? Just as you can make the best of the time you spend with any professional, maximize your time with your trainer. Your trainer will love your commitment.

Be on time for your sessions.

Time is money for your trainer. He or she has booked you for a specific time on a busy schedule. If you're late, that is your responsibility. Your trainer can not change his or her timetable on the spot.

Respect payment and cancellation policies.

If you miss a session without notifying your trainer sufficiently in advance so that they can use that time productively, you should pay for that time. Training is a service. Services are less tangible than products, but equally deserving of payment.

Respect your trainer's knowledge and expertise.

You are paying good money for the opportunity to work with a trained professional. Take advantage of your trainer's knowledge and experience. Listen to his or her tips. If you can't rely on your memory to remember your trainer's advice, write it down during your sessions. Or, ask your trainer to provide written handouts (find out if this is included in your fee).

Ask questions during your training sessions.

Use the time you have together with your trainer to clarify any questions you may have about your workout program. Learn how to perform exercises independently. Learn how to use equipment. Your trainer is a qualified professional. Take advantage of your access to that expertise.

Speak up if something isn't working for you.

Tell your trainer if a part of your program isn't working for you. Your trainer is skilled at making the exercises work for you. You don't need to be uncomfortable or do things that you do not like. Communicate and work together as you develop the best program for you.

Tell your trainer the truth.

Be honest with your trainer about your physical condition and your willingness to exercise. Your trainer will soon discover your abilities. To avoid injury, don't try to pretend that you are more fit than you really are. If you haven't exercised in twenty years, be honest. It's not a character flaw. You're with someone who can provide you with the advice and support you need. That advice, however, will only be as good as the information you share.

If it's not realistic for you to work out five times a week, tell your trainer. Don't agree to a program that you know you're not going to do. Work together to create workable solutions for your lifestyle and your goals.

Focus on your workout when you're together.
Many people develop great friendships with their trainers. This is a person who has a close relationship with you to achieve your personal fitness goals. Your trainer's expertise, however, is in exercise program design and development.

Do not spend your time together talking about all your personal problems. Focus on your workout. Ask workout questions. Evaluate your workout results. Keep your attention to your task at hand. Both of you will feel successful.

ALERT

Many trainers have given up clients because they feel that the client has become too personally dependent on them for emotional support. Don't let that happen in your training relationship. If you need a counselor, seek out a professional therapist.

If you're looking for a lifestyle coach, seek out a professional coach (see the following section). Remember that your personal trainer's expertise is in physical conditioning. There are certified coaches who can help with lifestyle issues.

Your relationship with your personal trainer can be just the thing you need to get started, get motivated, or focus on a specific training goal. Take advantage of the wealth of expertise in this growing profession. Regardless of whether you continue to work out on your own at home or at your local gym, time spent with a trainer will enhance your personal program.

You can even use this book as a reference while you work with a trainer. Take it with you to sessions and annotate the exercises that you like to do. Get pointers on modifications. Use all the resources available to you to enjoy a lifetime of weight training. It will be well worth the many rewards.

Look into using trainers on tape.
Some great personal trainers are available to you on videotape. If you enjoy exercising at home and can find enough room in front of your television set, exercise videos may work for you. Collage Video (✒ *www.collagevideo.com*) features over 500 exercise videotapes. Their catalog includes favorite selections by staff. Their staff consultants are friendly and are more than happy to help you with selections. Please note that their consultants are not certified trainers. Some of the videos feature people who are not certified trainers. Check qualifications of the trainers as well as personal opinions of the staff.

Professional Personal Coaches

A new profession that complements personal training is personal coaching. Coaching differs from personal training in significant ways. Your personal trainer develops and supports your physical training program. Your trainer guides your physical conditioning. How to set and achieve your conditioning goals and maintain your fitness is within your personal trainer's expertise.

In contrast, a personal coach helps you focus on what you want from the bigger picture of your life. For example, a personal coach can embrace your desire to change your lifestyle behaviors to ones that are healthier. Your personal coach would work with you to help you clarify which goals and dreams are important to you. Getting clear about what you want helps you move forward with intention, direction, and energy. Personal coaches also help identify your motivation and support you to make your vision a reality.

Personal coaches, therefore, have expertise in areas beyond personal training. A personal coach supports achievement of individual overall life goals. Today, some personal coaches combine coaching and personal training. It's important to note, however, that these are different services. Providers, therefore, will have different qualifications and experience.

Personal coaching works best for people interested in working on:

- Life planning
- Life vision and enhancement
- Spirituality
- Relationships (Singles, couples, families, etc.)
- Health and Fitness
- Creativity
- Financial Freedom
- Organization
- Children/Teens/College Students
- Attention Deficit Disorder

Kate Larsen, PCC, owner of Winning Lifestyles, Inc., in Minneapolis, Minnesota, is both a certified personal trainer and a certified personal coach. According to Larsen, "Working with a personal coach helps you create workable solutions to the obstacles in your life that prevent you from living the life that you want. As a personal coach, I help you identify what it is you truly want to achieve and how to achieve it. If I'm working with someone as a personal trainer, my role is to define a fitness program and support its execution."

People can work with a personal coach and not have a personal trainer. They can perform their exercise programs independently. Conversely, people can work with a personal trainer and not have a personal coach. It's important for you to know that these professionals are all available to help you achieve your personal goals, whatever they might be.

CHAPTER 19

Taking Group Muscle Conditioning Classes

Another alternative to performing your weight training on your own is to take group fitness classes. Group classes can either supplement your individual training or they can provide all of your weight training. It simply depends on what works out best for your personal needs.

Group Exercise

Group exercise as an industry emerged on the scene with dance aerobics back in the 1970s. Pioneers in the field included Jackie Sorenson and Judi Shephard-Missett. Jane Fonda brought group exercise into people's homes with her series of home exercise videos. What started out as modified dance moves set to popular tunes for a group to get a fitness workout has evolved into almost every manner of fitness activity imaginable for consumers.

Group exercise today spans weight training, aerobics, stretching, mind-body exercises, sports specific training, older adults, pregnant women, kids' fitness, and aquatic exercise, to name a few. Group exercise essentially consists of at least five or six participants up to as many as 100 who perform an exercise routine that is accompanied by music together under the leadership of one or more fitness instructors. There is so much variety available for so many different types of participants, there is no reason why a person cannot find a perfect match.

ALERT

Today's consumer needs to be aware of the available choices and how to evaluate the good from the bad. Many organizations that certify personal trainers also certify group exercise instructors. You can find a high-quality instructor and a high-quality program. You just need to know where to look.

Group Fitness Versus Personal Training

The essential difference between group fitness and personal training is that in a group setting, you are no longer under the individual supervision of a trainer. Group fitness, however, is distinct from small group personal training that typically consists of five participants or less. Most facilities have a minimum standard of five to six participants or more for a class to be considered a "group."

When you exercise in a group under the leadership of an instructor, the workout is no longer designed specifically to meet your individual needs. Instructors will do their best to provide suitable options for different people in a group setting. Clearly, however, there are limits to how broad a group can be to accommodate the varying needs of participants.

FACTS

As the group fitness market has grown, the types of classes available to participants have also expanded. Typically, group classes are no longer a "one size fits all" variety. You will observe that classes are designated to serve different levels of ability and different populations of people. For example, it makes perfect sense that a pregnant mom-to-be would not be doing the same workout as a teen-aged athlete.

Who Can Take Group Fitness Classes?

The great thing about group fitness today is that everyone can take classes. The health and fitness industry is expanding to meet the needs of different groups of people. Whether you are a complete beginner or a seasoned athlete, you can find classes that will suit your needs. Many facilities are also offering kids programming to supplement the fact that many schools are cutting back on physical education.

What Are the Benefits of Group Classes?

One of the strongest benefits of group classes is the opportunity that you have for social support in your classes both from your instructor and your classmates. Research studies show that friendships that involve exercising together and the social contacts from exercising in public places such as health and fitness clubs motivate continued exercise. The social benefits from exercising together are a very important indicator of the ability to adhere to an exercise program. So, if you're finding that you're having a hard time sticking with your exercise program or even in getting started, group classes may be a way to get you to keep it up.

In addition to keeping up with your program, when you exercise under the leadership of a qualified instructor, you will benefit from receiving a structured workout that should be safe and effective. Your instructor is available to monitor safety, provide individual alternatives, and to be a resource to you for your exercise questions.

ESSENTIALS Certified instructors receive training in CPR and should also be versed in emergency plan execution. When you work out in a group class, it should reduce your risk of injury.

Another benefit of group training is that when resources are pooled in a fitness facility, multiple equipment options are made available. Your group fitness class may use a variety of equipment including dumbbells, bands, resistive tubing, balls, medicine balls, bars, balance boards, and other devices. Your group instructor should be trained in the safe and proper use of this equipment. When you take group classes, you can learn proper technique for equipment use. You can also experience a broad variety that can later help make decisions when you decide to purchase pieces for your home use.

Group training is also lots of fun. Sharing your workouts with a roomful of your peers somehow makes it feel much more like fun and much less like work. You'll find that the group training environment can energize you to do more than you would on your own. There's something about sharing the "suffering" that makes it much more tolerable. And, it really isn't suffering, it's good and good for you. Remember, I've been a group trainer for over fifteen years, so I really do love it.

One more great benefit of group training is that while it can be a great place to begin, it's in no way an ending. As your strength improves, you will gain confidence to do more and more things both in the gym and in your life outside the gym. You should try new and different classes to experience more movement, such as ethnic dance classes or swing dancing or country line dancing. Often people in classes will organize outside activities together, such as participating in fund raising walks, runs or rides, or taking a cycling vacation across Europe.

Starting on the road to activity with group classes can be the beginning of a personal adventure in your life. You may meet even more people who share the new interest you're developing in enjoying a fit and active lifestyle. Keep an open mind and let the adventure happen as you get stronger over the years.

When to Start Taking Group Classes

You can start taking weight training group classes as soon as you find the right class for you. You don't already need to "be fit." So many people want to join a facility, but feel they need to get "in shape" first. The whole point about joining a facility is that it should be the place that can provide you with that opportunity. That is not to say that every facility is right for you.

First, you need to identify what you want from a class. For example, you want to start a weight training program and you're new to exercise. Then, you need to identify what locations and times will work for your schedule. Once you've established those details, you need to take the time to research different class offerings in your community to make sure they meet your needs. The key is to select the right class for your level and make sure you have the right personal equipment.

Selecting the Right Weight Training Class

First, to select the right group weight training class you need to be realistic about your level of conditioning and what you want to accomplish. If you are a beginner, you will not benefit yourself by enrolling in a class filled with recreational competitive athletes. It's not a character flaw to be a beginner. Be proud you're a beginner! You're ahead of the majority of people in America and many other developed nations of the world. Embrace your willingness to start something new and find the right match for your needs.

Next, all of the considerations that are relevant to finding the right facility are applicable to finding the right class. See Chapter 17, "Select the Perfect Gym for You," for further guidance on that topic. Assuming you have found the right facility for you, then you need to evaluate the group exercise schedule.

Most schedules will include a description of the classes. They may also include designations such as which classes are appropriate for what level of fitness. As you observe the types of members in any given facility, you will note that the group class schedule usually makes an effort to match those needs in the breadth of class offerings. For example, if the facility has kids and older adults, it's likely that the group program will include age-appropriate classes.

ALERT

People can be very sensitive about being labeled in a certain age group or at a certain level of ability. Keep in mind that these classifications are there not to insult you, but rather to facilitate you placing yourself in the right group.

Specialization and niche programming are the trends of the future. Be proud of who you are and what you can do. Put yourself in the right group. Take time to observe different classes and see who the majority of people are. If you feel that you can't find a group for you, make an appointment with the program director or coordinator to ask. Before you ask, be prepared by knowing what your physical limitations are and what types of movement you prefer. Do you like to dance? Do you like athletic styled movements? Do you enjoy pop music or do you prefer big band tunes? These are all relevant considerations for placing yourself in the right class for you.

In addition to finding the right level of class for a person of your age and ability, you also need to choose the right type of class. Traditional weight training in a group setting usually comes in the form of a group muscle conditioning class, circuit class, or interval class format.

Group Muscle Conditioning

Group strength-training classes can be listed under a variety of names. Some of these include body sculpting, body shaping, body shop, firm and tone, strong, and stretched. You get the idea. Other group weight training classes may be listed by body parts such as "south of the border" or "below the belt" for lower body training or healthy back or core conditioning for abdominal and back muscular training. An international fitness training company known as Les Mills has created a program that is known throughout the world as "Pump" or "Body Pump." This class has a universal format regardless of where you take the class in the world. You can check on the Internet for how to locate a class near you.

When in doubt about whether or not a class focuses on weight training, read the class descriptions. If you are unclear regarding what the class is, ask either the program director or coordinator.

Circuit Training

You can do circuit training on your own. However, these routines are also often offered as a group class in fitness facilities. A circuit class is typically organized around a series of weight machines. The instructor leads the group through a warm up and cool down together. During the weight training part of the workout, participants move from station to station at timed intervals, anywhere from thirty seconds to one or two minutes to perform training sets. Some circuits may include both cardiovascular stations as well as weight training stations. Other circuits focus entirely on weight training.

Circuit classes can be a great way to be introduced to the weight room if you cannot afford a personal trainer and need the motivation and support of an instructor to get you through a workout. Your instructor can also monitor the workout stations to make sure you perform your exercises with good technique to avoid injury.

Interval Training

Interval training can be similar to a circuit class except that it is usually not run on a group of weight machines. An interval-styled weight training class will often blend aerobic activities with toning exercises. For example, you may perform three minutes of cardiovascular step training movements. Then, the music changes, you grab the dumbbells you've hidden under your step and perform one to two sets of some type of strength-training exercise.

This type of class can be a nice change of pace from your usual training routine. It can provide variety and be fun. Observe or try a number of different classes to see what you like. As you become more experienced, revisit classes that may not have appealed to you when you were a beginner.

Variety is the spice of your training life. Keep your mind and your muscles fresh by trying out different exercises. Challenge your body in new ways to avoid staleness and to keep improving your fitness level.

Selecting the Right Instructor

Even if the curriculum of a certain class is perfect for you, the instructor may not be a good fit. While all certified instructors have safety training and should be knowledgeable about exercise technique, individual personalities influence the class experience. Instructors have playfully been divided into categories such as cheerleader or drill sergeant or Broadway entertainer and these descriptions are not too far off the mark. Some instructors are very serious, others incorporate lots of humor. Find a fit that works for you. If the instructor's personality doesn't suit you, find a different match.

Depending on how diverse your community is, you may find a broader variety among the instructional staff. It's not fair to assume that the instructor needs to conform to your personal preferences. If an instructor is on the schedule, it's likely indicative of the fact that the person appeals to a certain segment of the club's demographics. If you have a specific complaint or observation about the lack of safety or effectiveness of a particular instructor's teaching technique, then it's appropriate to mention it to the program director.

If, on the other hand, you simply do not appreciate the bubbly nature of the instructor's personality or the fact that he or she always likes to wear yellow, that is valid, but it's up to you to find a better match. That instructor does not need to change his or her personality or style to suit your individual style preferences.

In the Class

What to Wear to Class

Here again, what is appropriate to wear in the gym is generally appropriate to wear in group exercise classes. For most weight training classes, athletic shoes are required. If you like to wear open-toed athletic shoes, you should check with the facility rules to make sure it's accepted in the group exercise room.

In general, you want to wear athletic apparel that is comfortable, easy to move in, and breathes. You should also wear clean clothing to every class. Exercise clothing needs to be laundered after each use. Body odor is very individual and may not be apparent to you. However, it can be very noticeable among classmates. Be considerate and always wear clean gym clothes. It's also a good idea not to wear highly scented perfumes, deodorants, or after-shave lotions. Some participants may have allergies that will be triggered by highly scented products. These scents are magnified once you get active.

What to Bring

In most fitness facilities, you only need to bring yourself to class. You may want to bring a closed water bottle with you. Most facilities do not allow open cups in group training rooms as they can spill and create a slipping hazard. Be sure however to read the details of the class descriptions.

Some community-based classes or those offered in the workplace may require you to supply some of your own equipment. Alternatively, you may be required to purchase your own equipment and the instructor will bring it for you to the class. Check for these details. I have taught in instances when students have been required to bring their own resistance bands or to provide their own steps. Make sure you read up on all the details. It also doesn't hurt to ask the program director, coordinator, or the instructor.

Keeping Up with Everybody Else

This is often a big concern for people who are new to group exercise. Assuming that you have placed yourself in a class that is appropriate for people of your level, the instructor should be able to provide you with appropriate workout modifications. Typically, when demonstrating an exercise, a good instructor will show one or two options for more advanced or less advanced participants. We used to joke in the club environment because everyone wants to be advanced. So I would teach beginning-advanced, intermediate-advanced, and advanced-advanced options. That way we could all be advanced in our hearts. When offered with a smile, it seems to work for my class participants.

You Can Modify the Workout

A good qualified instructor can help you with exercise modifications. It's generally not a good idea to interrupt a large group session. If you find that you don't understand certain exercise instructions or you have particular needs such as you are prone to back pain, take the time to mention your concerns to the instructor. It's a good idea to either come a few minutes earlier or to stay a few minutes after class.

If you have very particularized individual concerns, then group exercise may not be appropriate for you. You may want to spend more time first with a personal trainer until you have a good understanding of your own movement limitations. When you feel ready to immerse yourself once again in the group environment, you can incorporate your specific understanding of your individual needs and modify your own exercises. If you already do this, it's generally a good idea to mention it to the instructor so he or she will know that you have some training and know what you are doing.

It's the instructor's responsibility to keep the experience safe, fun, and effective for a range of people. They cannot possibly know each and every person's unique concerns initially. To the credit of some instructors, if you stick with them over time, they will get to know you and can provide you with specific tips. This is a great situation to be in. To get to that level, however, you need to exchange information with your instructor and treat him or her as your partner in achieving your training success.

Group Class Etiquette

Similar to the principles discussed in gym etiquette, it's important ultimately to be respectful and considerate of both your group classmates and of your instructor. The group class environment is not personal training. You are receiving the benefit of trained instruction; however, the workout is not designed specifically to your individual needs. There is always a tension in that arrangement, however the benefit is that group fitness is much more cost-effective for you.

In addition to basic rules of respect and consideration, specific class rules include the following:

- Be on time to class. Do not enter a class late and disrupt the class. Not only is it not safe, since you have not participated in the warm-up, it can also distract other participant's at a critical moment that could lead to an injury. Remember, it's important to pay attention to form and technique when training.
- Avoid disrupting the class or bringing undue attention to yourself personally.
- If you want to do an entirely different workout than the rest of the group, do not participate in the class. It's one thing to modify exercises to suit your needs. It's another thing to create an entirely different workout that can distract others.
- Respect people's individual space. Whether you are new to a group or a confirmed "regular" none of you own any of the real estate in the group training room. Be flexible and accommodating to everyone's need for personal space. Do not dominate.
- If you have a personal complaint, do not voice it angrily and loudly at the instructor. Seek a more private opportunity to mention your concerns. If that's not possible, write a note to the program coordinator or manager. Conduct yourself responsibly and maturely.
- Get your own equipment and put your own equipment away. Remember that every movement you do during the day counts as activity. Be considerate of others and put all your equipment away.
- Unless it is a mommy or daddy and me class, do not bring your children into the group exercise room. The training room is not designed

to serve double-duty as childcare. Be sure to join a facility that provides childcare if you need it. Use the childcare services.

- Wear appropriate exercise attire that is clean. Avoid heavily scented products.
- Avoid spreading your gym bag out on the group exercise room floor. Most facilities will either provide cubbies for personal belongings or require that you lock them up in the changing room. Floor space can be at a premium. Any items on the floor can create a hazard as people may trip on them or not be able to see around them.
- Avoid loud conversations with your friends during class that can disrupt the workout. Of course, it's wonderful to exercise with your friends. At the same time, loud conversations can make it difficult for the instructor's cues to be heard. Be considerate of others.
- If you need to leave a class early, be responsible for your own cool-down. Also leave as quietly as possible with minimum disruption to other class participants.

Getting the Most out of Group Fitness

Group fitness offers so much to so many people, it's a shame not to take advantage of the skills of so many talented fitness professionals. Be flexible in your attitude towards group classes. Look for competent professional instructors. Try things you may not immediately think are right for you. Take your time and shop around.

Cathy Spencer, thirty-three years old, National Training and Program Director, Body Training Systems, recalls, "I've been weight training for twelve years . . . Weight training makes me feel 'able bodied,' like I can do almost anything. I have the strength and foundation to really enjoy all of the activities of life. I do many types of training; however, I really feel that it is weight training that keeps me injury free and strong enough to enjoy everything else. Aside from all of that it keeps me in great shape."

You may find that group weight training can provide you with all the weight training that you need. Or, you may discover that one class a week combined with one or two individual sessions a week works best for your schedule. Use the opportunity group classes provide to check out how to use different types of equipment and to learn new exercises. Group fitness classes are an excellent way to supplement your weight training program.

CHAPTER 20

Setting Up Your Home Gym

A dedicated home exercise space provides advantages. You are easily reminded of your exercise commitment each time you look at your equipment. It takes a minimal amount of time and effort to do your workout. Everything you need is already on display. It's convenient and efficient.

Define Your Space

Before you buy any equipment, you need to define your workout space. If you have enough space in your home to dedicate an entire room or a section of a room to your fitness program, that's great. A workout space does not require as much room as you might think. All you need is a section for a bench or sturdy chair, enough floor area to stretch out your body and reach all around you, and room to store your equipment.

Kate Larsen, forty-two years old, notes, "A positive impact of weight training for me is the ability to travel, lugging suitcases, computers, product, and such on and off airplanes and through airports without undue fatigue or pains, such as pulled back and neck muscles.

"I can take all kinds of exercise classes and keep up because my muscles are both strong and have good endurance. I can ski with my boys, golf or shoot hoops anytime without injury or concern.

"I think posture says a great deal about someone; the way a person stands reflects charisma, presence, and personal power. Having strong muscles allows me to maintain great posture. People sense and see strength in me because I can stand tall and maintain good posture even when I'm not thinking about it. (At least, that's what I hope.)

"The aspect of strength training I enjoy the most though, is the inner strength I feel being externally strong. I 'feel' my strength in my 'body' muscles which translates into courage, confidence and joy in my 'self-esteem' muscles."

Weight Training Choices

Your home gym can be as elaborate as money can buy. Typically, however, most people can't afford and would not select a full line of fitness machines like you would find in a fitness club. Manufacturers do design some weight machines, however, for the home market. Check out the following if you are thinking about equipping a home gym.

Multi-Station Units

Most home weight machines are styled as multi-station units. Some use weight plates. The majority feature alternative sources of resistance such as body weight, rubber straps, hydraulic pistons or even bending rods. Some of the higher-end machines are so versatile, you can perform more than twenty different exercises. The price of these home units generally runs from $1,000 to $3,500. A top-of-the-line fancy home gym with multiple features can run as much as several thousand dollars.

Before you purchase a multi-station unit, you should shop around and compare different products. Different body types will not be as comfortable on the same piece of equipment. Some machines are more suitable for petite women, whereas other machines meet the needs of large men.

Some machines feature very easy adjustments to convert from one exercise to another. Other machines have more complex features. Keep in mind that a multi-station unit will require some maintenance. You will periodically need to check the cables. You may also need to add lubricants. It's important to follow the manufacturers specific care directions that accompany the equipment.

Before you invest several thousand dollars, it's a good idea to check out the manufacturer's warranty for the product. Find out what type of customer service and support is offered. Some sporting goods store will include consultation and set up with your high-end equipment purchase. Ask if the store will help you if the machine breaks or whether you need to deal directly with the manufacturer. Go ahead and call the manufacturer's toll free number to find out what type of maintenance support is offered.

ALERT

Remember, you will get the best opportunity to find out what type of company you're working with before you make a major investment in equipment. Take your time to do your research thoroughly. It may save you a lot of headaches later.

Free Weights

Most home gyms are furnished with free weights. These are much more affordable, require less space, and are easy to maintain. For starters, you can buy a set of dumbbells in a range of weights. A typical set includes 3, 5, 8, and 10 pounds. If you are stronger, you may forego the 3-pound set and add heavier options such as 12-, 15-, and even 20-pound weights. Dumbbells come in quite a variety. Here is a sampling of some of the different types of products and their features.

Cast-iron dumbbells are minimalist both in style and cost. Cast-iron dumbbells are typically black or gray with a rough hewn look. These are more attractive to people who really enjoy the feeling of heavy metal in their hands.

Vinyl-coated dumbbells have a more feminine look and feel to them. They come in attractive colors such as pink, purple, and turquoise and have a soft, comfortable surface. These weights appeal more to people who are new to exercise as they are very friendly and unintimidating and come in light weights.

Plastic dumbbells tend to be less expensive. I do not enjoy the feel of plastic, but that is really up to your personal preference.

Chrome dumbbells are beautiful. These come in both the fixed weight variety or with weight plates so you do not have to buy several pairs. I prefer the weight plates as it takes less storage space. It's more time consuming, however, to adjust the weights as you switch from exercise to exercise. If you have space to store and the budget to purchase a variety of dumbbells, it does make for a faster workout.

You can pick up ankle weights for your lower body exercises. These come in adjustable sizes. You can purchase ankle cuffs that allow you to add weight in increments up to 20 pounds.

The PowerBlock is an interesting dumbbell product. The weights nest inside each other. By inserting a selector pin to the desired weight, you can adjust a single power block quickly and easily to range anywhere from 3 to 90 pounds. It's space efficient and much more economical than buying several pairs of dumbbells. This product satisfies the need for efficiency, comfort, and storage all in one product.

As you can see, there is a tremendous variety even among dumbbells. Check out a number of products in sporting goods or variety stores before you make your final decision. You're not likely to work out as much if you don't love your equipment. With so many choices available, you're sure to find something that will fit your particular needs.

Bands and Tubing

Elasticized resistance tools are great for variety and for traveling. They are easy to use, versatile, and very light weight. Physical therapists use these tools frequently when training people who are recovering from injuries. As a result, there are many varieties designed especially for exercise. Different manufacturers use different color coding systems to signify the level of resistance. As with all other equipment choices, try before you buy. Comfort is important, so you may prefer to use these tools with weight training gloves. Alternatively, you can buy products with padded handles for comfort. You can also purchase door attachments to increase the number of exercises that you can perform.

ESSENTIALS

Before you shop, call to see if they have the products you want to evaluate. Ask the salesperson if you can try out the equipment before you buy it. Actually perform a few exercises using different pieces of equipment. If you have any particular concerns or special needs, be sure to let the salesperson know.

Another option is to equip your home gym in consultation with a personal trainer. If you work with a trainer already, you can have your trainer select your equipment. Many trainers provide this service with only a minimal amount of mark up. This mark up is worth it if you consider the time and expertise the trainer has put into evaluating and selecting the right equipment. Alternatively, you can retain a trainer for the purpose of outfitting a home gym for you and creating a starter program. The fitness industry, like any other business, is complex. It pays to have a specialist's trained and experienced opinion.

Weight Bench or Sturdy Chair

To perform seated exercises, you will need either a weight training bench or a sturdy chair. In the beginning, a chair will be sufficient. The ideal chair is wooden and does not have any arms or upholstery. The chair should be very stable and not prone to tip over.

As you increase your exercise repertoire, a bench greatly increases your exercise options. You can buy a training bench from a sporting goods store that is padded and that can adjust from flat to incline positions. Benches can range from $100 to $300. If you don't want to buy a training bench, use any sturdy bench that can support sufficient weight. For example, you can use a piano bench if it's sufficiently strong and stable for your body.

A step bench that is popular for aerobic exercises can also serve as a weight bench. The step height should be at least 6 inches. You can use the step risers to alter the height of your bench and to create incline and decline positions. What's nice about using your step for weight training is that you can also use it as a step for aerobic exercises. This way it can serve a dual purpose for your exercise needs.

Mats

To improve your comfort when you are performing exercises on the floor, I recommend that you get a cushioned mat. Since you are likely to sweat when you workout, you should get a mat with a surface that can be easily cleaned. If it comes with a cloth cover, make sure it's removable so that you can wash it. Foam or rubber mats can be wiped clean.

Popular yoga "sticky" mats are useful to prevent your body from sliding during certain exercises. In general, however, they are not thick enough to cushion your spine against the floor for many exercises. Sticky mats work well on top of carpeted surfaces or when combined with a towel to increase the cushioning.

Foam mats come in different qualities. A denser mat is less likely to flatten out and lose its cushioning qualities quickly. A denser mat may be more expensive initially, but it's likely to provide longer and more comfortable use. A denser mat also provides better support, which can be important for certain exercises when you want to be sure you maintain neutral spinal alignment. A soft, cushy mat allows your body to sink into the mat where it conforms completely to your contours. This is not advantageous for monitoring your exercise form in certain positions.

Towels

A towel is another very useful weight training prop. Not only can you use it to wipe your brow when you are hot, but you also can use towels to improve your body position in certain exercises. For example, if the back of your neck is very tight and you have a thick back, you may need to use the towel under your head like a pillow when you lie on your back. You can also place a towel under your hips when you lie face down to support your back. A towel is also a great stretching tool.

FACTS

Play It Again Sports shops offer great deals on second-hand sporting equipment. If you want to try something out without making a huge investment, check out these stores. Look in want ads for moving sales. Wait until spring when everyone decides to sell equipment they bought at New Year's but never used.

Cardio Equipment

For total fitness, you need to supplement your weight training with aerobic exercise and stretching. Here again, space constraints, budget, and personal preference will be the determining factors in your choice. Most cardio machines offer low- or no-impact styles of training. Take the time to check out equipment just as you would for your weight training program. Remember, the most expensive piece of equipment in the world will not do you any good if you don't use it. Buy what you like and what you're likely to use.

You don't need to buy a fancy piece of cardio-training equipment. Maybe what is best for you is a good pair of walking or running shoes. Or, if you enjoy indoor workouts, try a jump rope, indoor rebounder, or a step bench for step aerobics.

Not all cardiovascular training machines are created equal. While all cardiovascular exercises feature large, rhythmic movements that use major muscles, some activities primarily challenge the lower body and others challenge the entire body.

It's a good idea to vary your cardiovascular exercises. They are all equally beneficial for your heart and lungs, but will train your other muscles in different ways.

MACHINE TYPE	ACTIVITY	PRIMARY MUSCLE GROUPS USED
stationary bicycle	riding a bicycle	lower body
treadmill	walking, jogging, or running	lower body
stair stepper	walking up stairs	lower body
elliptical trainer	walking	lower body
cross-country ski machine	cross-country skiing	upper and lower body
rowing machine	rowing a boat	upper and lower body
climbing machine	climbing a ladder	upper and lower body
cycle ergometer	pedaling a bike with your hands	upper body

CHAPTER 21

Special Considerations

While weight training routines can be appropriate for a wide variety of people, there are certain specific items that need to be addressed if you have special needs. If you have any special considerations, consult first with your health care provider before you start any exercise program.

Older Adults

While many of us are still very young at heart, our bodies are feeling the wear and tear of years of living. For purposes of this discussion, we will consider an older adult to be someone who is age fifty or above. Many people, particularly those who have exercised consistently since youth, may have a physiological age that is younger than their biological age. These guidelines refer to the average older adult.

Benefits of Weight Training for Older Adults

Research shows us that many of the attributes that we formerly associated with aging are really the result of disuse. If we use our bodies by engaging in regular exercise over the years, we can retain much of the resilience that we associate with youth. At the same time, however, research also shows us that the body has a remarkable capacity to get stronger and restore function with regular training.

Weight training for older adults can provide all of the previously mentioned benefits. In addition, weight training can enhance some of the specific concerns of older adults. Regular weight training can do the following:

- Improve muscular strength and endurance
- Improve daily functional ability to promote physical independence
- Improve bone mineral density to manage or prevent osteoporosis
- Improve digestion and relieve constipation
- Improve balance to prevent injury from falls
- Improve self-esteem and self-confidence
- Improve glucose utilization to reduce the likelihood of the onset of diabetes
- Decrease discomfort from arthritis
- Improve recovery during cardiac rehabilitation
- Reduce low back pain
- Improve feelings of depression
- May reduce resting blood pressure levels

All of these findings have been demonstrated in research studies.

How Old Is Too Old?

Adults over the age of ninety have experienced improvements in muscular strength and endurance through regular weight training. The key is to start very gradually. Older adults, in particular, should not start out with an overly aggressive program. Progression to more difficult levels should also be pursued in moderation.

Specific Modifications

For adults over the age of fifty, the ACSM recommends sets of 10 to 15 repetitions, instead of 8 to 12. One set of eight to ten exercises to train the major muscle groups is recommended. Training should be a minimum of two days a week to achieve results. Research shows that training two days per week produces 88 percent of the improvements in muscle strength and size as three training days per week.

Progression should be on the conservative side. When sets of 10 reps seem easy, choose to increase the number of repetitions up to 15 reps, before you choose to add more weight. This approach has less risk of injury than moving quickly to increase weight loads. When you do choose to increase your weight load, start out in increments of five percent of the weight load or less. Remember that gradual progression is equally important as good form and technique to prevent injuries.

ALERT

Remember that no pain equals no pain. Do not perform exercise that causes any sharp sensation of pain. This is usually a signal by your body that something isn't right. Learn to differentiate between feelings of discomfort and fatigue and feelings of pain. Any symptom of pain is a signpost to take notice.

Remember to combine your strength training with stretching. Flexibility training and aerobics are equally important components of an overall training program. While you may want to wait until you are stronger before you attempt any vigorous aerobic activities, you can start stretching the same day that you begin your weight training. Perform your exercises through your active range of motion. If some exercises cause noticeable discomfort, try to reduce the range of motion before giving it up altogether.

Most importantly, take the time to enjoy your training. Life is too short not to enjoy the process as well as the end results. Find a workout routine that is enjoyable to you. Look for good instruction and a comfortable workout atmosphere. Share your workout with friends so that it becomes a pleasurable part of your regular schedule. Consult frequently with your health care provider.

Kids and Teens

Believe it or not, even kids and teenagers can benefit from structured weight training programs. While weight training may still bring pictures to your mind of bulging men in skimpy body suits, remember that even body weight exercises constitute weight training. Your child's weight training or strength-training routine may consist of sit-ups, push-ups, and squats. It's not necessary for kids to use lots of heavy equipment to achieve results.

Before a child begins a structured strength-training program, the child needs to possess sufficient maturity to follow directions and should only train under a qualified supervisor. In addition, the NSCA recommends that children be evaluated by a sports medicine physician before undertaking a strength training program.

Benefits of Weight Training for Kids and Teens

The benefits of strength training for kids and teenagers is similar to adults and include the following:

- Improve muscle strength and endurance
- Improve body composition
- Improve self-esteem and self-confidence
- Enhance more lifestyle activity with improved energy to participate in games and other more vigorous activities
- Increase coordination, agility, and balance

- Improve social skills, interaction, and cooperation among youth who train together
- Reduce injury risk among athletic youth
- Improve sports performance
- Establish a healthy habit of regular exercise
- Build strong bones in youth to provide a healthy foundation for a lifetime

With growing concerns over the lack of physical activity among today's youth, a strength training program may be a great place to start exercising.

How Young Is Too Young?

Leading researchers in the area of strength training for youth include Avery Faigenbaum, Ed.D. and Wayne Westcott, Ph.D. In studies, they have found that children as young as age six have achieved positive results from strength training. An important factor in determining the starting age for training is the maturity of the child. A child can only successfully undertake training if he or she is disciplined enough to follow instructions.

Specific Modifications

Similar to older adults, youth achieve better results with lighter weights and more repetitions. Thirteen to 15 repetitions per set is recommended. No external resistance should be supplied until the child clearly demonstrates the ability to execute proper form and technique. If weight is added, it should be in small 1- to 3-pound increments only after the child can perform 15 repetitions with no additional weight. Children should never attempt to lift maximum or near maximum weight loads.

Children and teens should train only under the supervision of qualified adults. Training sessions should be kept short and should include both a warm up and stretching exercises. Two days a week are sufficient, particularly if the child is engaging in other sports activities. Each session should include eight to ten strength exercises. Progression needs to be conservative. Always increase reps before increasing weight. And, increase weight in small increments. It's very important for youth not to engage in overtraining.

It's always important to keep in mind that children are not simply miniature adults. Children are at a different developmental stage and are still growing. It's critically important to work with experienced teachers since inappropriate training can damage growth cartilage. This is serious as it can stop the bone from growing. Particular caution needs to be exercised. Children need to be taught that weights are not toys and that proper technique is essential to prevent injuries.

According to the American Academy of Pediatrics, "children and adolescents should avoid the practice of weight lifting, power lifting, and body building, as well as the repetitive use of maximal amounts of weight in strength training programs, until they have reached 'Tanner stage 5' level of developmental maturity."

"Tanner stage 5" for males and females means that they have passed their period of maximal velocity of height growth, during which the epiphyses, which is a part of bone, appear to be especially vulnerable to injury. This level of developmental maturity is reached at the mean age of approximately fifteen years in both sexes, with much individual variation. Therefore, it's important to include a physician in the decision making process regarding a teen's training program.

An additional important consideration for youth is that childhood is a time to develop habits for adult life. Fitness should be a fun experience. Young people need to enjoy the feeling of using their bodies and enhancing their body awareness. This foundation of pleasure in activity will serve them well as they age.

 **ESSENTIALS**

Fitness needs to be kept in perspective. Strength training and muscular development are only one part of an overall training program. Parents also need to keep competitive pressure in perspective and encourage goods sportsmanship behavior.

When youth increase their level of activity, they need to proportionately increase their rest. Sleep is the time for muscle tissue repair and growth. If your child is involved in training and sports, be sure to allow plenty of time for adequate sleep. It's particularly important for a growing body.

Many facilities do not allow youth under the age of sixteen to use weight training equipment. This is to reduce their risk of liability. Facilities such as the YMCA, however, do offer youth strength-training programs. Check in your local area or contact the YMCA of the USA for information on locator services.

One other important consideration for parents to keep in mind is that youth and teens are increasingly becoming subject to body image pressure. Pay attention to how your child feels about his or her training program. Listen to comments about his or her feelings about appearance. Youths may be subject to a lot of peer pressure, particularly if they are involved in the more aesthetic sports such as gymnastics, figure skating, dance, or synchronized swimming. Be sure to encourage healthy body image attitudes. If your child exhibits any eating or exercise disordered behavior, seek professional assistance.

Pregnant Women

Today's active woman can keep on being active. Neither wind, nor snow, nor sleet, nor hail can stop a determined woman from fitting in her workout. So, what do you do when you learn you're pregnant? Keep up the great work. All you need to do is make the appropriate modifications. The good news is that research studies support that women can weight train during pregnancy and increase muscular strength without adverse effects. All pregnant women, however, should discuss their intentions to train with their health care provider.

Benefits of Weight Training for Pregnant Women

Training during pregnancy can offer relief for some of the symptoms of being pregnant. If you have been involved in a regular exercise routine before becoming pregnant, you can derive many benefits from continued training.

- Maintenance of muscular strength and endurance
- Improved circulation and relief from swelling
- Relief from low back pain by stretching and strengthening abdominal and back muscles
- Eased gastrointestinal discomfort
- Improved energy levels
- Improved quality of sleep
- Improved balance
- Improved posture
- Reduced muscle cramps
- Improved feelings of well-being and self-esteem
- Increased body awareness
- More rapid recovery after you have given birth
- Fewer feelings of stress, tension, and anxiety

Exercise, including weight training, provides many benefits for the expectant mom. The most important point to remember is that training during pregnancy should be to maintain abilities and not to increase performance. Be conservative. You will have more than enough time after your child is born to get back into shape.

Specific Modifications

The American College of Obstetrics and Gynecology (ACOG) provides guidelines for exercise during pregnancy. The 1994 guidelines include the following points:

- Exercise regularly, preferably three times per week.
- Do not lie on your back after the first trimester.

- Modify intensity of your exercise. Do not exercise to the point of breathlessness. Use RPE to monitor intensity.
- Be careful of rapid shifts in direction. Do not jeopardize your balance.
- Avoid overheating. Wear proper clothes. Pay attention to the environment. Drink plenty of fluids.
- Always warm up and cool down properly
- Avoid excessive impact.
- Do not overstretch.
- Be sure to eat enough calories to cover both your pregnancy and exercise needs.
- Avoid spinal rotation when you lift your leg to the back or to the front.

When you are pregnant, there are certain instances when exercise is not recommended. According to the ACOG guidelines, you should discontinue exercise and seek medical advice if you have any of the following conditions during pregnancy:

- Pregnancy-induced hypertension
- Preterm rupture of membranes
- Preterm labor during the prior or current pregnancy or both
- Incompetent cervix
- Persistent second- or third-trimester bleeding
- Intrauterine growth retardation.

Weight training guidelines for pregnant women emphasize taking it easy. One set of eight to ten exercises twice a week is sufficient. Choose lower weights and higher repetitions such as 10 to 15 reps to avoid risk of injury. The hormone relaxin is circulating in the bloodstream. This hormone enables the ligaments to stretch so the pelvis can accommodate the size of the growing fetus. This can cause some instability in the ligaments throughout the body. Pregnant women should avoid lifting heavy weights because of this increased instability. Pregnant women also need to avoid holding their breath as this can cause the fetus to experience oxygen debt.

ALERT

When you are pregnant, you may be carrying anywhere from 10 to 25 more pounds than usual. This can cause additional fatigue. Decrease or stop exercise if you experience any discomfort or pain.

For exercises, focus on training upper back muscles to support the weight of growing breasts. Strengthen your abdominal and lower back muscles to support the weight of the growing fetus. Try side-lying exercises to strengthen your lower body. Avoid any exercises on your back after the first trimester as weight from the growing fetus can compromise blood flow to the brain and cause low blood pressure and feelings of faintness.

For best results, exercise during pregnancy under the supervision of a professional who is trained in how to work with pregnant women. Continue your program while maintaining a dialogue about your condition with your health care provider. Always choose more conservative options. Rest and take it easy whenever that feels like the right thing for you to do. In this manner, you should have a healthy pregnancy and delivery.

In any case, most, if not all, doctors do not recommend starting a new weight training program once you are pregnant. If you are already involved in a program, they will usually have you gradually eliminate certain exercises as you go along. Show your doctor what you are doing and be sure to ask questions!

Adults Who Are Larger-Sized

One of my fitness colleagues, Gayle Winegar in St. Paul, Minnesota, ran a "Take back the beach" campaign at her fitness facility to emphasize how body image obsession has made wearing a swimsuit a traumatic and unpleasant experience for many women. She created a "real" swimsuit calendar that featured the healthy and diversely shaped bodies of her club's members. What a great idea.

Along the same lines, everyone should "Take back the gym." Fitness facilities should not be the exclusive domain of the already fit and athletic public. Hopefully, there will be a day when all people, regardless of age, shape, size, or level of ability, can feel that they belong in a fitness club. Exercise offers too many benefits for too many people for us to keep it a hidden privilege.

The average American woman is 5 foot 4 inches tall and wears size 12 clothing. Only 2 percent of the American population can possess a supermodel's physique without resorting to unhealthy eating or exercise disordered behavior. The truth is the average American is a person who is larger sized.

Benefits of Weight Training for Adults Who Are Larger-Sized

One of the myths of exercise is that you should wait to do weight training until you are more fit. In fact, the reverse is true. A beginning training program for any person, including larger-sized adults, should include weight training. Some of the benefits for larger-sized adults of weight training include the following:

- Improved body awareness and understanding of how your muscles should feel when they work
- Reduced low back pain
- Increased muscle strength and endurance
- Increased energy levels so that other activities are easier and more appealing
- Enjoying the feeling of what your body can do when it gets strong
- Improved feelings of self-esteem and self-confidence
- Increased lean body mass and improve body composition
- Possibility of reduced blood pressure
- Improved glucose utilization
- Improved balance and coordination
- Improved quality of sleep

Remember that even elite athletes come in all shapes and sizes. Some people simply are naturally larger sized. The appearance of a strong and fit person is not necessarily ultra-thin. All people deserve to enjoy the pleasure of a strong and active body. Do your part to own your space in the gym, too. You can find fitness and wellness professionals who will provide you with support and resources.

Specific Modifications

You may need to modify certain exercises to accommodate the specific needs of a larger body type. Select big stable benches to support your body weight. Begin with seated exercises with back support first for stability. Progress to seated exercises without back support. When you've mastered these variations, then move to standing versions.

Weight machines that are designed for body building men can typically support a larger-sized person. If you want to work out on machines, select a gym that offers this type of equipment.

As long as you do not have any special medical considerations, your training regimen can be the same as that for other healthy adults. Perform one to two sets of eight to ten exercises for the major muscle groups at least two to three times a week. Choose a weight level that you can lift in the 8 to 12 repetition range.

Be particularly attentive to form and body positioning. Be sure not to use momentum or to swing your weights. Instead, tune into the working muscles and take the time to feel what it's like to make your muscles work up a sweat.

For exercises that you must do when standing, use the wall for support and extra stability. Try wall push-ups, standing calf raises, and standing toe raises. You can try wall squats against the wall. Work to a level of comfortable challenge for yourself.

Try performing exercises on the floor. If you're concerned about how to get down or how to get up, try these simple moves. To get down onto the floor: take a wide stance, put your hands on your thighs. Bend your knees and squat. Lower one knee to the floor, extend your hand out, lower your hips to the side and there you are.

When you're on the floor you can perform side-lying leg work for your inner and outer thighs. You can roll over onto your stomach and do leg lifts. You can do abdominal training on your back.

To get up from the floor: kneel face down, take a wide stance with your knees. Put your toes on the floor with your heels up. Walk your hands in and push off the floor with your hands. Roll your weight into your heels, walk your hands up to your thighs. Push yourself up into a standing position. You can perform your stretches while seated on a bench.

Remember that it's important to supplement your weight training with stretching and some form of aerobic exercise. If you want to avoid impact to protect your joints and back, try water exercise. If performed in shallow water, it's a great low impact exercise. If conducted in deep water, it's a great no impact workout. Water training is also great as your muscles get stronger working against water's resistance. Pretty soon, you'll be feeling so fit you won't even remember what it was like when you didn't exercise regularly.

People with Disabilities

It is particularly inspiring, and humbling, to see people who are able to continue their exercise programs in spite of disabilities. There are athletes who are blind, who have no legs, and who have no sensation in their legs. The resilience of the human spirit and adaptability of people to make the best of any condition or situation is impressive.

The ability to move our bodies is a joy and a privilege that we should not take for granted. If you have a condition that requires that you use a wheelchair or prosthetics to get around, exercise is an essential means to keep your body in condition. For people with fewer limbs and less access to mobility, exercise is even more essential to well-being.

Benefits of Weight Training for People with Disabilities

Weight training provides specific benefits to people with disabilities. Not only can you reap all of the rewards that have been previously mentioned, certain other benefits are critically important. Weight training can provide the following benefits:

- Improved muscle strength and endurance
- Enhanced circulation

- Increased ability to perform activities of daily living and increase physical independence
- Maintained range of motion and flexibility
- Prevention of muscle weakening or deterioration from lack of use
- Avoidance of contractures that can cause muscles to become fixed and rigid
- Improved balance and coordination
- Improved alignment
- Improved body awareness
- Improved feelings of well-being, self-esteem, and self-confidence

Specific Modifications

As there are many different types of disabilities, it's important that you consult with your health care provider when you start any training program. For people who have not had any weight-bearing forces placed on their skeletal system for some time, it's important to progress slowly and under the recommendation of a physician. If certain parts of the body have been nonfunctional, start very gradually and progress slowly.

With respect to sets and reps, start with one set of each exercise and perform between 8 to 15 repetitions. After a few weeks progress gradually to two sets per exercise. Remember to first increase the number of reps, then increase the number of sets. After you can comfortably perform at this level, you can gradually increase the weight no more than 5 percent. Do not rush to increase your weight level as that can increase your risk of injury. Take the time to condition your muscles and progress gradually.

Certain strength training machines can accommodate participants who are in wheelchairs. According to Jeff Jones, director of the Rehabilitation Institute of Chicago's Center for Health and Fitness in Illinois, "disability sports programs are growing across the country." You can check the Disabled Sports Organizations (DSOs) for access to a wheelchair friendly training facility in your neighborhood. Training programs may also be available in YMCAs, JCCs, and through organizations such as the United States Cerebral Palsy Association.

FACTS

The Americans with Disabilities Act (ADA) requires that all public access facilities make reasonable accommodation for all participants. You can contact one of the ten regional Disability and Technical Assistance Centers for additional leads on recreational business services in your community. These centers educate the business community on how to accommodate clients or employees with disabilities in accordance with the ADA. In 2000, the government issued technical guidelines that covered accessibility matters for recreational facilities.

Take the time to do a little research and you can find organizations that will support you to improve your physical conditioning. Remember exercise is a privilege that can be enjoyed by anyone who can move. Take advantage of all the resources that you need to meet your particular goals.

Appendix A

Glossary

Active stretching: A method of stretching that uses a muscle's active contraction to stretch the opposing muscle that must lengthen to accommodate the muscle contraction. No force is applied. A good example is when the shin is contracted, the calf muscles are stretched.

Activities of daily living: The physical activities you do every day as part of living your life.

Aerobic: with, or in the presence of, oxygen

Aerobic exercise: Aerobic exercise refers to moderate to vigorous exercise that uses large, rhythmic movements to elevate the heart rate for periods of time to condition the cardio-respiratory system. Examples of aerobic exercises include walking, jogging, hiking, cycling, swimming, and water exercise.

Amino acids: Compounds that are the building blocks or structural material of protein.

Anaerobic: without oxygen

Ballistic stretching: A method of stretching that uses high force bouncing movements. Ballistic stretching is fast and has a high risk of injury. This type of stretching may be appropriate for athletes in certain sports and for dancers that require dynamic flexibility.

Basal metabolic rate: The rate of energy consumption simply to exist is known as basal metabolic rate, resting metabolic rate, or metabolism.

BMI: The Body Mass Index or "BMI" is a table of measurements that rate weight in relationship to height. Your BMI is your weight in kilograms divided by your height in meters squared.

Body composition: Body composition refers to the percentage of fat and percentage of fat free body mass that makes up your total body weight. Fat free mass, also known as lean body mass, consists primarily of muscle tissue, bones and blood, essentially all the rest of your body that is not fat.

Bodybuilding: Bodybuilding is a competitive sport that uses weight training to achieve a physique that is judged based on muscle size, definition, and symmetry. The goal of competitive bodybuilding is to build large muscles.

Bone density: Bones are living tissue that provide structural support for our bodies, protect organs, and store calcium. Bone density refers to the thickness of bone and the amount of minerals it contains.

C

Calorie: A calorie is a unit of measure of energy. One calorie equals the amount of heat necessary to increase the temperature of one kilogram of water 1 degree Celsius. Calorie is also referred to as kilo-calorie.

Cardio respiratory fitness: The ability to engage in large rhythmic muscle movements for an extended period of time. It also refers to the ability of the heart to deliver oxygen to working muscles and to the muscle's ability to use the oxygen to produce energy for sustained performance.

Cardiovascular exercise: Cardiovascular exercise is the same as aerobic exercise or aerobics. It refers to moderate to vigorous exercise that uses large, rhythmic movements to elevate the heart rate for periods of time to condition the cardio-respiratory system. Examples of aerobic exercises include walking, jogging, hiking, cycling, swimming, and water exercise.

Carotid pulse: The carotid pulse is found at the side of the neck

Components of fitness: The components of fitness include muscle strength, muscle endurance, cardio respiratory endurance, flexibility, and body composition.

Connective tissue: Connective tissues includes fascia, a sheath that surrounds muscles, tendons that connect muscles to bone, and ligaments that connect bone to bone.

E

Ergogenic aids: Products or substances that enhance physical or athletic performance.

F

Fat free mass: The percentage of body mass that is not fat when you measure body composition. Fat free mass includes bones, blood, connective tissue, organs, and muscles. It is also known as lean body mass.

Fat mass: The part of body composition that includes body fat only.

Fat soluble: Fat soluble means that it can be dissolved in fat. This is relevant to vitamins in the body that are stored in body fat, primarily in the liver.

Flexibility: The ability to move a joint through a full range of motion without undue stress to the musculotendinous unit.

Flexibility training: An exercise program that is progressive over a period of time and results in an increase in the usable ROM of joint(s).

Food Guide Pyramid: A guide to daily food choices issued by the U.S. Department of Agriculture and the Department of Health and Human Services.

Functional fitness: Functional fitness is generally considered to be a person's ability to perform light, moderate, and strenuous recreational, household, daily living, and personal care tasks.

Functional flexibility: The ability to use a range of joint movement in the performance of a physical activity, including speed and angle.

Functional strength: Functional strength is the amount of strength necessary to perform your activities of daily living.

H **Heart rate:** Your heart rate is a measure of the number of beats of your heart in one minute.

I **Interval training:** A method of training that consists of bouts of high intensity exercise interspersed with rest intervals. The technique is used to improve cardio respiratory fitness.

Inverse Stretch Reflex: The response to stretch in musculotendinous unit, which leads to relaxation. Classic example—after holding a stretch, resistance suddenly releases, resulting in increased length.

L **Lean body mass:** Lean body mass is the same as fat free mass. It consists of the part of body mass that is not fat. This includes bones, blood, connective tissue, organs, and muscles.

Lifestyle: The way you live your life on a consistent basis.

M **Minerals:** Organic substances in foods that we eat that are essential for regulation of body functions such as energy metabolism.

Muscle endurance: Muscle endurance is the ability of a muscle to exert repeated contractions over a period of time.

Muscle strength: Muscle strength is the maximum amount of force a muscle or muscle group can exert.

O **Olympic lifting:** Olympic lifting is a competitive sport. Contestants are divided into weight classes depending on their size. Winners are determined by who lifts the most weight in two lifts: the snatch and the clean and jerk.

P **Passive stretching:** A method of stretching that uses an external force such as body weight, gravity, or a prop to lengthen a muscle. A static stretch is often also a passive stretch.

Physical fitness: The ability to perform physical activities with vigor.

PNF/CRAC stretches: PNF stands for proprioceptive neuromuscular facilitation. PNF is a method of stimulating muscle proprioceptors to develop the neuromuscular system. PNF stretching is a method that involves lengthening a muscle, contracting it, and then lengthening it again to achieve a greater stretch. CRAC stands for contract release antagonist contract. CRAC stretching is based on PNF.

Power: Power is the amount of work performed in a specific period of time. In it's simplest form, power = strength **x** speed. Most athletes seek to improve power, or the ability to exert force more quickly.

Power lifting: Power lifting is a competitive sport. Contestants are divided into weight classes depending on their size. Winners are determined by who can lift the most weight in three distinct lifts: the bench press, squat, and dead lift.

Proprioceptors: Part of the neuromuscular system, proprioceptors are located in muscles, tendons, and joints. Proprioceptors regulate a muscle's resting length and are stimulated when a muscle contracts or lengthens.

Q

Quality of life: Quality of life refers to an overall sense of well being and satisfaction in living.

R

Radial pulse: The radial pulse is found on the inside of the wrist.

Range of motion: The number of degrees that a joint will allow a limb to move, also known as ROM.

Rate of perceived exertion (RPE): The rate of perceived exertion is a method to determine the intensity of your exercise. This scale, created by Dr. Borg, is a subjective rating of intensity from six to seven, which is very, very light, to eighteen to twenty, which is very, very hard.

Reciprocal innervation: Muscles work in pairs. When the primary mover or agonist muscle contracts, the opposing muscle or antagonist relaxes. Reciprocal innervation, also known as reciprocal inhibition, is the name of the reflex action that triggers the relaxation of the opposing muscle. This reflexive action helps to facilitate coordinated muscle movements.

Resting heart rate: Resting heart rate is measured by taking your pulse for one full minute first thing in the morning, before you get out of bed. You also want to wake up naturally without a loud alarm clock that can startle you and send your heart soaring. Take your resting heart rate on several mornings in a row to determine an average for most accurate results.

S

Sedentary: Sedentary means not active. The 'couch potato' is the model of a sedentary lifestyle. It's used to refer to a lifestyle that does not include physical activity.

Static stretching: A low force method of stretching by holding a muscle in a lengthened position for periods of fifteen to thirty seconds.

Stretch reflex: The stretch reflex is stimulated by a sudden muscular elongation. If the nerve receptors sense a rapid stretch, the body's reflexive mechanism is to contract. This is the body's way of protecting joints from an excessive stretch.

V

Vitamins: Organic substances in foods that we eat that regulate energy metabolism. Vitamins are either water soluble or fat soluble.

W

Water soluble: Water soluble means that it can be dissolved in water. This is relevant to vitamins in the body.

Weight training: Weight training is a method of building muscle strength and endurance over time through the progressive use of resistance. Weight training is not bodybuilding.

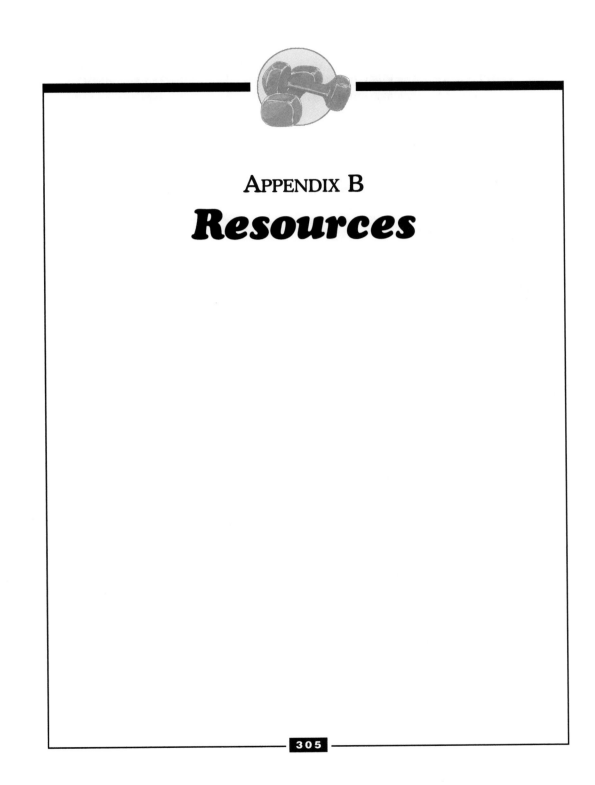

APPENDIX B
Resources

General Resources

Aerobics and Fitness Association of America (AFAA)
15250 Ventura Boulevard, Suite 200
Sherman Oaks, CA 91403
818-905-0040 or 800-446-2322
www.afaa.com

American College of Obstetrics and Gynecologists (ACOG)
409 12th Street, SW
Washington, DC 20023-2188
800-673-8444 or 202-863-2518

American College of Sports Medicine
P.O. Box 1440
Indianapolis, IN 46206-1440
317-637-9200
www.acsm.org

American Council on Exercise
5820 Oberlin Drive, Suite 102
San Diego, CA 92121-3787
or
P.O. Box 910449
San Diego, CA 92191-0449
858-535-8227
858-535-1778 (fax)
www.acefitness.org

American Dietetic Association (ADA)
216 W. Jackson Boulevard
Chicago, IL 60606-6995
800-877-1600
www.eatright.org

Aquatic Exercise Association (AEA)
3439 Technology Drive, Unit 6
Nokomis, FL 34275
888-AEA-WAVE
www.aeawave.com

Centers for Disease Control and Prevention (CDC)
1600 Clifton Road
Atlanta, GA 30333
Public Inquiries
404-639-3534 or 800-311-3435
www.cdc.gov

Cooper Institute for Aerobics Research
12330 Preston Road
Dallas, TX 75230
800-365-7050
www.cooperinst.org

Disabled Sports Organizations

The National Center on Physical Activity and Disability
Department of Disability and Human Development
University of Illinois at Chicago
1640 West Roosevelt Road
Chicago, IL 60608-6904
800-900-8086 (voice and TTY)
312-355-4058 (fax)
ncpad@uic.edu
www.ncpad.org

Disabled Sports, USA (DSUSA)
451 Hungerford Drive, #100
Rockville, MD 20850
301-217-0960
www.dsusa.org

HEALTHCLUB.COM
www.healthclub.com

IDEA Health & Fitness Association
6190 Cornerstone Court East, Suite 204
San Diego, CA 92121
858-535-8979
www.ideafit.com

International Coach Federation
1444 I Street NW
Suite 700
Washington, DC 20005
888-423-3131 or 202-712-9039
888-329-2423 or 202-216-9646 (fax)
cfoffice@coachfederation.org
www.coachfederation.org

International Health, Racquet, and Sportsclub Association (IHRSA)
263 Summer Street
Boston, MA 02210
800-228-4772
www.ihrsa.org

Medical Fitness Association (MFA)
915 Elmswood Avenue
Evanston, IL 60202
847-475-2332
www.medicalfitness.org

National Academy of Sports Medicine
123 Hodencamp Drive, Suite 204
Thousand Oaks, CA 91360
800-656-2739
805-449-1370 (fax)
www.worldhealth.net/whoswho/nasm

National Center on Physical Activity and Disability
800-900-8086
www.ncpad.org

National Heart, Lung, and Blood Institute
Information Center
P.O. Box 30105
Bethesda, MD 20824-0105
301-251-1222
www.nhlbi.nih.gov

National Strength and Conditioning Association
P.O. Box 9908
Colorado Springs, CO 80932-9908
719-632-6722 or 800-815-6826
719-632-6367 (fax)
http://nsca-lift.org

President's Council on Physical Fitness and Sports
701 Pennsylvania Avenue, NW
Suite 250
Washington, DC 20004
202-272-3421
www.fitness.gov

Rehabilitation Institute of Chicago
Center for Health and Fitness
710 North Lake Shore Drive
Chicago, IL 60611
312-908-4292
312-908-1051 (fax)
http://richealth.org

Weight-Control Information Network
1 Win Way
Bethesda, MD 20892-3665
202-828-1025 or 877-946-4627
202-828-1028 (fax)
win@info.niddk.nih.gov
www.niddk.nih.gov/health/nutrit/pubs/health.htm

U.S. Access Board
1331 F Street, NW
Washington, DC 20004-1111
800-USA-ABLE or 800-993-2822 (TTY)
www.access-board.gov

United States Cerebral Palsy Athletic Association (USCPAA)
25 West Independence Way
Kingston, RI 02881
401-874-7465
http://uscpaa.org

U.S. Department of Agriculture (USDA)
14th and Independence Avenue, SW
Washington, DC 20250
202-720-2791
202-720-2166 (fax)
www.usda.gov

U.S. Food and Drug Administration (FDA)
5600 Fishers Lane
Rockville, MD 20857
888-INFO-FDA or 301-463-6332
www.fda.gov

United States Water Fitness Association (USWFA)
P.O. Box 3279
Boynton Beach, FL 33424
561-732-9908
www.uswfa.com

YWCA of Canada
590 Jarvis Street, 5th Floor
Toronto, ON
Canada M4Y 2J4
416-962-8881
416-962-8084 (fax)
national@ywcacanada.ca
www.ymcanada.ca

YMCA of the USA
101 North Wacker Drive
Chicago, IL 60606
888-333-YMCA or 888-333-9622
or 800-872-9622
312-977-0031
www.ymca.net

Product Resources

Champion Sportswear
5 New England Drive
Essex Junction, VT 05452
www.championjogbra.com

Complete Guide to Exercise Videos Collage Video
5390 Main Street NE
Minneapolis, MN 55421, USA
800-433-6769
collage@collagevideo.com
www.collagevideo.com

Fitness Wholesale
895-A Hampshire Road
Stow, OH 44224
888-FW-ORDER (888-396-7337)
or 330-929-7227
330-929-7250 (fax)
fw@fitnesswholesale.com
www.fitnesswholesale.com

IntellBell PowerBlocks
1819 South Cedar Avenue
Owatonna, MN 55060
800-446-5215 or 507-451-5152
www.powerblock.com

Junonia (fitness apparel for plus sized woman)
800 Transfer Road, Suite 8
St. Paul, MN 55114
800-671-0175
www.junonia.com

M. Rose Sportswear Group, Inc. (fitness apparel for women)
1255 Activity Drive, Suite B
Vista, CA 92083-8517
877-86m-rose or 760-734-4090
760-734-4220 (fax)
m.rose@mrosesportswear.com
www.mrosesportswear.com

Reebok
1000 Technology Center Drive
Stoughton, MA 02072
617-341-4000
www.reebok.com

Water Safety Training

To learn how to swim or for training in basic water safety skills, contact the following organizations:

American National Red Cross
703-206-6000 or contact your local chapter

YMCA of the USA
312-977-0031 or 800-872-9622

The following organizations can help you locate water fitness classes, instructors, and trainers in your neighborhood. Contact them for further information.

Aquatic Exercise Association (AEA)
3439 Technology Drive, Unit 6
Nokomis, FL 34275
888-AEA-WAVE
www.aeawave.com

United States Water Fitness Association (USWFA)
P.O. Box 3279
Boynton Beach, FL 33424
561-732-9908
www.uswfa.com

YMCA of the USA
101 North Wacker Drive
Chicago, IL 60606
312-977-0031 or 800-872-9622
www.ymca.net

How to Find a Personal Coach

For a locator service to help you find a personal coach anywhere in the world, contact the International Coach Federation.

International Coach Federation
1444 I Street NW
Suite 700
Washington, DC 20005
888-423-3131 or 202-712-9039
888-329-2423 or 202-216-9646 (fax)
icfoffice@coachfederation.org
www.coachfederation.org

Exercise and Pregnancy
American College of Obstetrics and Gynecologists (ACOG)
409 12th Street, SW
Washington, DC 20023-2188
800-673-8444 or 202-863-2518

Exercise and Disabilities
United States Cerebral Palsy Athletic Association (USCPAA)
25 West Independence Way
Kingston, RI 02881
401-874-7465
http://uscpaa.org

**Disabled Sports Organizations
The National Center on Physical Activity and Disability**
Department of Disability and Human Development
University of Illinois at Chicago

1640 West Roosevelt Road
Chicago, IL 60608-6904
800-900-8086 (voice and TTY)
312-355-4058 (fax)
ncpad@uic.edu
www.ncpad.org

Disabled Sports, USA (DSUSA)
451 Hungerford Drive, #100
Rockville, MD 20850
301-217-0960
www.dsusa.org

Rehabilitation Institute of Chicago
Center for Health and Fitness
710 North Lake Shore Drive
Chicago, IL 60611
312-908-4292
312-908-1051 (fax)
http://richealth.org

The U.S. Access Board
1331 F Street, NW
Washington, DC 20004-1111
800-USA-ABLE or 800-993-2822 (TTY)
www.access-board.gov

Appendix C

Food Log

Photocopy the following log to record what you eat in a typical week. As you increase your awareness of your eating habits, you can start to move towards eating more healthfully. Compare your typical consumption with the recommendations in the Food Guide Pyramid. Use the notes section to record any emotions you may have related to your eating such as anger or sadness or physical feelings such as fatigue or headaches. This may increase your awareness of eating that is unrelated to your true physical needs for food or that is related to underlying physical conditions. You can share this log with your health care provider.

WEEKLY FOOD LOG

_____ TO_____

SUNDAY
breakfast
lunch
dinner

snacks
fluids
notes

MONDAY
breakfast
lunch
dinner

snacks
fluids
notes

TUESDAY
breakfast
lunch
dinner

snacks
fluids
notes

WEDNESDAY
breakfast
lunch
dinner

snacks
fluids
notes

THURSDAY
breakfast
lunch
dinner

snacks
fluids
notes

FRIDAY
breakfast
lunch
dinner

snacks
fluids
notes

SATURDAY
breakfast
lunch
dinner

snacks
fluids
notes

APPENDIX D
Your Body Mass Index

Body Mass Index (BMI) reduces the relationship between weight and height to one number. When you compare BMI value to charted ranges, BMI provides an approximation of body fatness, but is not a precise measure. The figure is not equal to a measurement of body fat percentage.

The value of knowing your BMI is that it provides a rough estimate of whether or not your body size indicates that you may or may not need to manage your weight more effectively.

Calculate Your BMI

The formula for calculating BMI is: BMI = your weight in pounds*/ (your height in inches)^2 x 703.

Or, try this simple three-step method:

1. Multiply your weight in pounds* by 703
2. Divide the answer by your height (in inches)
3. Divide the answer again by your height (in inches) to get your BMI

For example: If you are 5' 7" tall (or 67") and weigh 170 pounds, you would:
1. Multiply 170 x 703 = 119,510
2. Divide 119,510/67 = 1,785
3. Divide 1,785/67 = 26.6

BMI = 26.6; this BMI falls in the overweight category.
* Weight is measured with underwear but no shoes.

Body Mass Index

Here is a chart for men and women that gives the body mass index (BMI) for various heights and weights*.

	21	22	23	24	25	26	27	28	29	30	31
4'10"	100	105	110	115	119	124	129	134	138	143	148
5'0"	107	112	118	123	128	133	138	143	148	153	158
5'1"	111	116	122	127	132	137	143	148	153	158	164
5'3"	118	124	130	135	141	146	152	158	163	169	175
5'5"	126	132	138	144	150	156	162	168	174	180	186
5'7"	134	140	146	153	159	166	172	178	185	191	198
5'9"	142	149	155	162	169	176	182	189	196	203	209
6'0"	150	157	165	172	179	186	193	200	208	215	222
6'1"	159	166	174	182	189	197	204	212	219	227	235
6'3"	168	176	184	192	200	208	216	224	232	240	248

* Weight is measured with underwear but no shoes.

What Does Your BMI Mean?

The following categories of BMI will help you manage your weight.

Normal weight: BMI = 18.5–24.9.
Good for you! Try not to gain weight.

Overweight: BMI = 25–29.9.
Try not to gain weight. You need to manage your weight if you have two or more risk factors for heart disease and:

- Are overweight, or
- Have a high waist measurement.

Obese: BMI = 30 or greater.
You need to manage your weight. Lose weight slowly, about ½ to 2 pounds a week. See your doctor or a nutritionist if you need help.

Source: Clinical Guidelines on the Identification, Evaluation, and Treatment of Overweight and Obesity in Adults, National Heart, Lung, and Blood Institute, in cooperation with the National Institute of Diabetes and Digestive and Kidney Diseases, National Institutes of Health, June 1998.

Index

THE EVERYTHING TOTAL FITNESS BOOK

By Ellen Karpay

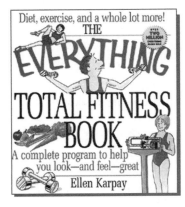

Diet, exercise, and a whole lot more!
THE **EVERYTHING TOTAL FITNESS BOOK**
A complete program to help you look—and feel—great
Ellen Karpay

Trade paperback, $12.95
1-58062-318-2, 304 pages

The Everything® Total Fitness Book features complete information and instructions on the best exercises for aerobic and muscular fitness, from outdoor sports for all seasons to the latest machines at the gym. The step-by-step illustrations of exercise, weight training, and stretching techniques will help ensure that your workouts are safe and effective. With dozens of helpful hints, tips, and excuse-busters, you'll quickly develop a routine that works for you. You'll learn to build time for rigorous and effective exercise into even the busiest schedule.

OTHER *EVERYTHING*® BOOKS BY ADAMS MEDIA CORPORATION

Everything® **After College Book**
$12.95, 1-55850-847-3

Everything® **American History Book**
$12.95, 1-58062-531-2

Everything® **Angels Book**
$12.95, 1-58062-398-0

Everything® **Anti-Aging Book**
$12.95, 1-58062-565-7

Everything® **Astrology Book**
$14.95, 1-58062-062-0

Everything® **Astronomy Book**
$14.95, 1-58062-723-4

Everything® **Baby Names Book**
$12.95, 1-55850-655-1

Everything® **Baby Shower Book**
$12.95, 1-58062-305-0

Everything® **Baby's First Food Book**
$12.95, 1-58062-512-6

Everything® **Baby's First Year Book**
$12.95, 1-58062-581-9

Everything® **Barbecue Cookbook**
$14.95, 1-58062-316-6

Everything® **Bartender's Book**
$9.95, 1-55850-536-9

Everything® **Bedtime Story Book**
$12.95, 1-58062-147-3

Everything® **Bible Stories Book**
$14.95, 1-58062-547-9

Everything® **Bicycle Book**
$12.00, 1-55850-706-X

Everything® **Breastfeeding Book**
$12.95, 1-58062-582-7

Everything® **Budgeting Book**
$14.95, 1-58062-786-2

Everything® **Build Your Own Home Page Book**
$12.95, 1-58062-339-5

Everything® **Business Planning Book**
$12.95, 1-58062-491-X

Everything® **Candlemaking Book**
$12.95, 1-58062-623-8

Everything® **Car Care Book**
$14.95, 1-58062-732-3

Everything® **Casino Gambling Book**
$12.95, 1-55850-762-0

Everything® **Cat Book**
$12.95, 1-55850-710-8

Everything® **Chocolate Cookbook**
$12.95, 1-58062-405-7

Everything® **Christmas Book**
$15.00, 1-55850-697-7

Everything® **Civil War Book**
$12.95, 1-58062-366-2

Everything® **Classical Mythology Book**
$12.95, 1-58062-653-X

Everything® **Coaching & Mentoring Book**
$14.95, 1-58062-730-7

Everything® **Collectibles Book**
$12.95, 1-58062-645-9

Everything® **College Survival Book**
$14.95, 1-55850-720-5

Everything® **Computer Book**
$12.95, 1-58062-401-4

Everything® **Cookbook**
$14.95, 1-58062-400-6

Everything® **Cover Letter Book**
$12.95, 1-58062-312-3

Everything® **Creative Writing Book**
$14.95, 1-58062-647-5

Everything® **Crossword and Puzzle Book**
$14.95, 1-55850-764-7

Everything® **Dating Book**
$12.95, 1-58062-185-6

Everything® **Dessert Cookbook**
$12.95, 1-55850-717-5

Everything® **Diabetes Cookbook**
$14.95, 1-58062-691-2

Everything® **Dieting Book**
$14.95, 1-58062-663-7

Everything® **Digital Photography Book**
$12.95, 1-58062-574-6

Everything® **Dog Book**
$12.95, 1-58062-144-9

Everything® **Dog Training and Tricks Book**
$14.95, 1-58062-666-1

Everything® **Dreams Book**
$12.95, 1-55850-806-6

Everything® **Etiquette Book**
$12.95, 1-55850-807-4

Everything® **Fairy Tales Book**
$12.95, 1-58062-546-0

Everything® **Family Tree Book**
$12.95, 1-55850-763-9

Everything® **Feng Shui Book**
$14.95, 1-58062-587-8

Everything® **Fly-Fishing Book**
$12.95, 1-58062-148-1

Everything® **Games Book**
$12.95, 1-55850-643-8

Everything® **Get-A-Job Book**
$12.95, 1-58062-223-2

Everything® **Get Out of Debt Book**
$12.95, 1-58062-588-6

Everything® **Get Published Book**
$12.95, 1-58062-315-8

Everything® **Get Ready for Baby Book**
$12.95, 1-55850-844-9

Everything® **Get Rich Book**
$12.95, 1-58062-670-X

Everything® **Ghost Book**
$14.95, 1-58062-533-9

Everything® **Golf Book**
$12.95, 1-55850-814-7

Everything® **Grammar and Style Book**
$12.95, 1-58062-573-8

Everything® **Great Thinkers Book**
$14.95, 1-58062-662-9

Everything® **Travel Guide to The Disneyland Resort®, California Adventure®, Universal Studios®, and Anaheim**
$14.95, 1-58062-742-0

Everything® **Guide to Las Vegas**
$12.95, 1-58062-438-3

Everything® **Guide to New England**
$14.95, 1-58062-589-4

Everything® **Guide to New York City**
$12.95, 1-58062-314-X

Everything® **Travel Guide to Walt Disney World®, Universal Studios®, and Greater Orlando, 3rd Edition**
$14.95, 1-58062-743-9

Everything® **Guide to Washington D.C.**
$12.95, 1-58062-313-1

Everything® **Guide to Writing Children's Books**
$14.95, 1-58062-785-4

Everything® **Guitar Book**
$14.95, 1-58062-555-X

Everything® **Herbal Remedies Book**
$12.95, 1-58062-331-X

Everything® **Home-Based Business Book**
$12.95, 1-58062-364-6

Everything® **Homebuying Book**
$12.95, 1-58062-074-4

Everything® **Homeselling Book**
$12.95, 1-58062-304-2

Everything® **Horse Book**
$12.95, 1-58062-564-9

Everything® **Hot Careers Book**
$12.95, 1-58062-486-3

Everything® **Hypnosis Book**
$14.95, 1-58062-737-4

Everything® **Internet Book**
$12.95, 1-58062-073-6

Everything® **Investing Book**
$12.95, 1-58062-149-X

Everything® **Jewish Wedding Book**
$12.95, 1-55850-801-5

Everything® **Judaism Book**
$14.95, 1-58062-728-5

Everything® **Job Interview Book**
$12.95, 1-58062-493-6

Everything® **Knitting Book**
$14.95, 1-58062-727-7

Everything® **Lawn Care Book**
$12.95, 1-58062-487-1

Everything® **Leadership Book**
$12.95, 1-58062-513-4

Everything® **Learning French Book**
$12.95, 1-58062-649-1

Everything® **Learning Italian Book**
$14.95, 1-58062-724-2

Everything® **Learning Spanish Book**
$12.95, 1-58062-575-4

Everything® **Low-Carb Cookbook**
$14.95, 1-58062-784-6

Everything® **Low-Fat High-Flavor Cookbook**
$12.95, 1-55850-802-3

Everything® **Magic Book**
$14.95, 1-58062-418-9

Everything® **Managing People Book**
$12.95, 1-58062-577-0

Everything® **Meditation Book**
$14.95, 1-58062-665-3

Everything® **Menopause Book**
$14.95, 1-58062-741-2

Everything® **Microsoft® Word 2000 Book**
$12.95, 1-58062-306-9

Everything® **Money Book**
$12.95, 1-58062-145-7

Everything® **Mother Goose Book**
$12.95, 1-58062-490-1

Everything® **Motorcycle Book**
$12.95, 1-58062-554-1

Everything® **Mutual Funds Book**
$12.95, 1-58062-419-7

Everything® **Network Marketing Book**
$14.95, 1-58062-736-6

Everything® **Numerology Book**
$14.95, 1-58062-700-5

Everything® **One-Pot Cookbook**
$12.95, 1-58062-186-4

Everything® **Online Business Book**
$12.95, 1-58062-320-4

Everything® **Online Genealogy Book**
$12.95, 1-58062-402-2

Everything® **Online Investing Book**
$12.95, 1-58062-338-7

Everything® **Online Job Search Book**
$12.95, 1-58062-365-4

Everything® **Organize Your Home Book**
$12.95, 1-58062-617-3

Everything® **Pasta Book**
$12.95, 1-55850-719-1

Everything® **Philosophy Book**
$12.95, 1-58062-644-0

Everything® **Pilates Book**
$14.95, 1-58062-738-2

Everything® **Playing Piano and Keyboards Book**
$12.95, 1-58062-651-3

Everything® **Potty Training Book**
$14.95, 1-58062-740-4

Everything® **Pregnancy Book**
$12.95, 1-58062-146-5

Everything® **Pregnancy Organizer**
$15.00, 1-58062-336-0

Everything® **Project Management Book**
$12.95, 1-58062-583-5

Everything® **Puppy Book**
$12.95, 1-58062-576-2

Everything® **Quick Meals Cookbook**
$14.95, 1-58062-488-X

Everything® **Resume Book**
$12.95, 1-58062-311-5

Everything® **Romance Book**
$12.95, 1-58062-566-5

Everything® **Running Book**
$12.95, 1-58062-618-1

Everything® **Sailing Book, 2nd Ed.**
$12.95, 1-58062-671-8

Everything® **Saints Book**
$12.95, 1-58062-534-7

Everything® **Scrapbooking Book**
$14.95, 1-58062-729-3

Everything® **Selling Book**
$12.95, 1-58062-319-0

Everything® **Shakespeare Book**
$14.95, 1-58062-591-6

Everything® **Slow Cooker Cookbook**
$14.95, 1-58062-667-X

Everything® **Soup Cookbook**
$14.95, 1-58062-556-8

Everything® **Spells and Charms Book**
$12.95, 1-58062-532-0

Everything® **Start Your Own Business Book**
$14.95, 1-58062-650-5

Everything® **Stress Management Book**
$14.95, 1-58062-578-9

Everything® **Study Book**
$12.95, 1-55850-615-2

Everything® **T'ai Chi and QiGong Book**
$12.95, 1-58062-646-7

Everything® **Tall Tales, Legends, and Other Outrageous Lies Book**
$12.95, 1-58062-514-2

Everything® **Tarot Book**
$12.95, 1-58062-191-0

Everything® **Thai Cookbook**
$14.95, 1-58062-733-1

Everything® **Time Management Book**
$12.95, 1-58062-492-8

Everything® **Toasts Book**
$12.95, 1-58062-189-9

Everything® **Toddler Book**
$14.95, 1-58062-592-4

Everything® **Total Fitness Book**
$12.95, 1-58062-318-2

Everything® **Trivia Book**
$12.95, 1-58062-143-0

Everything® **Tropical Fish Book**
$12.95, 1-58062-343-3

Everything® **Vegetarian Cookbook**
$12.95, 1-58062-640-8

Everything® **Vitamins, Minerals, and Nutritional Supplements Book**
$12.95, 1-58062-496-0

Everything® **Weather Book**
$14.95, 1-58062-668-8

Everything® **Wedding Book, 2nd Ed.**
$14.95, 1-58062-190-2

Everything® **Wedding Checklist**
$7.95, 1-58062-456-1

Everything® **Wedding Etiquette Book**
$7.95, 1-58062-454-5

Everything® **Wedding Organizer**
$15.00, 1-55850-828-7

Everything® **Wedding Shower Book**
$7.95, 1-58062-188-0

Everything® **Wedding Vows Book**
$7.95, 1-58062-455-3

Everything® **Weddings on a Budget Book**
$9.95, 1-58062-782-X

Everything® **Weight Training Book**
$14.95, 1-58062-593-2

Everything® **Wicca and Witchcraft Book**
$14.95, 1-58062-725-0

Everything® **Wine Book**
$12.95, 1-55850-808-2

Everything® **World War II Book**
$14.95, 1-58062-572-X

Everything® **World's Religions Book**
$14.95, 1-58062-648-3

Everything® **Yoga Book**
$14.95, 1-58062-594-0

*Prices subject to change without notice.

EVERYTHING® **KIDS'** SERIES!

Everything® **Kids' Baseball Book, 2nd Ed.**
$6.95, 1-58062-688-2

Everything® **Kids' Cookbook**
$6.95, 1-58062-658-0

Everything® **Kids' Joke Book**
$6.95, 1-58062-686-6

Everything® **Kids' Mazes Book**
$6.95, 1-58062-558-4

Everything® **Kids' Money Book**
$6.95, 1-58062-685-8

Everything® **Kids' Monsters Book**
$6.95, 1-58062-657-2

Everything® **Kids' Nature Book**
$6.95, 1-58062-684-X

Everything® **Kids' Puzzle Book**
$6.95, 1-58062-687-4

Everything® **Kids' Science Experiments Book**
$6.95, 1-58062-557-6

Everything® **Kids' Soccer Book**
$6.95, 1-58062-642-4

Everything® **Kids' Travel Activity Book**
$6.95, 1-58062-641-6

Available wherever books are sold!
To order, call 800-872-5627, or visit us at everything.com

Everything® is a registered trademark of Adams Media Corporation.